# THE ELEVEN COMMANDMENTS OF 21ST CENTURY MANAGEMENT

# THE ELEVEN COMMANDMENTS OF 21st CENTURY MANAGEMENT

## MATTHEW J. KIERNAN

**PRENTICE HALL**
Englewood Cliffs, New Jersey 07632

**Library of Congress Cataloging in Publication Data**

Kiernan, Matthew J.
    The eleven commandments of 21st century management : what
cutting-edge companies are doing to survive and flourish in today's chaotic
business world / Matthew J. Kiernan.
      p.  cm.
    ISBN 0-13-532433-5 (case)
    1. Management.   2. Strategic planning.   I. Title.
HD31.K4627   1996                         96-10551
658.4—dc20                               CIP

© 1996 by Prentice Hall Inc.

*Printed in the United States of America*

*10 9 8 7 6 5 4 3 2 1*

ISBN 0-13-310855-4

---

**ATTENTION: CORPORATIONS AND SCHOOLS**

Prentice Hall books are available at quantity discounts with bulk purchase for educational, business, or
sales promotional use. For information, please write to: Prentice Hall Career & Personal Development
Special Sales, 113 Sylvan Avenue, Englewood Cliffs, NJ 07632. Please supply: title of book, ISBN number, quantity, how the book will be used, date needed.

---

**PRENTICE HALL**
Career & Personal Development
Englewood Cliffs, NJ 07632
A Simon & Schuster Company

**On the World Wide Web at http://www.phdirect.com**

Prentice Hall International (UK) Limited, *London*
Prentice Hall of Australia Pty. Limited, *Sydney*
Prentice Hall Canada, Inc., *Toronto*
Prentice Hall Hispanoamericana, S.A., *Mexico*
Prentice Hall of India Private Limited, *New Delhi*
Prentice Hall of Japan, Inc., *Tokyo*
Simon & Schuster Asia Pte. Ltd., *Singapore*
Editora Prentice Hall do Brasil, Ltda., *Rio de Janeiro*

*"Wealth is created by the capitalization of innovation."*

PROFESSOR LESTER THUROW
MASSACHUSETTS INSTITUTE OF TECHNOLOGY

*"There is at least one point in the history of every company when you have to change dramatically to rise to the next performance level. Miss the moment, and you start to decline."*

ANDREW S. GROVE
CHAIRMAN AND CEO, INTEL CORPORATION

# ACKNOWLEDGMENTS

Like any writer, I have acquired numerous intellectual and experiential debts, few of which I have any realistic hope of adequately repaying. Happily, such debts are much more agreeable than the financial variety, at least for the debtor.

Many of the book's conceptual seeds were initially sown in Geneva, where I had the privilege of working for eighteen months on a special project with ceos and senior executives from some of the world's leading industrial companies. That unique organization, the Business Council for Sustainable Development, founded and led by the extraordinary Swiss industrialist Stephan Schmidheiny, served as the principal business and industry advisor to Maurice Strong, Secretary General of the historic Earth Summit in Rio de Janeiro in 1992. Stephan and his colleagues taught me an enormous amount about both the possibilities and the necessity of creating large-scale business paradigm shifts. Maurice has been both a friend and a hero of mine for over fifteen years, and continues to astound, educate, and inspire me.

In my previous incarnation as a strategy consultant, my partners, colleagues and clients at KPMG Peat Marwick were instrumental in tutoring me about the day-to-day realities of running competitive businesses under extraordinarily challenging circumstances. I am particularly grateful to Greg Doyle, Cam Mackie, Ian Gillies and Michael Decter in this regard.

More recently, I owe a debt of gratitude to my publishers, Neal Goff and Gene Brissie, and to my literary agent Beverly Slopen for believing that the "wake-up call" which the book provides is both timely and necessary. Catherine Harris and David Oliver, my eminently capable and talented research assistants, expertly provided both facts and their own insightful opinions, and were unfailingly able to distinguish between the two. In many respects they should really be viewed as co-authors. The CEOs and officials of many of the firms profiled here gave generously of their time and insights to help me develop a richer understanding of their companies' strategic architecture. One of them, Hubert Saint-Onge, custodian and grower of the intellectual capital base at CIBC bank, was especially helpful in sharpening my thinking in that area. My editors, Tom Power and Brian Scrivener, proved to be first-rate, value-adding colleagues, without whose contributions the book would have been considerably impoverished.

Last but by no means least, my wife Catherine and my children Susannah and Patrick all sacrificed at least as much as the author did to bring this project to fruition. They also teach me something new about strategic management on a daily basis. It is to them, and to my parents, that this book is dedicated.

# CONTENTS

# THE FORTUNE 500 IS OVER

*"The Fortune 500 is over."*
PETER DRUCKER

Talk about understating the obvious!

I have a personal rule of thumb about these matters: Any time the business world gets sufficiently complex, volatile and unfathomable that even a certified financial genius like billionaire George Soros can lose $600 million in a single day (February 14, 1994), I figure that's God's way of telling normal mortals like you and me that the business world has changed irrevocably, and is becoming a pretty scary and unmanageable place.

The era of the unshakeable corporate franchise appears to be well and truly over. The phenomenal mortality rate among Fortune 500 companies—and their erstwhile CEOs—over the past five years is testimony enough to the accelerating volatility of the international business environment.

As the swamps of the corporate Industrial Age begin to dry up in earnest, the broad contours of the 21st century competitive landscape are becoming visible. It is not a pretty sight for those who have grown overly comfortable with the old terrain. This brave new corporate world will be virtually unrecognizable and it will require entirely different survival skills. Many, if not most of today's Jurassic Park CEOs will be nowhere nearly up to the task.

I firmly believe it's possible to divide corporate executives into two distinct camps: Those who have an almost visceral predisposition towards changing, reforming and improving things, and those who do not. For most of this century, the tide has been running strongly in favor of the latter group; the virtues of stability, size, experience and hierarchy have been unquestioned and seemingly self-evident for decades. The leitmotifs of Alfred Sloan's and Frederick Taylor's "scientific management" were sufficiently robust that they have gone largely unchallenged and unexamined.

Sadly for the modern executive, however, these canons of scientific management turn out to be infinitely better suited to the challenges of mass producing black Model Ts in the 1920s than to managing the global, diversified and frequently "virtual" corporations of the 21st century. Today, what were once unalloyed virtues have become the new corporate carcinogens. "Economies of scale," "critical mass," "functional specialization" and their inescapable companions—rigid hierarchies, stoutly defended departmental borders and hidebound job descriptions—have paralyzed many companies' abilities to think, to act and, most importantly, to *learn.*

Even the almighty market survey, the staple of 20th century capitalism, may have outlived its usefulness. Market research is well suited for analyzing relatively static, well-defined markets in search of incremental improvements or advantage. It is *not* well suited for providing quantum leaps of innovation, insight or inspiration. The list of breakthrough products that were created with almost no market research is truly impressive: the Chrysler minivan, the Sony Walkman, 3M's yellow sticky Post-it Notes, the microwave oven, and on and on. You could even throw in Gutenberg's printing press; with European literacy rates in low single digits at the time, his market research numbers would have looked appalling! It's all well and good to be market driven and customer focused, but tomorrow's world of global "hyper-competition,"[1] will demand much, much more. Companies will need to be market *driving* and to create their own markets, customers and futures.

The root of the problem is that, whereas the business world has been turned completely upside down, most of the people running it are still operating with assumptions and formulae that were designed to cope with another era altogether. This is perfectly understandable; most of today's business "leaders" received all their formal education and most of their business experience in a world that, for the most part, has ceased to exist. The business landscape of the mid-90s is littered with corporate Cold Warriors, fighting yesterday's battles and using the day before yesterday's conceptual and managerial weaponry.

Many, if not most, of what today's CEOs grew up believing to be unquestioned assets have become liabilities. Chief among them are experience and "proven approaches." After all, in a world that reconfigures itself about every two weeks, how much value should we really accord to having twenty years' experience manufacturing the latter-day equivalent of buggy whips, particularly if it's being done in an organizational context more reminiscent of the Soviet Red Army than of the virtual companies of tomorrow? Experience may have been the dominant currency of yesterday's business world. Tomorrow's will be flexibility, agility, skepticism and an insatiable lust for learning, improvement and change.

In these pages, I shall propose—with some trepidation—11 Commandments for 21st century strategic management. They are designed to help companies construct the innovation infrastructure they will require to remain competitive amidst the approaching maelstrom. The Commandments are focused almost entirely on aspects of corporate value potential that are generally invisible to the naked eye: attributes such as organizational learning and innovation ability. These elements of a company's strategic architecture are rarely, if ever, captured on conventional corporate balance sheets, but they will have far more to do with the company's ultimate competitive success in the 21st century than any factors that are currently analyzed.

There's only one thing: Whereas the original 10 Commandments were printed on stone tablets, my eleven were first drafted on the backs of Heineken beer coasters in an assortment of airplanes, hotel rooms and airport lounges. You can draw your own conclusions about the respective staying power of the two sets of prescriptions. But to be fair, Moses didn't have to contend with the revolution in information technology, twenty-four-hour global derivatives trading, or the rise of Bahrain and the British Virgin Islands as the new financial superpowers.

The examples I have selected to illustrate my 11 Commandments are an unabashedly eclectic lot: from Silicon Graphics in California to an innovative oil company in Siberia, and from Mick Jagger and his distinctly capitalist Rolling Stones' Voodoo Lounge World Tour to the formerly Communist Ho Chi Minh City People's Committee in Vietnam. But they all have one thing in common. Each of the companies and organizations profiled is constantly pushing the envelope. They instinctively understand that there is no such thing as the status quo anymore, that change is a constant and that necessity must now become the mother of reinvention.

These companies and organizations have much to teach us, yet it all basically boils down to only one thing: Get Innovative or Get Dead!

# LEARNING TO LOVE TURBULANCE
## THE 11 COMMANDMENTS OF 21ST CENTURY MANAGEMENT

*"Everything is in a state of change; nothing endures.*
*We do not seek permanence."*
MASATOSHI NAITO/ MATSUSHITA CORPORATION

Businesses all over the world are entering a period of unprecedented and seemingly permanent volatility and turbulence. Companies from Zurich to Taipei to San Francisco are coming face to face with the bewildering impact of at least ten "frame-breaking" global megatrends:

*The explosive and accelerating power of the information and communications technologies.* Call it what you want—the Digital Revolution, the Multimedia Revolution or the Information Superhighway. The bottom line is this: These newly converging technologies are shattering organizational and political barriers, empowering new players and completely rewriting the rules of international business competition for both individual companies and entire countries.

Satellite and wireless communication have rendered national boundaries and governments virtually irrelevant. Computer and fiber optic technologies are breaking boundaries within and among companies, allowing tiny companies (and countries) to compete with massive ones, and catapulting enormous global capital flows beyond the reach of even the most powerful governments. What's really scary is that the experts tell us that less than *one-millionth* of the potential communications power of the new technologies has so far been placed in the hands of customers.[1] Just wait until they get their hands on the rest.

1

*The rapid globalization of markets, competition, trading patterns, finance capital and management innovation.* One knowledge-based industry—publishing—nicely captures the increasingly cosmopolitan nature of the new global marketplace. An academic journal I read is a typical product of the new economy: it is edited by seven professors in three different American universities, published out of Amsterdam, printed in India and administered in Switzerland. Its readers, and its competitors, come from anywhere on earth. Welcome to the new global knowledge economy.

But this new, globalized marketplace is being constructed at a price: unprecedented volatility. The explosion and convergence of computing, communications and financial technologies have created a world of instantaneous interdependence. Debt, equity and currency markets have all become so profoundly globalized and interconnected that when the Mexican peso catches a cold, the American dollar, Swedish kroner and Italian lira immediately begin sneezing loudly as well.

In addition to technology drivers, globalization is being propelled by another factor: the nearly worldwide triumph, at least for now, of the ideology of economic liberalism and "free" markets. The opening up of formerly closed economies from Beijing to Buenos Aires has thrown over two billion new consumers onto world markets, igniting ferocious competition for both consumers and foreign investment opportunities. This, too, demands speed, innovation, flexibility and the ability to adapt to the imperatives of an infinitely more complex and competitive international marketplace.

*The fundamental shift from a world economy based on manufacturing and natural resource exploitation to one based on knowledge-value, information and innovation.* All around the world, competitive advantage based on natural resource endowments and "economies of scale" manufacturing capacity is eroding dramatically, both for individual companies and for entire countries. It is of more than trivial significance that the cost and value of the information technology currently embedded in the average car has now outstripped the value of the steel. Even formerly specialized, high value-added goods like computers are rapidly becoming bulk commodities, and their price levels have plummeted accordingly.

Business academic James Brian Quinn has captured this mega-shift nicely: "With rare exceptions, the economic and productive power of a modern corporation lies more in its intellectual and service capabilities than in its hard assets—land, plant, and equipment...Virtually all public and private enterprises are becoming predominantly repositories and coordinators of intellect."[2] Sadly, very few executives and financiers seem to have figured this out. They persist in devoting most of their attention to managing the more tangible and familiar assets of the "old" economy.

Today, the only reliable way to make the proverbial better mousetrap is to embed more knowledge-value in it than your competitor does, and to be prepared to come out with a new, improved and even more knowledge-rich version before the competition has figured out your last one.

*The accelerated decoupling of the "real" global economy from the "virtual" economy of synthetic financial instruments and transactions.* The global market for financial derivatives has *doubled* to $35 *trillion* in only two years. Less than 10 percent of the world's daily capital flows are now actually related to increasing productive assets or value-based wealth. The rest, over $1 trillion of "hot" money, crosses national borders every day in search of the next microscopic edge in the computerized global casino of foreign exchange trading. These astonishing capital flows, which have more than quadrupled in the last decade, are almost entirely unconnected to the production of real value or wealth. They are also beyond the reach and effective control of both individual governments and international institutions. Central bankers, even acting in concert, have been unable to defend their currencies (and therefore their fiscal and monetary policies) from the assaults of the traders and speculators—the new, all-powerful mercenaries from cyberspace. Even the new World Trade Organization (successor to the GATT) can realistically hope to influence only the 10 percent or so of world capital flows which are directly related to trade. The WTO has no representation in financial cyberspace, where the real financial and investment decisions get made every day.

The net effect of this decoupling of the real and synthetic economies is a dramatic increase in the volatility, instability and complexity of global financial markets and, therefore, of the entire international business environment.

The stunning 1995 bankruptcy of California's Orange County provided a sobering reminder of this volatility. Previously one of the richest local governments in the world, Orange County suffered catastrophic losses trading in derivatives—the epitome of the new, synthetic economy. Also, consider the role of currency traders and speculators in the Mexican peso's spectacular free fall in early 1995. In the space of a month, the peso lost fully 50 percent of its value, causing massive turmoil in global money markets and necessitating an emergency international rescue package of nearly $50 billion. All of this occured with almost no change in the underlying fundamentals of the Mexican economy. The currency traders and speculators managed to inflict more damage on the Mexican economy in thirty days than successive governments have been able to produce in thirty years of systematic mismanagement.

*Geopolitical rebalancing: the emergence of a new world economic order.* Double-digit real GDP growth rates in Taiwan, Singapore, South Korea and China, among others, coupled with the relative stagnation of the OECD economies, has created a whole new international economic architecture. The balance of economic power and dynamism has shifted unmistakably and probably irreversibly. The hegemony of the OECD countries is well and truly over, and Southeast Asia's seems about to begin. For now, we live in an economic triad: North America, Asia and Europe. In ten years, who knows? The advent of new fiber optic and ATM (Asynchronous Transfer Mode) switching technologies will have a profoundly democratizing effect. Formerly Third World countries such as India can use them to leapfrog over decades of economic and technological evolution. Skeptics need only check out bustling Mahatma Ghandi Road in Bangalore, the epicenter of India's bourgeoning software industry, to see the new economic geography for themselves. And the new technologies have also leveled the playing field between large countries and small: At the rate some of the new international banking centers are growing, the next financial superpowers could turn out to be Liechtenstein, Bahrein, and the British Virgin Islands.

*The "twilight of government."* The globalization of markets and capital, massive privatizations, and the financial and credibility crisis of governments worldwide have all severely reduced the capacity of national governments to control their own economic and political destinies.[3]

With the end of the Cold War and the disintegration of the former Soviet Union, it has become fashionable to argue that we are now living in a world with only a single superpower, the United States. In point of fact, however, even the American government is impotent in the face of even larger superpowers: the major credit agencies such as Moody's and Standard and Poor's. In a world of massive government indebtedness, the faceless rating agencies that evaluate the creditworthiness of that debt wield at least as much power over economic policy as the elected governments which they scrutinize. Anyone who doubts this has only to sit in on the cabinet discussions of any G7 country at budget time. Their single greatest consideration is invariably the potential reaction of the international bond markets—the holders of most of the country's debt. The merest hint of an adverse reaction from the credit-rating agencies is enough to turn even the bravest finance minister's backbone into jelly.

At the same time, the proverbial twenty-five-year-old currency trader in red suspenders has proved to be a more potent force than even the G7 central bankers in setting exchange rates and shaping the international currency environment.

And it isn't just the capital markets that have weakened the sovereign power of governments. In a world of globalized commerce, transnational industrial corporations have also become far more potent instruments of social and economic change than governments. Their superior international infrastructure—not to mention credibility and clarity of purpose—enables them to project power and resources around the world much more rapidly and effectively than even the strongest governments.

*Sectoral and industrial convergence.* We are witnessing an unprecedented convergence and blurring of the formerly sharp distinctions between the public and private sectors. Governments everywhere are being squeezed by acute and protracted fiscal restraint, and are being forced to place new emphasis on bottom lines and "businesslike" management. At the same time, companies in the private sector are also now obliged to respond to the demands of an increasingly broad range of external stakeholders—not altogether unlike government. These days, it's getting harder and harder to tell the two sectors apart. Indeed, much of the action and momentum has already shifted to a different place altogether—the rapidly-growing "third sector," comprised of civil society and a bewildering variety of citizens' groups. Empowered and interconnected by technologies such as the Internet, this third force represents an increasingly powerful response to the perceived limitations of both government and the private sector.

Within the private sector itself, there has been a rapid convergence and blurring of once distinct industries into a fluid, constantly changing gestalt of competitors, suppliers and strategic alliances. A quintessential illustration of this trend is the progressive blurring of the telephone, cable TV, wireless communications, software and entertainment industries into a powerful but as yet ill-defined new paradigm called multimedia. Today, competition (or, for that matter, collaboration) between a telephone utility in New York and Walt Disney Studios in California scarcely raises an eyebrow. Just two years ago, it would have been unthinkable—and illogical.

Under present circumstances, it is increasingly difficult to determine precisely what business one is in. Of even greater concern, it is now prodigiously difficult, if not impossible, to predict who your competitors are or even from which industry they'll emerge. Managing international companies has become even more daunting than it already was.

***The emergence of unprecedented new forms of business organization, both within and between firms.*** The explosive centrifugal power of information and communications technologies has catapulted both knowledge and power beyond the boundaries of hierarchical institutions and Industrial-Age social systems. Boundaries are blurring everywhere: between different functional departments within the same firm, and between the firm itself and its suppliers, customers and even competitors. Among the most conspicuous examples of these new organizational forms are the development of non-hierarchical, interdisciplinary teams, the proliferation of strategic alliances, the rise of the "virtual" organization, and the emergence of megacompetition between rival alliances in industries as disparate as automobiles, aerospace and computer chips.

The organizational architecture of German industrial giant Daimler-Benz is becoming increasingly typical: "the company" now includes not only its permanent in-house employees, but also strategic alliances (IBM, Mitsubishi), joint development and production initiatives (Thomson and Fiat), and cross-stakeholdings (Deutsche Bank, Saab, Banque Nationale de Paris). It's increasingly difficult to tell where companies begin and end, and there's less and less point in trying to do so.

*A shift in the economic "center of gravity" of the business world from large, multinational companies to smaller, nimbler and more entrepreneurial companies.* Technological change has obliterated the traditional balance of power between established corporate behemoths and tiny, but innovative upstarts. Corporate mass and size have even turned from a competitive advantage into a serious liability, as the beleaguered executives—and former executives—of companies like IBM, Sears and American Express can attest.

*The geometric increase in the social, political and commercial significance of environmental considerations in both OECD and industrializing countries.* A number of senior industrialists consider this transformation to be so profound and far-reaching that they have called it an "Eco-Industrial Revolution." In less than a decade, a company's environmental performance has moved from the status of a peripheral irrelevancy to a potentially make-or-break competitive issue. Just ask any of the dozens of CEOs whose companies suffered multi-hundred-million-dollar, environmentally driven losses last year, or who personally served jail time. On the upside, "the environment" is also well on its way to becoming a $700 billion per year international growth industry within the OECD countries alone, and it's growing even faster in the newly industrializing countries.

The cumulative power of these megatrends has created the most dramatic and pervasive transformation of them all:

*An exponential increase in the velocity, complexity and unpredictability of change.* Together, all these trends are creating a hypercompetitive international business environment that bears little resemblance to the one that existed five years ago—or that awaits us two years hence. It is a world in which competition has become so ferocious, multifaceted and unpredictable that no competitive advantage can possibly endure, but must be constantly recreated.

Anyone who doubts we are living in a world of unprecedented volatility need only ponder the fate of Barings PLC. On January 1, 1995, Barings was a prestigious, 233-year-old British merchant bank whose clients included the Queen of England and Prince Charles. Its corporate history included financing Britain's participation in the Napoleonic wars. Barings even predated that upstart banking family, the Rothschilds. Two months later, Barings was pronounced clinically dead, the victim of catastrophic losses in derivatives trading in Asia. Official reports project the losses at roughly US$1 billion. Insiders in the City of London quietly whisper that the real amount may be closer to $4 billion. Even frantic efforts by the Bank of England and the Sultan of Brunei couldn't save Barings, though not for lack of trying. From corporate icon to bankruptcy in sixty days. Sic transit gloria!

Given that most contemporary corporate executives received their training and experience, and formed their world view in a bygone era, a major problem emerges. Almost all of our business organizations were built to function in the much more stable and predictable environment of the Industrial Age. As a result, the current pace of organizational renewal is simply inadequate to cope with both the velocity and complexity of change created by the advent of the new era of knowledge-value.

I place the date of our official emergence from the corporate equivalent of the Palaeolithic era at roughly 1991, the first year that total, global investment in the "new economy"—things like telecommunications and information technology—outstripped our collective investment in the "old" one—things like machinery, natural resource extraction and physical plant. At the same time, it became glaringly obvious that, while the old management paradigms were pretty much discredited, no compelling, new business theology had yet emerged to replace them.

The table on the next page sets out some key distinctions between the old management paradigm and the new one, now clearly visible if not yet fully complete. Each element of the right-hand, 21st century column is a direct response to the imperatives created by the combined impact of the aforementioned megatrends, as they begin to dominate the final half-decade of the 20th century.

## THE ICEBERG OF CORPORATE VALUE POTENTIAL

Corporate value potential is like an iceberg; only 10 percent of it is readily apparent above the waterline. The other 90 percent—the *intellectual* capital base of the corporation—remains largely hidden from the view of accountants, financial analysts and executives alike, and is desperately undermanaged as a result.

The central thesis of this book is the following: Senior executives currently spend roughly 90 percent of their time focused on the 10 percent of their asset base which shows up on their balance sheets and profit and loss

### *Organizational Paradigms: The Torch Passes*

| 20th Century | 21st Century |
| --- | --- |
| Stability, predictability | Discontinuous change, continuous improvement |
| Size and scale | Speed and responsiveness |
| Top-down "command and control" | Empowerment; leadership from everybody |
| Organizational rigidity | "Virtual" organizations, permanent flexibility |
| Control by rules and hierarchy | Control by vision and values |
| Information closely guarded | Information shared |
| "Rational," quantitative analytics | Creativity, intuition |
| Need for certainty | Tolerance of ambiguity |
| Reactive; risk-averse | Proactive; entrepreneurial |
| Process driven | Results driven |
| Corporate independence and autonomy | Interdependence; strategic alliances |
| Vertical integration | "Virtual" integration |
| Internal organizational focus | Focus on competitive environment |
| Consensus | Constructive contention |
| Domestic market orientation | International focus |
| Competitive advantage | Collaborative advantage |
| Sustainable competitive advantage | Hypercompetition, constant reinvention of advantage |
| Competing for today's markets | Creating tomorrow's markets |

## The Iceberg Balance Sheet

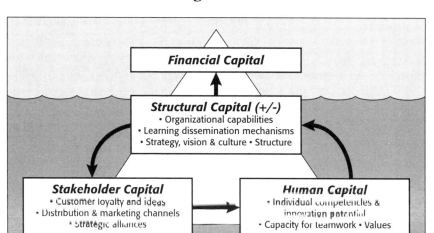

statements. They spend virtually none on their companies' *intellectual* capital base and innovation infrastructure, which are the real sources of its future competitiveness.

Stated that boldly, this proposition sounds outrageous, and no self-respecting CEO would ever admit it. But it's true. For a whole set of thoroughly understandable reasons, CEOs and their financiers have grown used to focusing on balance sheets, profit-and-loss statements, and the other artifacts of an Industrial-Age business civilization, when key assets actually could be captured reasonably accurately by accountants. There's just one problem: Those days are well and truly over.

As we move deeper and deeper into the era of knowledge-value, conventional balance sheets and profit-and-loss statements will capture and reflect less and less of a company's true value and potential, as will stock prices, which are driven almost exclusively by the same narrow, short-term financial accounting metrics.

What is needed instead is a new, more dynamic "iceberg balance sheet,"[4] which focuses senior management attention where it belongs: on the underlying sources of the company's *future* value-creation capabilities and unique comparative advantages. There are three basic components to a company's intellectual capital base:

- Human capital
- Stakeholder capital
- Structural capital

The first of the three core components of intellectual capital is *human capital:* the competencies, knowledge, values and innovative potential of the individuals within the organization. The second might be called *stakeholder capital,* including a company's distribution and marketing channels, its network of strategic alliance partners and the loyalty and idea-generating capacity of its customers. The real key, though, is the third kind of intellectual capital: *structural capital.* Structural capital, the central focus of this book, is at the heart of what we would call the *innovation infrastructure* of the firm. It is the means by which both human and stakeholder capital are harnessed, leveraged and ultimately converted into financial capital and profitability. Structural capital includes the organization's innovation, learning and team-building ability, its strategies, vision, culture, information systems and myriad other intangibles that are the true sources of value potential and comparative advantage.

This is the company's real intellectual capital base. How well it is constructed and mobilized will determine how much of it can be converted into the financial capital that analysts, accountants and stockholders scrutinize so carefully.

A company's capacity to generate real, sustainable value is almost entirely a function of its ability to create synergies out of the interplay among the three elements of its intellectual capital base. Thus:

*Intellectual Capital = Human + Stakeholder Capital ± Structural Capital*

It is crucial to note that structural capital can either add to or detract from a company's intellectual capital base. The entire raison d'être of this book is to ensure that addition occurs; hence, my 11 Commandments of 21st century strategic management. Individually and as a group, the Commandments are designed to strengthen companies' structural capital and thereby build an innovation infrastructure that is both powerful and sustainable.

---

## BUILDING THE INNOVATION INFRASTRUCTURE OF 21ST CENTURY COMPANIES

---

The 11 Commandments are focused almost entirely on the intellectual capital base of the company—the 90 percent of the corporate value iceberg normally hidden from view. If executives were to devote even a fraction of the time to uncovering and leveraging their intellectual capital that they currently spend on managing their financial capital, their companies would be infinitely better positioned for the future.

As with any major paradigm shift, the process of building this new innovation infrastructure will be neither painless nor instantaneous. The principles of "scientific management" may be widely discredited, but they are by no means clinically dead or off life-support systems. As a secular theology, they have dominated Western business thought for over sixty years and their influence will not evaporate overnight. Even if it were possible to construct a new business religion out of whole cloth, there would remain the untidy problem of dealing with the intellectual and human residue of the earlier one. Both Wall Street and the accounting profession, among others, have enormous intellectual, emotional and financial stakes in perpetuating the myth that balance sheets and P&L statements can provide meaningful insights into corporate value and potential. As time passes, this view will become increasingly outdated, even fraudulent.

But there is hope. If the experience of the innovative, leading-edge companies profiled in this book is anything to go by, the 11 Commandments will give you a significant leg up—for now.

## THE 11 COMMANDMENTS

1.  *Don't play by the dominant competitive rules of your industry.* Invent your own and make others follow you! Create *new* competitive space; zero-sum battles over static markets are yesterday's game.

2.  *Get innovative or get dead!* Develop conscious strategies and mechanisms to promote consistent innovation. Resting on your laurels is simply not an option; the best companies are innovating and surpassing themselves *constantly.*

3.  *Reexamine your company for hidden strategic assets, then leverage the hell out of them.* Exceptional companies find value potential that others overlook, and then liberate and leverage it. Sometimes the hidden value is within the firm, sometimes outside it. Either way, the real innovators will find it or create it.

4.  *Create a bias for speed and action in your company.* Analysis and reflection are all well and good, but you're nowhere without implementation—and it had better be fast. These days, it's far better to be 80 percent right and quick than 100 percent right and three months late.

5. *Be proactive and experimental.* The days of depending on corporate size and reputation to drop opportunities in your lap are over. You need to go out and make things happen.

6. *Break barriers.* 21st century, "virtual" companies are dismantling the internal barriers that so often separate people, departments and disciplines. The boundaries between firms and their outside suppliers, customers and sometimes even competitors are also under severe pressure.

7. *Use all of your people, all of their skills, all of the time.* The business school profs at Harvard, Stanford and INSEAD (France) call it "empowerment. Normal human beings simply call it giving both authority and resources to their front-line people closest to the action and letting them get on with it.

8. *Globalize your perspective and knowledge base.* The fastest growing markets in the world today are not only outside North America, they're outside the OECD countries. Even General Electric can't survive on a single country market any more. You certainly won't.

9. *Admit that the eco-industrial revolution is well and truly upon us.* All over the world, the links between environmental performance, competitiveness and bottom-line financial results are growing tighter every day. Leading-edge companies are turning superior environmental performance into a powerful competitive weapon. Managing environmental risk and investment opportunities effectively can make the difference between outperforming your business and investment competitors and lagging behind.

10. *Turn organizational learning into a corporate religion.* At the end of the day, the only truly sustainable competitive advantage will be your ability to learn faster and better than your competitors, and to turn that learning into new products, services and technologies before your competitors can imitate your last innovation.

11. *Develop strategic performance measurement tools.* Any bozo can measure the last quarter's production or profit figures, but at best he or she will give you a static, superficial snapshot of yesterday's news. By concentrating instead on key strategic and profitability drivers, ones that reveal the underlying dynamics of your business, you can focus your energy on what *really* drives the future success of your business.

The remainder of this book is devoted to an elaboration of these Commandments, and to strengthening the innovation infrastructure and intellectual capital base of your firm. And, on the off chance that a skeptic or two remains among you, I have also included a liberal smattering of short case studies and real-life vignettes showing the 11 Commandments in action around the world. The examples are drawn from companies based in twenty different nations and a wide variety of sectors. While these illustrations do not (and cannot) provide definitive proof of the eternal validity of the 11 Commandments, they do suggest the Commandments have an increasing number of adherents in an unprecedented variety of countries and industrial contexts. This augurs well for the half-lives of both the companies and the Commandments themselves, though I can give no absolute guarantees in either case. The business world has become far too unpredictable and unforgiving for that.

### CHAPTER TWO

# MAKE YOUR OWN RULES
## BETTER STILL,
## INVENT YOUR OWN GAME

*"A different, and I think more powerful, way to compete
is to avoid competition altogether."*
PAUL COOK/ CHAIRMAN/ RAYCHEM

## THE ART OF STRATEGIC REFRAMING

The revolution in information and communications technologies has fundamentally and permanently altered the international business landscape. One of the most far-reaching consequences of these tectonic changes is a massive shift in the corporate balance of power. For the first time in the history of commerce, ten-person boutiques can now take on multinational giants and win. In one fell swoop, competition has become more ubiquitous, intense, unpredictable, democratic and, in a word, difficult.

Collectively, these technological changes ushered in the era of the strategic reframer. It has become tougher and tougher to generate competitive advantage by simply doing the same old things a little bit better. Now, almost anybody can do that. Beating one's brains out in direct, head-to-head competition for an extra half-point of market share will yield only Pyrrhic victories if it yields victories at all. Increasingly, competitive advantages and profits will belong to innovators who *transcend* the existing parameters of competition altogether. These strategic reframers force their competitors to play by new rules of the game, rules they themselves have largely devised. Not only does this throw the competition off balance, but the reframers create a temporary monopoly over the critical success factors for their industry. This ability to completely transcend or bypass competition might be considered the business equivalent of Edward de Bono's celebrated concept of lateral thinking.

There are three basic varieties of strategic reframing. First, creating an entirely new industry; second, reinventing how an existing industry operates; and third, setting the de facto world standard for an emerging industry that others are creating. Let's look at all three.

## INVENTING BRAND NEW INDUSTRIES

### *Starting From Scratch: Apple Computers*

Arguably the purest form of strategic reframing (and certainly the most ambitious) is to construct an entirely new industry from scratch. In the four years between 1977-1981, the computer company which began in Steve Jobs' and Stephen Wozniak's garage in California did precisely that. By 1994, Apple Corporation had grown from a two-man private company to an $8 billion per year multinational corporation employing some 15,000 people directly and spawning literally hundreds of new spin-off and supplier companies. Apple's story is instructive in the extreme.

By commercializing the personal computer, Apple effectively democratized the computer industry, transforming it from a business supplying large, expensive, inflexible products to highly trained specialists in large corporations, to one focused on individual users in homes, small businesses, and schools. Apple's revolutionary goal of adapting computers to human needs rather than forcing users to learn arcane computer languages has remained a hallmark of Apple's strategy and success to this day. The pirate flag fluttering over Apple's headquarters in Cupertino, California was an apt metaphor for the company's iconoclastic, in-your-face culture.

Apple's approach didn't just win the company new customers. It also forced competitors to play by *its* rules. Apple's use of brightly colored icons appealed to pros and technophobes alike, and the company's rebellious image attracted nonconformists, creative free thinkers and agents of change. Although its competitors, including long-time rival IBM, eventually began to support more user-friendly products themselves, Apple has retained its distinctive reputation as an innovator specializing in user-centered computing. Its competitors have been forced to play technology catch-up for more than a decade, and for the most part even Microsoft continues to do so.

Most important of all, Apple essentially created an entirely new industry from scratch. The personal computing industry—both hardware and software—has become one of the three largest industries and wealth creators on the planet. Before Apple, the industry essentially didn't exist. Today, thanks in large part to the trail blazed by Apple, companies such as Microsoft, Intel, and Sun Microsystems are corporate superstars, creating thousands of new jobs and billions of dollars of new value.

Sadly, however, the Apple saga does not have an entirely happy ending. Steve Jobs' visionary, iconoclastic, but undisciplined leadership gave way in 1985 to the buttoned-down, "professional" management of ex-Pepsi executive John Sculley. By 1993, it had become apparent that Sculley's appointment of himself as Apple's chief technology officer was a less than inspired one, and the company tiller was turned over to chief operating officer Michael Spindler. Unfortunately, the company's slide continued unabated. By early 1996, Apple was experiencing declining market share, operating losses, and the wholesale defection of talented executives. Business pundits were writing the company's obituary,[1] and Apple's board jettisoned their CEO yet again, dumping Spindler in February and replacing him with turn-around artist (and patent-holding physicist) Gilbert Amelio, the former CEO of National Semiconductor. How had it all come undone?

In a nutshell, Apple had been unable to convert its undeniable technical leadership into *market* dominance. While the immediate cause of Apple's demise was the ascendency of Microsoft's Windows operating system, the seeds of decline had been sown much earlier by Steve Jobs himself. While Jobs' iconoclasm had unquestionably provided enormous dynamic energy to his company, its downside was the technological hubris that utterly disdained making the MacIntosh compatible with other technology platforms. In the final analysis, this effectively blocked Apple from becoming a dominant player outside of the niche markets of educational software and desktop publishing. The opportunity to dominate the industry which it had created virtually single-handedly had passed Apple by.

Critics may carp that Apple's decline repudiates and invalidates this book's constant insistence on the competitive power of innovation. I beg to differ. What it *does* illustrate, however, is that even the most sweeping innovations have increasingly short half-lives, and that the inescapable price of commercial leadership has become consistent and *repeated* innovation. After almost 20 years, the power of Apple's initial series of breathtaking product and technical breakthroughs had evaporated, and *nothing of comparable potency had emerged to take their place.*

The lesson of Apple, then, is that merely inventing a new industry is no longer any guarantee that you can dominate it *sustainably*. In the new, Darwinian universe of global hypercompetition, the cry has become "what have you done for me *lately*," and lately can now be measured in weeks, not years. In the words of one 18-year Apple veteran: "The jig is really up this time. We just can't do business the same way anymore."[2] You got *that* right!

## *Decibels R Us: The Story of* MTV

One-upping Ted Turner is no easy task, and very few have pulled it off. Robert Pittman did it fifteen years and two careers ago. (He is currently CEO of the Century 21 real estate empire, following a stint as CEO of Time-Warner Enterprises.) Whereas Turner's genius lay in extending the geographic and programming reach of an existing medium—television—at MTV Pittman managed to synthesize two previously separate media to create an entirely new art form: Music Television.

In 1981, the precocious Pittman was, at twenty-four, already head of programming at Warner subsidiary, The Movie Channel. Pittman recognized the enormous potential of bringing together the two most potent cultural forces of his generation, television and rock music. Pittman was not the first to have this insight, just the first to make it work with devastating effectiveness. Previous attempts had foundered in trying to contort the music idiom to fit the form of television. Pittman recognized two things intuitively. The first was that precisely the opposite would be necessary; TV's normal format of flowing narrative would have to be abandoned to fit the more urgent and staccato requirements of the music. The second and more fundamental point was that he was creating an entirely new industry, and would therefore need to reinvent much of the current industry's infrastructure as well, notably its advertising and distribution channels, and its financing.

Conventional industry wisdom held that Pittman was seriously delusional and that MTV was doomed from the word go. For openers, the jury was still out as to whether cable could become a commercially viable distribution medium. (With the 20/20 hindsight of the billion-dollar cable acquisitions of the mid-90s, this concern now seems a trifle misplaced.) In addition, "everyone knew" that national advertisers would never support a medium with cable's limited geographic coverage. And anyway, who would actually pay to produce the rock videos? Ever the iconoclast, Pittman argued that he was not simply creating a new product or program, but a veritable leitmotif for an entire youth culture. And this particular youth culture happened to have the greatest disposable income in demographic history.

In the final analysis, Pittman convinced the record companies that producing rock videos for MTV would be the single most effective way for them to sell more records and compact discs. Advertisers flocked to MTV in droves, attracted by both demographics and Pittman's ability to deliver a single integrated, thematic package of graphic look and feel, something conventional TV could deliver only rarely. Encouraged by the success of MTV, Ted Turner decided to create a video music station of his own. He signed up 400,000 subscribers, but Pittman quickly counterattacked, launching VH-1, an MTV spin-off. VH-1 not only attracted two million subscribers, but it did so at considerably lower cost by leveraging MTV's existing infrastructure. Thirty-four days later, Ted Turner was off the air, his career as a rock video impresario over before it began.

The moral of the MTV story: If you're going to defy conventional wisdom and create an entirely new industry, don't use half-measures. Having a brilliant, timely and resonant business concept is a terrific starting point, but nowhere near sufficient by itself. Entrepreneurs must also look at the entire "value system" and infrastructure required to actually bring the concept to life. Nine times out of ten, trying to superimpose a radically innovative new concept on an existing implementation infrastructure won't work. As MTV demonstrates, the infrastructure itself (distribution, finance, marketing, etc.) needs to be reinvented too.

## REINVENTING EXISTING INDUSTRIES

### *Switzerland's Swatch*

Strategic reframing need not be limited to relatively new industries such as computing and multimedia. The story of Swatch's meteoric growth in the centuries-old watch industry in Switzerland provides a compelling illustration of the power of innovation to revolutionize the most mature, even ossified, industry.

In the early 1980s, the Swiss watch industry remained highly craft oriented, producing watches in small numbers and at relatively high costs. These small-scale watchmakers proved to be no match for the sophisticated mass-production techniques of Japanese firms such as Seiko and Citizen, who delivered highly accurate digital watches for low prices. These new watches proved enormously popular with customers worldwide, who were beginning to see watches as no longer just a once in a lifetime, coming-of-age gift, but as a low-cost consumer product that could be readily replaced as the owner's tastes changed.

Little in the Swiss business culture had equipped it to deal with this Japanese onslaught. Most Swiss industries had been operating in stable, protected, oligopolistic markets for decades, if not centuries. This was not exactly a textbook environment for incubating the sort of innovation, flexibility and dynamism the late 20th century would demand. The new Japanese products cut through the Swiss watch industry like a hot Swiss army knife through butter, devastating the economic base of entire valleys that had been dependent on watchmaking.

While most of Switzerland's clubby senior-business fraternity were content with wringing their hands over this deteriorating situation, only Nicholas Hayek had both the creativity and the conviction to do something about it. He would fight back with a qualitatively new product: the Swatch. Designed by Ernst Thomke, the Swatch combined the traditional prestige and reliability of a Swiss watch with heavily automated process innovations that enabled rapid-fire new product lines, all in trendy and highly affordable formats.

Swatch's real genius, of course, lay in reinventing the very concept and functionality of the watch itself. By turning watches into sporty, whimsical *fashion* accessories, as well as reliable timepieces, Hayek changed the rules of the game completely and captured an entirely new market of younger consumers. No longer did customers have to choose between an elegant but expensive Swiss watch and a functional yet cheap Japanese model. Swatch's low-cost competitors such as Timex were simply overwhelmed by the sheer volume and speed of Swatch's introduction of new products and designs.

Not content with simply reinventing the product itself, Hayek also reinvented its distribution system, moving Swatches out of exclusive jewelry stores and into the much higher volume department stores. The results astounded Hayek's critics: by 1992 the company had sold over 100 million Swatches. Employment in the Swiss watch industry actually began to rise again in 1985 after fifteen years of steady decline, despite the heavy automation of the Swatch production process.

Nor has Hayek been content to stand still and rest on his considerable laurels. Recently, he began hiring well-known artists to design new Swatches and encouraging collectors through a strict policy of never repeating a design. Next, Swatch's trademark strengths in fashion, design and marketing were leveraged horizontally into entirely new product lines such as telephones and fax machines. And finally, in February 1994, the company took another quantum step: it announced the launch of an environmentally friendly Swatch *car*, to be developed in collaboration with Volkswagen AG.

The mind-set that drives a Jobs or a Hayek is clearly quite different from the linear thinking that has traditionally dominated Western business practices. Western executives are generally trained to diagnose, analyze and fix problems that already exist. They tend, however, to be much less adept at generating and harnessing the truly creative possibilities and alternatives that do not yet exist. (This helps to explain both the uselessness of conventional market research in generating truly innovative products and services—and, regrettably, its continued popularity.) Most of what passes for contemporary competitive strategy focuses doggedly on what exists—what industry competitors are doing, and what products and services they offer—in the hope of attaining an incremental improvement over what is already available. This approach dramatically limits a manager's ability to step back and ask more fundamental, difficult and ultimately useful questions, such as: Is this product the best possible way of satisfying my customers' wants and needs? Is there any other way of meeting that need that our company is uniquely positioned to deliver? Are there other needs the customer doesn't even know he or she *has* yet?

The problem with such lateral thinking is that it's difficult, far more difficult than simply trying to do what everybody else is already doing, only better. Quite frankly, in my experience, most corporate CEOs simply aren't up to it. They have neither the intellectual capacity, the training, the energy nor the guts to invent something radically different. And, in an earlier, kinder, gentler business era, they didn't have to. Now they do.

## *Selling Ideology and Social Conscience: England's The Body Shop*

The cosmetics industry has done an extraordinarily good job of convincing us to buy $5 worth of pleasantly aromatic, nicely packaged ingredients for $65. Clearly, the $60 increment is generated not by selling cosmetics per se but by selling dreams, hope, illusion and romance. Body Shop founder Anita Roddick's real genius lies not so much in challenging this huge discrepancy between retail price and the cost of ingredients, but in choosing to fill it with something radically different. Instead of selling the dreams, illusions and romance of L'Aire du Temps or Giorgio, Roddick sells ideology.

As with other cosmetics shops, customers at The Body Shop are offered much more than mere shampoo and shower gel. What is genuinely innovative about The Body Shop is that its customers are also implicitly buying the sensation that they have actually helped to make the world a better place. Social and environmental responsibility are the core of the value set that is The Body Shop's ultimate product. The company's wares must adhere to rigid standards: absolutely no animal testing, minimal packaging and labeling, refillable bottles of cosmetics and products derived from sources that encourage the sustainable use of natural resources. She may not have invented it, but Anita Roddick turned consumers' willingness to reward corporate social responsibility into an absolute art form—and a stunningly successful international business.

Two of Roddick's favorite causes are environmentalism and the empowerment of indigenous peoples. Through her work in Brazil, she combines the two. Roddick argues that the root cause of at least some of the destruction of the Amazonian rain forest is the abject poverty of its native inhabitants, which in turn compels them to destroy natural resources for fuel and other basic necessities. The solution? Give them jobs and incomes, working as suppliers of ingredients for natural products—to The Body Shop, of course. As a direct result of Roddick's travels to places like the remote jungles of Amazonia, The Body Shop now features a number of distinctive products made specially for the company by local inhabitants from Brazil to Nepal to the Sahara desert.

As a company, The Body Shop is a generous financial supporter of non-profit organizations working on environmental and other social issues. In addition, Roddick encourages individual shops to devote time and money to local causes that the shop's employees deem worthwhile and important, such as child care, inner-city education and AIDS hospices.

Consistent with its emphasis on social responsibility, The Body Shop provides customers with a wealth of background product information, instead of advertising hype. The company's incredibly successful marketing, which involves *no* direct paid advertising at all, centers on Anita Roddick, who campaigns ceaselessly for the causes she (and by extension, the business) considers important. Her issues are wide ranging, including the environment, AIDS, human rights in Tibet, Amazonia and Kurdistan, and Romanian orphans. And there can be no doubt her concerns are genuine.

To say that Roddick's approach has worked would be a massive understatement. The Body Shop has expanded at a breakneck pace, growing from a tiny storefront in Brighton, England in 1976 to a $250 million business with over 850 shops in 41 countries worldwide by 1994. Despite her insistence that wealth is not important to her—"I have no doubt that wealth is corrosive"—Anita Roddick and her husband Gordon are now one of the richest couples in Britain, worth an estimated $350 million. One senses this is mildly embarrassing to Ms. Roddick, though you and I would probably find ways to assuage our psychic angst were we in her place.

Inevitably, The Body Shop's formula has attracted imitators. However, she who invents the new game and writes the first set of competitive ground rules usually stakes out an unassailable position and everyone else is relegated to playing catch-up. (At the Harvard Business School they call this "first-mover advantage.") None of the "competitors" in the industry Anita Roddick created has come close to rivaling her success. For one thing, none of them has figured out what The Body Shop is really selling. If and when they do, most customers will probably still prefer the real thing.

## *Store Wars: Canada's Loblaws*

Until recently, the retail grocery business had not exactly been a hotbed of innovation and excitement. (One struggles to recall a grocery retailing breakthrough since the legalization of Sunday shopping.) Recently, however, we have begun to witness a quiet revolution in the industry, driven in large part by a new phenomenon called "private label" or "store brands." This has radically altered the dynamics of the master-servant power relationship that historically prevailed between powerful, nationwide retail brands such as Coca-Cola and Cheerios and the local stores carrying their products.

Few companies have done more to create and accelerate this trend than Loblaws, the $7 billion-per-year, Toronto-based supermarket chain. To many Canadians (and increasing numbers of Americans) the chain is closely associated with the face of Dave Nichol, the originator and tireless promoter of the "President's Choice" private-label brand line. He has single-handedly changed the rules of how store brands should behave.

Traditionally, no-name brands offered lower prices for a (usually) lower quality product with minimal packaging. Nichol's new store brand offered something innovative: products of equivalent and often superior quality to the name brands, but providing far better value for money. President's Choice cereals, cookies, soft drinks and even good quality wines emerged and now compete head to head with some of the world's most powerful brands.

Nichol knew that many established brands demanded a substantial premium, or "brand tax," as he described it. This brand tax was based on years of heavy advertising and perceived product reliability. However, Nichol believed that this premium was often excessive, and that by building up his own high-quality line, he could create his own value and appropriate some of that ill-gotten brand tax for *his* shareholders. (It didn't hurt that Nichol was launching this strategy during a global recession so severe that even bank presidents' wives were joining the ranks of cost-conscious shoppers.) But Nichol also created and captured other benefits too. First, advertising President's Choice products created a unique and special image in customers' minds for the Loblaws stores themselves. Second, not only did his new brand actually attract new customers, but having a private label on the shelf gave Loblaws further leverage in negotiating prices with the established brands. As Nichol himself puts it: "What is involved here is a massive power shift from the national brands to the store. That's being accomplished by branding the store."

Another Loblaws innovation was to turn those strategic insights into a service business outside its own stores. Loblaws began working with other retailers—for a fee—helping them introduce private labels in their own stores as counterweights to the dominant national brands. Foreshadowing a trend that will grow as we move through the 90s, Loblaws provides not simply a product but an integrated package of *services*. Loblaws supplies not only the new private-label products, but a whole constellation of services including marketing and merchandising advice. For the icing on the cake, Loblaws will also work with other retailers, showing them how to capture and interpret the wealth of customer and sales data that they already possess, but have yet to leverage and exploit.

Loblaws has subsequently "exported" its President's Choice product line and service philosophy to the United States, where they have met with great success. The proportion of Americans loyal to well-known brands is falling steadily, from 64 percent in 1985 to 57 percent in 1992. Nichol predicts that store brand products, which now control 14 percent of the market, will eventually control 40 percent. He sees the David and Goliath struggle between private labels and the huge national brands as the equivalent of a moral crusade against the forces of darkness, and places his faith in the smaller competitors' superior "ingenuity quotients." Australia and the United Kingdom are next on his agenda. Dave Nichol has seen the future—and it is definitely in attacking the franchises of "big name" grocery players who have grown fat, sassy, and complacent. We are all in his debt.

## REINVENTING THE WAY BUSINESS IS DONE

The opportunities for creating new competitive battlegrounds are by no means limited to developing entirely new products or attacking new market segments. Equally rewarding are the opportunities to those innovative enough to reinvent not so much the industry they are in, but the *way* business is done within existing markets and industries.

### *David vs. Goliath: Nucor and the Minimills*

Like so many other economic sectors, the American steel industry thrived in the postwar economic boom. As in other industries, conventional wisdom dictated that the only way to increase efficiency was through economies of scale, so steel mills got bigger and bigger. The larger they got, however, the less adaptable they became. Weakness in the American car industry, foreign competition and the shift in North America towards "lean production" delivered severe body blows to the large, integrated mills. Poor management, including an appalling labor relations record, overly generous pay increases and slow adoption of new technology, left these mills highly uncompetitive. The industry responded in the early and mid-1980s by reducing capacity by one-third, and employment by fully 60 percent. The somber term "rust belt" became an apt metaphor for the economic decay that radiated out from Pittsburgh across much of the American eastern seaboard.

But not all steelmakers had fallen on hard times. During this crisis, a new breed of steelmaker was coming to the fore, with ideas that would change the steel landscape permanently.

When Ken Iverson took the helm at Nucor, the Charlotte, North Carolina-based minimill company, in 1968, he could not have imagined his company would grow to become the fourth biggest steelmaker in the nation, with annual sales of over $2 billion by 1994. Like the other innovators profiled in this chapter, Iverson turned conventional industry wisdom on its head: He proved that, through more flexible production and innovative management techniques, small can indeed be beautiful—and profitable.

Nucor achieved lower costs partly because its smaller minimills could locate closer to markets and locally available scrap steel than the bigger integrated mills. Even more importantly, its smaller electric arc furnaces were highly automated and much more flexible than the huge blast furnaces of the integrated mills, allowing Nucor to make higher value-added steel products. But according to many analysts, the major success factor for Nucor has been its CEO. Ken Iverson instituted a flat management structure (only four levels), encouraging decisions to be made as close to the action as possible. Long before the word "empowerment" had been discovered by pointy-headed business academics, Iverson was practicing it. A legendary open-door policy, combined with high pay and fair treatment of workers, kept the unions at bay, allowing Nucor to maintain its flexibility.

Nucor has continued to generate competitive advantage through the strategic use of technology. Until recently, minimills were confined to producing bar steel, which restricted them to roughly 50 percent of the overall steel market. After years of research, Nucor developed a method to produce sheet steel, formerly the exclusive preserve of the large integrated mills. The new method uses sophisticated computer technology to control the rush of molten metal into narrow mould openings. The thinner slabs formed by this method require less expensive rolling than the thicker ones produced at the integrated mills. The procedure allows Nucor to make a ton of sheet steel in forty-five minutes, as opposed to three hours for the large integrated producers. This translates into a $50–$75 saving on a $310 ton of sheet steel. Nucor is well on its way to quadrupling its production of sheet steel between 1992 and 1995.

Even more importantly, Nucor has taught the business world at least two important lessons. First, even firms in mature and declining industries like steel can be both highly innovative and profitable. And second, a small, nimble, resourceful competitor can often run rings around a bigger, better financed opponent who lacks the necessary flexibility, agility and openness to new approaches.

And Nucor isn't done yet. Like all truly innovative companies, Nucor is not content to sit back, even though they've already reinvented their industry once. In the spring of 1995, Nucor put together an ambitious new alliance with American steel and industrial gas company, Proxair. If successful, Nucor's latest initiative will create even larger shock waves than its first. For seventy years, steel companies have been searching for their industry's philosopher's stone: direct steelmaking. Conventional steelmaking involves intermediate steps such as blast furnaces and cooking ovens, which are enormously expensive and environmentally destructive. Nucor believes it can make steel directly from iron carbide, which it currently produces at its plant in Trinidad—the world's first. If successful—and Chairman Ken Iverson rates his chances at no less than 50-50—Nucor could cut the cost of producing liquid steel by fully one third. Even if the new process doesn't work, the iron carbide can still be used as a more dependable and cost-effective replacement for scrap iron as a steelmaking input. But don't bet against Nucor on the home-run gamble, either.

## *Dell Computers: Reinventing Marketing and Distribution*

By the time Texas-based Dell Computers arrived on the scene in 1984, the personal computer industry had been well established by Apple, IBM and their imitators. Most of the major product innovations in the industry had either already occurred or would be the preserve of the early leaders, who had built up formidable barriers against competition. Surveying this scene from his college dorm in the mid-1980s, Austin wunderkind Michael Dell (a venerable nineteen year old) recognized that an entirely different approach and focus would be required for an upstart firm like his to make an impact. And he found it: He would reinvent the PC industry's distribution and marketing system.

Before Michael Dell, computer manufacturers generally sold their products through their own retailers, or through retail chains. Face-to-face customer service was deemed an essential part of the computer sales business. However, Dell had discerned an industry trend that would soon make him rich: PCs were becoming increasingly commoditized. Dell recognized that, apart from technical specifications, there was little differentiation in PCs, so customers should easily be able to purchase them by mail or over the phone from competent sales reps. His response was to pioneer the concept of direct-to-consumer marketing for computers. Instead of bricks-and-mortar stores, Dell invested in an extensive battery of telephone lines and a network of courier trucks that could deliver products the next day. To reduce customer unease, Dell offered unlimited calls to a 1-800 number for technical support, a thirty-day money-back guarantee, and free on-site service for the first year of ownership. Although the costs associated with this level of service meant that Dell was not the low-cost producer in its industry, the quality of service allowed the firm to build up an incredibly loyal following. Says Michael Dell:

"Our telephone sellers aren't nerds with telephones. Most aren't supertechnical people, but they *do* understand that everything starts with the customer."

Dell's telephone/mail-order strategy means the firm has considerably lower sales and marketing expenses than its competitors. In 1993, Dell's selling and administrative expenses accounted for just 14 cents out of every sales dollar, compared with 24 cents at Apple and 30 cents at IBM. The company can also customize machines faster because its production is more centralized; conventional computer retailers have to order from the factory and wait for delivery. Dell's inventories are kept down because its computers are all kept in one place rather than scattered in dealer warehouses across the country.

Michael Dell considers himself more of a marketing and distribution pioneer than a computer guru. Like many pioneers, however, it took some time for his own industry to notice him. Said Dell in 1992: "If I read the trade magazines, I'd say that the industry still doesn't take us very seriously. But when some of our competitors put in their own [1-800] telephone lines nine months ago, it was an indication that they're no longer ignoring us." Competitors are certainly noticing now, with Dell's sales exceeding $2 billion in 1993.

Of course, in the world of commerce, imitation has always been the highest form of flattery. Aspects of Dell's once unique strategy are now being copied by IBM, Apple and Digital, among others, creating the first real test of Dell's staying power. If there is one lesson to be emphasized above all others in this book, it is this: *A single innovation or advantage is never enough. You must keep generating new innovations faster than your competitors can copy your last one.* Michael Dell understood this intuitively. He recognized that, aside from making him a multi-millionaire, reinventing the marketing and distribution dimensions of the PC industry had really only bought him a few years' breathing space before rivals would replicate his innovation and perhaps even surpass it.

Not wanting to be written off as a corporate has-been before his thirtieth birthday, Dell has already launched the next wave of innovation. To keep ahead of his new competition, the company has launched an entirely new and much broader suite of products (DellWare) that includes software, PC games and computer peripherals like modems and printers. Dell's goal is to become a mail-order computer superstore, still featuring its trademark top-quality servicing network and "factory direct to you" distribution.

## The Virtual Fashion Company: Italy's Benetton

Another leading exemplar of dramatically reinventing the way an existing industry is conducted is the Italian firm, Benetton. No one in the $2 billion company would dream of arguing that Benetton invented the clothing or fashion industries. What it did do, however, was literally reinvent how the industry worked.

Founded in Italy in 1965 by Carlo, Giuliana, Gilberto and Luciano Benetton, the company bearing their family name is today a household word in over 110 countries. The key to Benetton's success is its refusal to play by the prevailing rules of the clothing and fashion industries. Conventional wisdom said that a clothing company should design, manufacture, advertise and sometimes even retail its own products. Instead, Benetton concentrates on the areas where it can achieve technological economies of scale: design, cutting, dyeing, quality control and above all, advertising. It farms out almost all its manufacturing and retailing, thereby minimizing its own capital requirements.

Benetton provides production planning, raw materials, technical assistance and financial aid to roughly 350–400 small, ultra flexible clothing manufacturers near its head office north of Venice. Its system of centralized buying allows the company to achieve massive economies of scale in its raw materials (it is the world's largest wool purchaser). Because Benetton operates as a "system of systems," the core company remains small, nimble and flexible: a key attribute for the fast-moving world of fashion. In this sense, Benetton is the archetype of the 21st century "virtual" corporation—quarterbacking a complex and constantly shifting set of partners on the periphery, monopolizing at the center only those parts of the product value chain where it can excel and can add real value. Says Giancarlo Chiodini, Benetton's top logistics executive: "Our logistics system *has* to be this responsive because the fashion markets change so quickly."

On the retail side, Benetton avoids the costs, headaches and distractions of the real estate business by selling through independent shop owners, who agree to carry Benetton products exclusively. In return, Benetton offers quick delivery and a massive (4.7 percent of sales in 1992) advertising campaign. Its controversial advertising, including pictures of a dying AIDS patient, a newborn baby and the blood-soaked uniform of a Bosnian soldier, has created one of the most powerful brand images in the world. The Benetton name can be seen on everything from Formula 1 racing cars to watches and sunglasses.

Benetton is now responding to the new challenges created by the flight of significant clothing manufacturing capacity to low-wage countries in the Third World. Part of Benetton's response is to make strategic new technological investments in its Italian subcontractors. That, however, is just the beginning. In preparation for its planned doubling of sales over the next seven years, mainly through expansion into developing countries, the company is also forming new joint ventures with Chinese, Turkish, Indian and

Mexican partners. The true test of Benetton's ability to reinvent the fashion industry value chain is yet to come. Will the company be able to replicate on a global basis the logistics wizardry it refined to such devastating effect in northern Italy? Only a fool would bet against them.

---

## SETTING NEW INDUSTRY STANDARDS

---

*"Money is made by setting de facto standards."*
BILL GATES, CHAIRMAN, MICROSOFT [4]

Take it from Bill, he ought to know. The next best thing to inventing a new industry outright is creating the standards everybody in that industry has to meet—or else. In fact, as Mr. Gates has convincingly demonstrated, sometimes it's even better. After all, Gates didn't invent the computer industry. But through a felicitous combination of luck, skill and timing, Gates acquired and improved what would become the DNA of the exploding computer era: the MS-DOS operating system. Over time, MS-DOS became the *de facto* world standard, and the center of a worldwide web of dependencies among both customers and manufacturers of hardware, software and components. At the centre of this web? You guessed it: Mr. Gates and the corporate juggernaut he built by creating the world standard. Since then, all Gates' competitors have been playing catch-up, while Bill amuses himself dreaming up new ways to leverage fresh value out of the global computing franchise he has built.

The high-profile battle between Sony and Matsushita to set the de facto standard for consumer videotapes was a similar, if less spectacular, example. In less than two years, Matsushita's technically inferior VHS format had crushed Sony's Betamax system, turning it into the video-age equivalent of the Edsel. Today, other high-stakes battles are being played out in such fields as HDTV (high-definition television) and computer chips. Few of these battles will be more interesting or more far-reaching than the looming struggle to set the world standard for our next emerging megaindustry: multimedia.

### *General Magic: The Artful Conjurers*

Friday, February 10, 1995 was a very good day indeed for General Magic, a 1990 Apple Computer Inc. spin-off. That was the day of its initial public stock offering. Share prices opened at $14, but within minutes had skyrocketed to US$32. By the end of its first day of trading, General Magic shares had become the fifth most active issue in American equity markets, closing at US $26⅝ on Nasdaq, up 90 percent from its initial offering price. This, from a company with almost $60 million in costs thus far, zero profits, "substantial" losses predicted at least to 1997,[4] and a technology with absolutely no track record. How did this software upstart come so far so fast? It mixed together a heady brew of vision, crème-de-la-crème talent, shrewd marketing and strategic partnerships with companies looking to cash in on the biggest bonanza in computer history. General Magic had convinced the world that it could create the de facto standard for multimedia technology.

The personal philosophy of Marc Porat, president and chief executive of General Magic, is to "Make sure there is a vision in the company—a shared vision—that is so powerful that once a person joins the family, they barely have to be reminded of what to do,"[5] And what a family! Porat's cofounders of General Magic are software development icons Andrew Herzfeld and William Atkinson, two of the original creators of the legendary Apple Macintosh.

And what a vision! In 1990, Porat predicted that, by using his fiber-optic and wireless communications software invention called Telescript, we would be able to send electronic "agents" to do our shopping, make our hotel, restaurant and travel reservations and oh, so much more for us. (In fact, about the only thing these electronic messengers won't be able to do is run the White House. On second thought . . . .)

But Porat did not bet the bank on just one technology to beat. General Magic is already pushing the envelope by trying to create the de facto industry standard in a second area: personal handheld communicators, otherwise known as "personal digital assistants" or PDAs. Undeterred by the dismal performance of the Newton, Apple Computer's initial entry into this area, Porat and Company have developed an operating system for PDAs called Magic Cap. It can be used in transit or in situ on rival, personal computer operating systems and employs a unique interface which is not just user-friendly, but a positive love-in.

When Porat initially went to raise cash for General Magic, he didn't look to venture capitalists. For one thing, they're too greedy. For another, despite their name, a lot of them just aren't venturesome enough for a truly innovative, path-breaking concept like Porat's. And for a third, they tend to have the attention span and patience level of the average fruit fly. Nope, this project called for a commitment of patient, long-term capital. Accordingly, Porat took his vision (and top-drawer talent) to future users and propagators of General Magic technologies, including Apple Computer, AT&T, Matsushita Electric, Motorola, Philips, Toshiba and Sony—and raised $77 million from strategic partnerships with them. These partnerships almost certainly guarantee Magic Cap built-in corporate customers, and effectively preempt competitors by locking up the most attractive dance partners.

Five years after General Magic's inception and one month after its successful public offering, where stands the vision today? Where can you access General Magic's amazing services? Well, nowhere really. At least not in its fully conceived state. To date, only AT&T has actually based a service on Telescript. On the strength of their compelling vision, their technology track records in previous incarnations and some shrewd alliance building, Porat and his partners have succeeded in becoming the acknowledged industry-standard setters for a technology that few consumers have actually tried. Porat's feats of conjuring economic value out of (so far) thin air suggest that General Magic is perhaps more aptly named than even its founders intended. But general reality is about to kick in.

General Magic will face stiff competition from competitors such as IBM, Microsoft and Silicon Graphics, who are bent on knocking it off track in the race to dominate future information technologies. The stakes are enormous: The ability to monopolize at least a couple of lanes of the information superhighway. But don't sell General Magic short. With its heavy-hitting investor partners committed to using its technologies, General Magic has launched a huge preemptive strike in the race to set the standard for one of the next monster industries.

## The Boys From Netscape: Microsoft's Worst Nightmare

There can be no more dramatic or contemporary illustration of the financial power of setting *de facto* industry standards than the phenomenal recent success of Netscape. The California company went public on August 9, 1995 at $28 per share. Notwithstanding its virtually nonexistent revenues, Netscape's shares skyrocketed to $75 in a matter of hours. By December, its stock price had broken the $170 barrier, before settling back to the merely stratospheric level of $140 in early 1996. The company's current stock market valuation is currently roughly five *billion* dollars. If anything, or anyone, can pose a realistic threat to Bill Gates' mantle as the J.D. Rockefeller of the postindustrial world, it is surely Netscape and its brain trust of chairman Jim Clark and technology wizard Marc Andreeson.

Clark, a former Standford University professor, had already made his reputation (and his first fortune) as one of the original founding fathers of Silicon Graphics. His $500 million paper profit on the day Netscape went public and the billion-dollar current value of his Netscape stock are simply icing on the cake. Andreeson, today a multimillionaire before his twenty-fifth birthday, is only a few years removed from his job writing software code at an Illinois university for the princely sum of $6.85 per hour. Think of him as a mid-90's version of Horatio Alger, albeit one with a voracious appetite for pizza, Oreo cookies, and taco chips.

In the beginning, there was the Internet. Initially created in 1969 by U.S. Defense Department scientists for use as a small-scale, internal communications tool, by mid-1996 the Internet had become the *lingua franca* of the entire information technology revolution. Its most important progeny, the World Wide Web, had originally emerged from the European Particle Physics Lab near Geneva. Developed by Tim Berners-Lee, the Web significantly increased the coherence, accessibility, and utility of the Internet, and moved it firmly beyond the esoteric preserve of particle physicists and their ilk. But even so, at that point the Web lacked the ability to access or transmit either sound or video images. This was a major barrier to opening up the Web and the Internet to a broader, mainstream audience—and to their true commercial potential. That task would ultimately fall to Mark Andreeson and his colleagues, most of whom were barely old enough to shave.

The key to unlocking the power of the World Wide Web turned out to be an access program called Mosaic, created in an inspired orgy of code-writing by Andreeson and his intellectual sidekick Eric Bina at the University of Illinois' National Center for Supercomputing Applications between January and March of 1993. Elegant, spare and parsimonious (a mere 9,000 lines of code, compared to Windows 95's 11 million) Mosaic would ultimately make it possible, for the first time, for anybody with a PC and a bit of new software to harness the almost unimaginable information power of the Internet.

Following Andreeson's graduation in December 1993, the University of Illinois was gracious enough to invite him to stay on at the supercomputing center—on one condition: that he abandon the Mosaic project. Not unreasonably—particularly in retrospect—he declined, and decamped instead to Silicon Valley. There he attracted the attention of Valley legend Jim Clark, the man who had virtually invented 3-D computer graphics and founded the wildly-successful Silicon Graphics company described elsewhere in this book. Clark hired Andreeson, Andreeson hired Bina, and the rest, as they say, is history—albeit a history that is still unfolding as this book is being written.

Working out of cheap, cramped quarters in Mountain View, California, Andreeson, Bina, and a half-dozen other young programmers poached from their former Illinois group set to work creating a more advanced, robust, and commercially useable version of Mosaic, which ultimately became the Netscape Navigator. While it wasn't in their original business plan, Clark and Andreeson hit on the then-novel software marketing strategy of giving their product away. That's right: *giving* it away. The idea was that, having enticed the customer into the game with a freebie, they could then sell him a virtually endless stream of related, value-added products and enhancements. To say that the strategy worked would be the height of understatement: within a few months Netscape captured a 70% share of the Web browser market, and it remains the frontrunner today.

But what *really* solidified Netscape's claim on world commercial history was its integration and close alliance with Java, the newly dominant programming language for the World Wide Web. Just as Bill Gates and Paul Allen had previously galvanized the entire personal computer market by creating their Basic programming language, Java was to be the key to unlocking the power – and the full commercial potential—of the World Wide Web and the Internet. Created by Sun Microsystems' software genii Bill Joy and James Gosling, Java and Netscape became the *de facto* standards for accessing the Web. Software programmers designing Web "sites" for their corporate clients naturally began designing them specifically to capitalize on Netscape's particular features. This created precisely the same sort of virtuous circle of dependency which Mr. Gates had exploited so successfully under the "old" paradigm of proprietary operating systems and desktop-centered computing.

By tying Netscape to Java, Clark and Andreeson not only ensured their place at the epicenter of the Web's rapidly-expanding commercial universe, but they may well have also permanently dislodged Bill Gates from his familiar perch as Supreme Being of the Information Age. Suddenly, the foundations of the world as we know it were being shaken. Dismissed by Gates only months earlier as inconsequential, the Internet now held the potential to undermine the very basis of his entire corporate franchise. The power and importance of the individual PC and its operating systems were being eclipsed, superceded by an historically unprecedented capacity to access directly the full informational power and resources of the estimated thirty *million* computers currently hooked into the Internet. This created, for the first time, the very real prospect of a widespread users' emancipation from the entire mainstream (Microsoft-dominated) computing paradigm, predicated as it is on individual desktop PCs and proprietary, noncompatible operating systems. In the apocalyptic words of technology guru George Gilder, "Your computer will never be the same. From now on, the relevant computer is the *network*, and the computer becomes a peripheral to the Internet and the Web. The ascendant software is Internet software . . . owning the operating system becomes irrelevant."[6]

All of this is bad news indeed for Mr. Gates, who for the first time in his life finds himself playing catch-up. Now, it's still a bit early to write Bill Gates' commercial obituary; after all, you can play a helluva lot of catch-up with 50 billion dollars and tens of thousands of bright people. But the boys from Netscape sure have made things interesting, and have demonstrated emphatically that *two* can play the game of setting the *de facto* standards for computing.

## CONCLUSION

Each of the companies profiled in this chapter has one thing in common: Their approach represented a *fundamental* departure from the status quo in their industry. Indeed, for companies like the early Apple and MTV, it was more a question of creating an entirely new industry. In future, the accelerating pace and ferocity of global competition will mean that more and more companies will need to do likewise—or go out of business.

Precisely because strategic reframing goes against the grain of conventional business thinking, it will become even more important in the coming decades. Increasingly, corporate leadership will be based on improvement that is not merely continuous and incremental, but frequently nonlinear and exponential. In the past, much of this improvement was driven by technological change. But as old technologies become commonplace and commoditized, a constant supply of new ideas and approaches will also be needed to gain competitive advantage.

This will require a truly fundamental paradigm shift for business leaders. Rather than slugging it out for miniscule, and increasingly temporary advantage in well-delineated markets and industries, tomorrow's winners will be creating entirely new industries and competitive space for themselves.

As I have demonstrated in this chapter, there are many different ways to create this new competitive space. You can create a whole new industry à la Apple and MTV, or, like Netscape and General Magic, attempt to set the *de facto* standards for an emerging one being built by others. Alternatively, you can completely reinvent the way an existing industry works, the way Dell and Nucor have done, or create entirely new value out of apparently familiar commodities like watches and soap, the way Swatch and The Body Shop have done.

The point is simply this: Competing for existing markets is rapidly becoming yesterday's game. At best it is still today's. Companies aspiring to make any kind of impact tomorrow must realize they are really playing an altogether different game: Competing for the future.[7]

### CHAPTER THREE

# GET INNOVATIVE OR GET DEAD

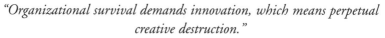

*"Organizational survival demands innovation, which means perpetual creative destruction."*

PETER DRUCKER

It has been argued persuasively that "the essence of strategy lies in creating tomorrow's competitive advantages faster than competitors can mimic the ones you possess today."[1] If this is true, and I devoutly believe it is, then surely the essence of strategy must therefore lie in building an infrastructure for consistent innovation (along with its close relative, organizational learning).

In this century, we have already seen the basis of competitive advantage shift at least three times: from price and volume to quality, then to speed, and finally to "mass customization." Each era has incorporated the attributes of its predecessors and then added new and progressively more challenging requirements. In what promises to be an even more volatile and demanding 21st century, the competitive ante will be jacked up even higher. Factors that were once genuine competitive advantages are now simply the minimum admission requirements for staying in the game. The premium has shifted to the ability to manage major, strategic change effectively and almost continually—in short, to innovate consistently.

For decades, bloated companies such as IBM, AT&T and Sears could simply coast, relying on their sheer mass and market muscle to achieve steady, if unspectacular, profitability. Innovation was not a competitive necessity—and this was just as well, because the cultures and structures of the behemoths militated strongly against it. Today, however, with competition coming from a dizzying range of unanticipated sources, a "steady as she goes" business strategy has become a recipe for oblivion. Companies must innovate and innovate continuously to have any hope of survival, let alone dominance. And while innovations in technology, production, marketing and finance all remain essential, it is innovation in *management and strategy* that is most desperately in short supply.

The main problem, in my view, is that corporate CEOs have been seduced by a false god. At the risk of unfairly vilifying business-school professors and their ilk, academics have done executives an unspeakable disservice by holding out the false promise of the corporate Holy Grail: The attainment of *sustainable* competitive advantage.

It was one thing to strive for sustainable advantage in the era of the buggy whip, or even the transistor radio. You simply made them better or cheaper than the next guy—and occasionally you even did both. In today's era of hypercompetition, you need to be better, cheaper, faster, flexible, responsive and creative *just to get into the game!* What's more, once you're in the game, you can rarely tell which direction your next adversary is coming from, or even from which industry. Today's competitive environment is to classical business strategy what high-energy quantum physics is to Sir Isaac Newton and falling apples.

In such a turbulent business environment, it not only becomes nonsensical to talk about sustainable competitive advantage, it becomes positively dangerous. Companies subscribing to the sustainability myth misdirect their intellectual and financial energies into attempting to build impregnable competitive fortresses. Strategies constructed and executed in pursuit of sustainable advantage are likely to be far too mechanistic, inflexible and sclerotic for contemporary circumstances. The half-life of monolithic, strategic fortresses has shrunk to almost nothing, and their legacy is a hardening of companies' neural pathways, leaving them incapable of rapid response to changing competitive circumstances.

So what is to be done? To be blunt, there are only two choices: Get Innovative or Get Dead![2] It's that simple, and that complicated. The first step is to abandon the pernicious notion that *any* advantage can be sustained for long, and instead to build the corporate capacity to innovate repeatedly. That will be what separates the corporate winners from the losers in the early 21st century.

Unfortunately, merely resolving that your company will henceforth become innovative is clearly nowhere near sufficient. And, while there is no unanimity in the strategy literature about precisely how to go about actually delivering innovation, there is a consensus that the problem lies more in the lack of innovation in management than in technology, finance or production.

We can discern a number of common characteristics among truly innovative companies. For starters, they tend to pursue a multiplicity of smaller initiatives rather than putting all of their innovation eggs into one or two large baskets. They favor early and frequent "reality testing" of new products, services and ideas, and are eager to incorporate the resulting feedback into new and improved iterations. They consciously structure their incentive and reward systems to encourage successful innovations and to celebrate and broadcast them forcefully to colleagues. Incentives can include money (which is often, perhaps surprisingly, not the most effective method), sought-after new assignments, and the opportunity to create entirely new "intrepreneurial" vehicles within the company. With corporate hierarchies compressing dramatically, innovative companies are beginning to devote serious attention to developing *horizontal* fast tracks for the careers of their brightest people.

But incentives and rewards aren't everything; setting exacting expectations is also critical. At 3M, for example, continuous innovation is promoted by a sacrosanct company policy: 30 percent of annual revenues must come from products less than four years old. And just to add a bit more incentive, executive compensation is explicitly tied to the achievement of those targets.

Some leading Japanese innovators go 3M one better, pushing the concept of raised expectations to what must surely be its outer limits. Sony and Mitsubishi, for example, use the technique of "systematic abandonment" with devastating effectiveness. Whenever they introduce a new product, they simultaneously set a sunset date at which they will deliberately abandon that same product. This immediately triggers work on developing a replacement offering. The object is to create three new products for every one they phase out: an incrementally improved old product, a new product spin-off from the original, and an entirely new innovation. In the distinctly un-Japanese words of one senior American executive: "It's far better to eat your own lunch than to have one of your competitors do it for you!"

Perhaps most important of all, innovative companies make a fetish out of consciously linking innovation with organizational learning. In part, this is a matter of refusing to confine the responsibility for creativity and innovation to the organizational ghetto of a single department: R&D, the chairman's office or anywhere else. Leading world-class companies encourage, expect and reward innovation from everybody: executives, managers, secretaries and the people on the loading dock. At their best, outstanding companies transcend the innovation itself, learning *how* to innovate successfully, and then disseminating that learning throughout the firm.

For those with the energy and commitment to pursue it, a culture of corporate innovation can be consciously created and maintained—but only if the CEO genuinely believes it is a real competitive necessity in his or her industry. Sadly, remarkably few do. Let's look at some exceptions, companies with a superior track record of repeated and consistent innovation.

## 3M: The Grand-daddy of Innovation

3M's legendary reputation for innovation is richly deserved. The corporate culture of 3M has historically embraced product innovation with an almost evangelical fervor. (Without it, we might still be living in a world devoid of sticky Post-it Notes—a prospect I, for one, would rather not contemplate.) This is the spirit that made 3M into the $14-billion-a-year consumer and industrial goods giant it is today. But simply declaring your company's intention to be innovative is nowhere near enough; the road to bankruptcy is often paved with innovative intentions. So how do they actually do it?

3M did it by creating the organizational culture, structures and human resource pool necessary to support and nourish a climate of consistent creativity and innovation. At its heart is a characteristic extremely rare in multi-billion-dollar-a-year corporations: 3M is actually flexible. New ideas and new tactics are embraced, celebrated, developed and tested. If they don't work, 3M quickly pulls the plug and moves on. This flexibility starts at the top and suffuses all levels of the company's organizational structure.

3M's strategic architecture of innovation has a number of key components. Perhaps the most celebrated is the corporate fiat mentioned above: that fully 30 percent of all revenues must be generated by products introduced in the previous four years. (It used to be 25 percent and five years.) Talk about a structural incentive to innovate!

Of course, many companies can and do set such lofty goals, but few achieve them with such stunning and repeated success. So how does a company with the girth of a 350-pound Super-Bowl lineman (85,000 employees worldwide) move with the speed and agility of a wide receiver to stay ahead of the competition? The answer is both simple and complicated. From senior management on down, 3M hires the best people and then respects, supports and, in fact, insists on their efforts to think, learn and create—in short, to innovate. And in business, that in itself turns out to be a real rarity.

At 3M, technicians are given the freedom to spend anywhere from 15 to 50 percent of their time researching their own pet projects. Particularly promising concepts are awarded up to $50,000 in Genesis Grants to help develop them to the next stage. Individual creativity is then further enhanced through collaboration among different disciplines. Salespeople are in continuous dialogue with customers to find out what they need or want, preferably before even the customer knows it. Then the salespeople dialogue with the technicians to initiate the creation of new products. This emphasis on a team mentality and the concommitant sharing of ideas is a fundamental tenet of 3M's culture.

The story of the creation of Post-it Notes has become almost a corporate cliché but bear with me; it illustrates the coming together of 3M's best practices. 3M employee Art Fry needed a convenient way to mark individual pages of his hymn book at church for quick reference—a simple little problem needing a potentially money-making solution. He discussed his thoughts with a guy in a different department, Spence Silver, who had already developed a new adhesive for 3M. You know the rest. 3M sold over $100 million of Post-it Notes in 1994. Mark Twain once said that an expert "is just some damn fool from someplace else." 3M's genius was to recognize that the damn fool needed for the company's next blockbuster product might just be sitting in an office in another department. All 3M had to do was remove the barriers.

What's in it for the employees who share their ideas and help generate big profits for 3M? Well, financial incentives and being lionized at glitzy company extravaganzas aren't a bad place to start. But what many people value even more is the knowledge that 3M won't abandon them lightly when the going gets tough. In 1991, the icy fingers of the recession had touched even 3M's robust corpus. The company hadn't been able to raise real prices on products in four years. At other megacompanies, CEOs were responding to the times by cutting thousands from their staff, many of whom had been with the company the longest and were thus potentially the richest repository of ideas to rescue their company from the doldrums. Did 3M CEO L. D. (Desi) DeSimone embrace this no-brainer solution? That isn't DeSimone's way and it certainly isn't the 3M way.

Instead of laying people off, DeSimone increased the R&D budget and raised his expectations of his people's innovative capacities even higher. The old 25 percent new products rule became 30 percent, and the time frame shortened by a year. The results? Fifty new products were identified and over half were brought to market—several of them in record time. One of these was new-market-contender Scotch-Brite scrubbing pads which, in their first two years, captured almost 25 percent of the $100 million yearly market from their competitors. These new products alone will put $1 billion onto 3M's bottom line by the end of the decade.

Human-resource professionals take note: 3M's innovation-driven corporate culture has another major benefit. It breeds almost fanatical loyalty and staying power in the company's employees. In the words of one observer: "The Mafia gets more resignations than 3M!"

## *Silicon Graphics: Pushing the Envelope in Cyberspace*

In selecting case examples for this book, Silicon Graphics was an obvious choice. The only problem was where to put it. In the chapter on consistent innovation? On speed? On setting industry standards? This is a company that has achieved them all in great measure. In the end, I settled on the innovation chapter because everything this company does, it does with one goal in mind: Keeping Silicon Graphics ahead of the competition. "Our philosophy," says President Ed McCracken, "is that the key to achieving competitive advantage isn't reacting to chaos; it's producing that chaos. And the key to being a chaos producer is being an innovation leader."[3]

Silicon Graphics was ahead of the crowd from day one. In 1982, founder James H. Clark brought us the world's first silicon chip embedded with a graphics code. This chip provided the necessary speed for 3D visual computing. Since then, Silicon Graphics has maintained its preeminent position by totally rejecting mainstream computer industry orthodoxy.

Established (and endangered) companies like IBM and DEC traditionally pursued mass markets and economies of scale to manage recessionary hard times. This, however, has led to a deadly spiral of low margins, decreased R&D spending and a resultant diminished capacity to innovate. Silicon Graphics chose an entirely different strategy. It attacked a high-end, value-added, almost customized market niche to produce computer workstations for scientists, engineers and other professionals on the cutting edge of R&D. With sales of $1.5 billion and a profit margin 10 percent higher than its major competitors, Silicon Graphics has enjoyed the luxury of spending 12 percent of revenues on R&D.

This is not to say the company isn't interested in mass markets. In 1993, it introduced the Indy, a computer for the consumer market costing less than $5,000. McCracken has been cautious in taking Silicon Graphics in this direction—in fact, too cautious for chairman and founder Clark. When he thought they should push faster into low-end markets, McCracken stuck to his guns. Consequently, Clark left in 1994 to start his own company—again. He has to be the only person in Silicon Valley who thinks Ed McCracken moves too slowly. (In Clark's defense, that new company turned out to be Netscape. Since, as we have seen (pp. 30–32), Netscape put $500 million in Clark's pocket on the day it went public, it's difficult to be *too* critical of his departure.)

To ensure that Silicon Graphics' hardware always sets the industry standard, the company consciously targets the most demanding, sophisticated, "lighthouse" customers it can find for input on what the current equipment *can't* do and what the next generation *should* make possible. This way, Silicon

Graphics doesn't respond to market trends, it dictates them. To reinforce this strategy, Silicon Graphics' engineers incorporate the most recent customer feedback as close to the end of their development cycle as possible, to ensure their technology is perpetually on the cutting edge. Company policy also aims for twelve- to eighteen-month planning cycles. Even Hewlett-Packard has only been able to manage a two-year planning cycle, which is itself considered lightning fast among mammoth computer companies. The ability to crank out state-of-the-art innovations repeatedly is McCracken's most formidable weapon in his ongoing campaign to create chaos for his competitors. It seems to be working.

Silicon Graphics keeps its employees constantly pumped up by creating a culture of fun and freedom, and almost a mythology of elitism. The message is: "If you're the best in your field, we're the right company for you." Says team leader Pavan Nigam: "To us, engineers are gods. Engineers are the creators, and everyone else, including managers, are there to serve them."

Constant innovation inevitably leads to the cannibalization of existing product offerings, which is just fine with McCracken. He says: "We don't pay a lot of attention to whether or not a product is still gaining market share when we decide to launch a new product. This approach is the only way to ensure that no one gets to the market first with a faster, better, cheaper product. When someone beats us to the market, which has happened only a very few times, we are embarrassed."[4]

It may be hard to believe that a company barely more than a decade old has already needed to reinvent itself, but such is life in the 21st century world of global hyper-competition. Like many other companies, Silicon Graphics had concentrated on selling to the American defence department, which used SG's million dollar 3D computers to simulate the testing of military hardware. When the Berlin Wall came tumbling down and defence budgets were cut, the company was forced to look for other markets with deep pockets for its high-end technology. It turned to the greatest simulator of them all: Hollywood. Silicon Graphics' 3D technology gave films such as *Jurassic Park, The Mask* and *The Flintstones* much of their box office draw capacity, and will give visitors the magic carpet ride of their lives in Aladdin exhibits at Disney theme parks.

The entertainment industry has not only given the company huge new sources of both revenue and leading-edge, demanding clients, it has given them an entry into mass markets and the glamour the Pentagon never could. When American President Bill Clinton and Vice President Al Gore held their technology conference in Silicon Valley in 1994, Silicon Graphics was the only technology company they visited personally.

Silicon Graphics has striven mightily to preserve the virtues of staying small, even as it grew. Any work not considered a core competency is quickly contracted out. Partnerships with Time Warner and Nintendo have let SG enter the interactive TV and video games markets without adding substantially to its own bulk. However, Microsoft Corporation's bid to dominate the market for computer-generated images by taking over Canada's computer graphics software leader, Softimage, has forced Silicon Graphics to rethink its small is best policy. In 1995, it merged with Alias Research Inc. of Canada and Wavefront Technologies Inc. of Santa Barbara so that, in Ed McCracken's words: "We can build the digital studio for the 21st century for the entertainment industry, because that is the future of film, television commercials and video games."[5]

But no one, not even Silicon Graphics, will get a free ride to the future. There are industry rumors SG's ultra-fast development cycles are slowing to speeds comparable to, say Hewlett-Packard's, one of Silicon Graphics' biggest, and I do mean biggest, competitors. Can the creators of *Jurassic Park*'s dinosaurs grow to the size of Tyrannosaurus Rex while still maintaining the speed and agility of the small (but vicious) Velociraptor? I, for one, would hesitate to bet against them.

## Canon: Where Craziness Is a Virtue

There is much in Japanese business practices that North American executives would do well to emulate, but seething cauldrons of innovation they normally ain't. Which makes the case of Canon Inc. doubly interesting. By any standard, Canon has demonstrated a willingness to reinvent itself and take risks often enough to earn a place in the pantheon of noteworthy corporate innovators. Perhaps this was inevitable, given its corporate culture. Canon President Hajime Mitarai views risk taking as the only logical response to the velocity of technological advancement, which makes the obsolescence of today's technologies a certainty. Or, as he has put it: "We should do something when people say it is crazy. Crazy is praise for us. If people say something is good, it means that someone else is already doing it."[6]

Twenty years ago, Canon was "just" a household name in cameras. Canon management recognized the self-limiting nature of its business—and the need to innovate if its company was to survive. This type of forward thinking was unusual. Canon's major Japanese competitors in the camera business, Nikon and Minolta, did not come to the same conclusion, and have recently run into major financial difficulties as a result.

Risking R&D money to diversify out of cameras and into picture taking of a different sort, Canon built on its core competency of precision mechanics and fine optics. The result was the development of a low-cost disposable drum for minicopiers and the addition of microelectronics and electronic imaging to its arsenal of core competencies. Canon then proceeded to capitalize on the market for small personal copiers, a market niche unrecognized (or undervalued) by its competitors. And it had a very precise, focused goal: Take on and thrash copier giant Xerox. Within a few short years, Canon successfully dominated the personal copier market.

Not content to rest on its laurels, however, Canon continued to take risks. It leveraged its increasingly sophisticated and diverse core competencies into new markets. In a single decade, Canon doubled its revenues to over $18 billion in 1994, and dominated the world market in low-end copiers, color copiers and laser-printer engines. The magnitude of the risk Canon took can be better understood against the backdrop of the times: It diversified into laser-printers before anyone was using personal computers on a significant scale.

Canon achieved its triumphs using techniques not unfamiliar to Western companies, but certainly innovative and unorthodox by Japanese standards. In order to raise money for R&D in new areas, Canon licensed some of its best established technologies (good old Japanese know-how) to American companies, including its chief rival, Xerox. Guarding your technologies fiercely may work for many large, established companies, but sometimes being innovative means simply doing what you have to do to survive at any given point in time. To quote that guru of Japanese business thought, country singer Kenny Rogers: "You gotta know when to hold 'em, and know when to fold 'em."

Also against the grain of mainstream Japanese business practice, Canon abandoned traditional cradle-to-grave employment practices, and now receives promising new employees with open arms. Like Raychem and 3M, Canon places high expectations on its employees to innovate. Technicians *must* apply for three to four patents a year.

The road to world dominance is not without hazard, but Canon shows flexibility and creativity in this area too. Canon management recognizes no-go situations, pulls the plug early and learns from its mistakes. One particularly innovative example of this was the response to its early inability to stay ahead of the competition even though Canon was first on the scene with a new technology. It correctly analyzed the problem as operational and fixed it. Canon restructured its management into three separate systems for development, production and marketing. The reasoning was that the mind-sets and skills required for development, for example, were essentially the same regardless of the specific product under consideration. By grouping these skills together in the same unit, specialized experience and insights could be effectively consolidated and leveraged to the benefit of the entire range of Canon products.

This flexibilty and willingness to move quickly have ensured that organizational structures are in place to support Canon's innovation strategy. Combining its core competencies in laser and ink-jet technologies with its newly acquired personnel talent in printer marketing and computer software, Canon is poised to challenge Hewlett-Packard's dominance in the growing laser and ink-jet color printer markets, just as it successfully challenged Xerox in the copier market almost two decades ago. Meanwhile, Canon continues to innovate in markets other companies won't touch, such as ferroelectronics.

Ironically, a past failure may provide Canon with the competitive platform for one of its most promising new markets yet. In 1989, Canon introduced a multifunction system combining PC, printer, fax and phone. But the world wasn't ready for this advanced technology and Canon dropped it in 1992. With the move to digitally controlled office environments just around the corner, the world now appears ready. If Canon had not been willing to dream and to risk—to innovate—ten years ago, it would not hold the second best strategic position to catapult into this new market. Who holds the best position? That's right: Once again, Canon has Xerox clearly focused in its sights. Smile for the camera, Xerox!

## Raychem: Attacking Competition by Preempting It

To paraphrase that noted capitalist entrepreneur Leo Tolstoy: "Successful businesses are all alike; every unsuccessful business is unsuccessful in its own way." Probe deeply into the hearts of today's successful businesses and you will invariably find a conscious core commitment to innovation, and a common pattern to their successful innovation strategies.

Raychem CEO Paul Cook has pursued a philosophy of systematic innovation with outstanding results since he founded the company in 1957. Says Cook: "There is no secret. To be an innovative company, you've got to ask for innovation. You assemble a group of talented people who are eager to do new things and put them in an environment where innovation is expected. It's that simple—and that hard . . . We get innovation at Raychem because our corporate strategy is premised on it. Without innovation we die."[7]

By identifying core technologies (such as shape-memory alloys, liquid crystal displays and cross-linked gels) that Raychem could excel at and nobody else was doing, Raychem has not just kept ahead of the competition, it has virtually eliminated it. Cook says: "A different, and I think more powerful, way to compete is to avoid competition altogether. The best way to avoid competition is to sell products that rivals can't touch."[8] Shades of Sun Tzu! For Cook, staying ahead of the competition means exercising a consistent willingness to make obsolete Raychem's most highly and continuously successful products in order to create demand for its new technologies—thus forcing the competition into a constant game of catch-up. In 1990, Raychem began cannibalizing one of its most popular products, a splice-sealing system for telephone cables, which then accounted for more than 10 percent of the company's total sales. Raychem had developed a superior technology called SuperSleeve to replace it. Even though the replacement meant a period of lower margins and a hard sell to customers happy with the old system, the company aimed for 100 percent conversion within two years. Raychem could have contented itself with marginal improvements to the still popular twenty-year-old technology—but then so could the competition. By the time Raychem's competitors catch up with SuperSleeve, Raychem will probably have cannibalized it and moved on to something else.

But Paul Cook is a far cry from the mad scientist working in his lab, oblivious to the requirements of the real world. He is acutely aware that innovation must be economically compelling and that customer needs, the marketplace and the capabilities of competitors determine what is economically practical.

Raychem works hard to achieve the right balance between technical excellence and marketplace savvy. Cook has been so committed to finding the right employees to fit the Raychem corporate culture that, before his retirement as president in 1993 (he stayed on as chairman) he personally committed up to 20 percent of his own time to staff recruitment. Raychem's technologists are the best in their field, and Raychem is outstanding among technology companies for the number of business types it hires to add commercial reality checks to the technological wizardry of the company's scientists.

Raychem uses some of the same techniques as companies like 3M to keep the creative juices flowing, but puts its own unique spin on them. Everyone at Raychem, from janitors to senior executives, from secretaries to technologists, is pressured to innovate—both individually and in teams. Cook himself works the phone and fax machine to keep in constant touch with employees around the world who are working on new ideas. Employees receive financial bonuses commensurate with their *effort* to innovate; they don't necessarily have to be successful as long as the idea was new and showed promise. Teamwork wins recognition in the form of trophies that proudly declare: "I stole somebody else's idea, and I'm using it." Whoever came up with the idea gets a certificate that says: "I had a great idea, and [colleague's name] is using it."

One of Cook's most effective tools for keeping the innovation pot boiling is to act as an internal venture capitalist. It is all too common for high-tech firms to lose bright inventors who take their innovation and try to go it alone. Cook doesn't lose these people, he *funds* them! Typically, Raychem retains a small equity interest in the spin-off. That way, Cook doesn't really lose an employee, he gains a networked colleague and an equity stake in a promising new business.

According to Paul Cook, however, innovation is the easy part of business. New discoveries are exciting. Managing the drudgery of developing the product to market readiness is the real challenge. This is what management sage Peter Drucker aptly terms "the discipline of innovation." Cook believes we could take a page from Japan's book. Japan may not come up with the brilliant ideas in the first place, but it sure has mastered the art of buying the technology licences and getting them to market most efficiently. Cook's response: Don't let them have the licences in the first place. Raychem doesn't succumb to the lure of quick money and thereby lose long-term earning power; it guards its intellectual property zealously. Worldwide, Raychem holds over 4,000 patents with some 9,000 pending, and it enforces them aggressively. Some of the core technologies identified at Raychem thirty years ago, such as radiation chemistry, are still spinning off new ideas and profits.

As in the case of companies like 3M, Raychem's philosophy of innovation is underpinned by a steadfast commitment to R&D. Cook has faced down stiff opposition from both Wall Street and within Raychem itself in order to spend up to 11 percent of sales, even in lean years, on developing projects that may not show returns for years. In fact, Raychem has spent up to twenty-five years developing technologies that are only now beginning to show profits, such as in the area of shape-memory alloys. Projections indicate that profits from this technology are going to be very, very big indeed. And when a company has a track record of eventually yielding very big profits, even Wall Street can occasionally find it in its collective heart to be patient.

## *Honda: The Virtues of "Constructive Contention"*

Honda Motor Company has been called the best managed company in the world. Yet, ironically, Honda has achieved this status by employing an innovative organizational system that might be best termed *anti*management.

Embodied in the Honda Motor Company's operating principles are the goals "Learn, Think, Analyze, Evaluate and Improve," and "Listen, Ask and Speak Up." Now, if all 60,000 Honda employees lived up to company expectations simultaneously, it could get pretty noisy, not to mention contentious.

And that is precisely the point. The constant questioning of ideas, decisions and management is encouraged, even demanded of each employee. Which is precisely why Honda has become one of the world's exemplary practitioners of what one business writer has termed the art of "constructive contention."[9] Honda cofounder Takeo Fujisawa put the case nicely when he said: "There are discordant sounds within a company. As president, you must orchestrate the discordant sounds into a kind of harmony. But you never want too much harmony. One must cultivate a taste for finding harmony within discord, or you will drift away from the forces that keep a company alive."[10]

In a Japanese social and business culture dominated by conformity and unquestioning respect for one's elders and superiors (usually one and the same), Honda's culture of self-criticism and intellectual diversity stands out conspicuously. But it was precisely these values that allowed Honda to transform itself in just twenty-five years from a small, local motorcycle manufacturer to the auto manufacturer that replaced Chrysler among the Big Three.

It is not just management who hears the babel. This innovative enshrining of discord is systemic at Honda. Differing perspectives among Honda's various functional departments are actively encouraged, with the view that intellectual competition will only sharpen and improve the end product. (The German philosopher Hegel would be right at home.) Design and development teams are deliberately staffed with engineers from peripheral disciplines who are unfamiliar with the core technology under development. This is designed to ensure that problems will be approached from different and innovative perspectives, and that conventional wisdom will be challenged and tested.

Young engineers are given extraordinary responsibilities at Honda, and are encouraged to question their seniors sharply in regular *waigaya* sessions, or debates. Years ago, one lowly bench engineer almost took this license too far. He had the audacity to get into a heated argument with company cofounder Soichiro Honda over the relative merits of water and air-cooled engines. So resolute was he that he actually went on strike for a month, withdrawing to a Zen monastery. Impressed by the young man's passionate conviction, Mr. Honda reconsidered and ultimately changed his mind, to the company's subsequent benefit. The young engineer who convinced him was Tadashi Kume, and today he is Honda's CEO. This story is still told today, and forms an important reinforcement of the company's culture of constructive dissent. (The bad news for North American executives is the desperate shortage of Zen monasteries from which to launch successful crusades of "constructive contention" in their own country.)

The management style of Honda's founders remains very much in evidence today. Honda cofounder Takeo Fujisawa always believed his time and influence were best spent rallying the troops. (This was "management by wandering around" long before Tom Peters had even coined the term.) He visited employees at their desks, learning about their work, asking questions, contributing to problem solving, inspiring them. This practice conjures memories of the Paul Cook style of management. But, whereas Raychem's Cook used the phone and the fax to stay in touch with employees after the business outgrew his ability to meet with them personally, Fujisawa empowered other senior executives to play the roving ambassador role when Honda became too large for him to do it alone. For the employees at both companies, the message is the same: their work matters. And Honda executives are not afraid to get their hands dirty—literally.

Fujisawa's approach, however, also had some unusual and unexpected ramifications for senior management, starting with executive perks—like desks. So convinced was he of the effectiveness of this style of management that he insisted that work spaces be designed to enforce it. Even today, no senior executive can get too comfortable behind the proverbial big desk, because there aren't enough desks to go around. Honda's forty senior executives work in a common open area and share six desks. Most work side by side at conference tables, which encourages interaction, facilitates problem solving and discourages "cocooning" at headquarters. Compared with the North American business ethos, where successfully climbing the greasy pole of senior management is generally rewarded with the isolating grandeur of a corner office, Honda's style of management is breathtakingly different.

But innovation at Honda goes well beyond management style and the configuration of furniture. It is systemic, suffusing all the company's operations. It was at Honda that the practice of holding an Idea Contest first began. Twice a year, employees are encouraged to present personal projects developed with the support of time and money from Honda. The prototypes judged to be the most promising are then funded for further development. Few if any of them would have emerged from "normal" product development channels, even in a constructively contentious environment like Honda's.

Innovation at Honda is also demonstrated by a willingness to make obsolete old systems which, while they may have been wildly successful in the past, show signs of being unable to weather new challenges. The Japanese *shusa* system of new product development gave Honda an organizational structure that played a major role in its past successes. In this system, total responsibility for a program was given to a chief engineer, who tended to be more creative with an auto design line than with the bottom line. However, times change and, at Honda at least, systems must change with them if preeminence is to be maintained. Recently, the ultimate responsibility for projects was taken away from the chief engineers and put into the hands of "large project leaders," who tend to bring a more holistic, interdisciplinary perspective to the table. Explains Honda executive Tomoyuki Sugiyama: "We spent more money on the 1990 Accord than we had ever spent in the past, so the profit was not as high as we wanted. We learned a lesson from that."[11]

Honda's extraordinary capacity for innovation and organizational learning was demonstrated again in January 1995, with the announcement that Honda had done what the Big Three automakers had steadfastly declared to be impossible: designed an ultra-low emission vehicle (ULEV) powered by a conventional, internal combustion engine. Leveraging its legendary core competence in engine design, Honda has added bells and whistles such as new cylinder heads and catalytic converters, and new, ultra-high-performance microprocessors to adjust the fuel mix to minimize pollution. The bottom line? In 1997, Honda will become the first major car maker to meet California's ULEV air-quality standards with an essentially conventional engine. Given that California's standards are the toughest in the world, this portends a new competitive advantage for Honda not only in the U.S., but in such environmentally conscious markets as Europe and Japan.

While American automakers were busy hiring high-priced lawyers and lobbyists to complain loudly that the new environmental standards were ruinous and impossible to meet, Honda simply went out and did it.

## Hewlett-Packard: A Silicon Valley Original

What goes around, comes around. Business pundits often talk about the principle of innovation as if it were invented in the 1990s. But hey—the Roman Legions conquered the world using innovative attack techniques and very big shields. And how about the introduction of the longbow in the 14th century? But we really needn't go that far back in history to study the introduction of new methods of conquering the world. In 1938, in the proverbial garage in Silicon Valley, in the throes of the great Depression, Hewlett-Packard was founded on the simple principle of innovation.

William Hewlett and David Packard started their business with little more than five hundred dollars and no products. Their plan was "to use technology in new ways." That's it. Can you imagine raising capital for a new venture with a business plan like that today? You and I almost certainly couldn't. But fifty-seven years later, H-P is a $20 billion company that has just about conquered its world by continuing to operate on that same, simple principle of innovation. Few companies have been able to reinvent themselves more consistently or successfully.

Until the 1970s, Hewlett-Packard was primarily committed to engineering instruments. As it diversified into computing technologies, it bet on the proliferation of personal computer use and positioned itself as an industry leader in its most important adjunct: printers. What we look back on now and call a safe bet, was still called risk in 1980. And the risk paid off, big time.

Using Canon laser-printer engines, H-P sold over 10 million laser printers. Then it took the only logical step open to a company bent on innovation. It went into competition with itself and effectively began the cannibalization of its own laser-printer business. Using Canon's own, cheaper, ink-jet technology, H-P beat Canon to market by a year, capturing a 60 percent share of the new, $1.6 billion per year market for lower-end printers.

It further leveraged its knowledge base and reputation in the printer market to corner an astonishing 88 percent share of the color ink-jet market, and is now positioned to dominate the color laser-printer market as well. Today, its $7-billion-per-year PC printer division is H-P's leading source of growth and revenues.

CEO Lewis Platt believes it is H-P's ability to render obsolete its own technologies, before the market does, that has saved it from the fate of companies like IBM and DEC. Platt says: "We have to be willing to cannibalize what we're doing today in order to insure our leadership in the future. It's counter to human nature, but you have to kill your business while it is still working."[12]

You also have to move fast enough to respond quickly to market imperatives and competition from small, upstart rivals. So how did this behemoth of a computer company move fast enough to not just survive but thrive, while its erstwhile peers suffered at the hands of smaller companies? In the first place, H-P didn't behave like a behemoth. It organized itself into a group of largely autonomous smaller divisions which, left free of unwieldy top-down management, were able to act and react with the swiftness of small companies.

To get an idea of just how swiftly these little Hewlett-Packards can move, compare their new product development time frame to that of 3M, which is itself considered a veritable jack rabbit. 3M demands that 30 percent of sales be from products developed in the last four years. Well, fully 70 percent of Hewlett-Packard's orders are for products introduced or changed in the past two years.[13] These numbers make 3M look like it's in the terminal stages of narcolepsy. Such is the nature of the computing industry, which demands this velocity of change as the price of survival.

But H-P's ability to produce consistent innovation is not restricted to its traditional core businesses. At the beginning of the decade, defence cutbacks threatened its traditionally reliable market: supplying precision measuring devices to the Pentagon. Hewlett-Packard swiftly deployed its devastating combination of anticipating trends, cannibalizing products before the market does, and synthesizing core competencies in measurement instrumentation, computing and communications. H-P recognized early on that the huge American video industry would eventually move from analog to digital technologies. In a few short years, H-P has entered this entirely new field and become a player. With this new core competency complementing its original ones so beautifully, it is now poised to grab a significant share of the interactive television market.

So, if your company's philosophy is based on innovation and you find an operations structure that catapults it from seventh spot to number two in the American computer market, what do you do? You change it, of course, because Lewis Platt's dictum on cannibalism doesn't only apply to product lines. It applies to organizational structures as well.

Platt concluded that, as effective as the operational model of small autonomous divisions was, there was too little collaboration between sectors to maximize synergies and capitalize on H-P's core competencies. The result was the formation in 1993 of a committee known as HP = MC$^2$; the MC$^2$ standing for the three core competencies of precision Measurement instruments, Communications and Computing. The committee was comprised of representatives from all sectors of the company. So far, this multifaceted think tank has facilitated greater collaboration between H-P's scientific and computing competencies to produce such high-end technologies as physician workstations. In March 1995, H-P announced production of the first wireless printers. Aimed at the burgeoning mobile computing market, the printer uses new infrared technology.

What does the future hold for Hewlett-Packard? If the past is any indication, the only prediction one can safely make is that probably the only thing we'll recognize about it is its name.

## CONCLUSION

Innovation in business is a lot like excellence in any other field of endeavor: Difficult but manageable to do once, infinitely harder to produce consistently. Think about all the one-shot-wonders who had a single hit record, novel or fifty-goal hockey season and then vanished without a trace. What separates the Beatles, Hemingways and Wayne Gretzkys of this world from their more mortal contemporaries is their ability to pull off feats of brilliance repeatedly. And that's no accident.

So it is in business. What separates truly great corporate innovators from the competitors they leave in the dust is their ability to create conscious mechanisms to innovate consistently.

In the good old days, you didn't really need to innovate consistently. The pace of competition was sufficiently leisurely that a single innovation could often stand up for twenty years and enable a bloated corporate infrastructure to coast for decades. In almost every industry, however, those halcyon days are either over or are coming to an end. Today's global hypercompetition leaves nowhere to hide, and repeated innovations have become a competitive necessity.

Companies like Honda do it by promoting a culture of "constructive contention" that ensures new initiatives have benefited from systematic criticisms from the best minds in the company. Others, like 3M, do it by constantly "raising the bar" of performance expectation and by providing their employees with the tools and incentives they need to get on with the job. Still others, like Silicon Graphics, consciously seek out pathbreaking or "lighthouse" customers to spur them on to new heights of innovation and performance. A few exceptionally gutsy, "in your face" companies, like Sun Microsystems, actually license their best, state-of-the-art technologies to their competitors! This really puts the innovation fat in the fire, and absolutely forces the company to keep innovating and adding value to stay ahead. It's definitely not a technique for the complacent or faint of heart. But whatever the mechanism of choice, all truly innovative companies have at least two cardinal traits in common: An almost fanatical desire to get out front and stay there; and a determination that, if anybody is going to render their product or service obsolete, it's going to be them.

### CHAPTER FOUR

# LEVERAGING HIDDEN VALUE POTENTIAL

*"Developing latent value potential is the essence of corporate dynamism."*
PROFESSOR CUNO PUMPIN/
UNIVERSITY OF ST-GALLEN SWITZERLAND

While each of the 11 Commandments in this book is challenging and difficult, none demands more imagination and creativity from senior management than Commandment Number 3: Thou shalt uncover and leverage every ounce of hidden value potential in your organization.

In its broadest sense, "value potential" can refer to any organizational asset that has yet to be exploited to the fullest extent possible. In this book, however, I use the term in a narrower sense, to refer to lateral shifts in thinking where one of two things happens: Either a previously latent resource is suddenly recognized and harnessed, or else an existing asset is used in a qualitatively different context or application that gives it new and additional value. By our definition, corporate efforts that simply try to do "more of the same" or "more with less" do not qualify as leveraging hidden value potential. Downsizing and "rightsizing" efforts, which may reduce the corporate headcount by ten thousand with little or no reduction in the volume of output, are invariably heralded as triumphs of productivity and shareholder value. This may or may not be the case—and usually it isn't—but it is light-years away from what I mean by leveraging value potential. That actually takes *talent*. And *thinking*.

Value potential comes in an almost infinite variety of forms. One of the most commonly recognized is what business school profs delight in calling economies of scope—for example, leveraging existing investments in production capacity, R&D, distribution networks, management talent, or brand-name recognition to create and market wholly new products and services. The recent expansion of Cartier and Gucci into wholly new lines of luxury products provides a good example of capturing the economies of scope available from strong brand recognition. Ditto for leveraging the macho image of Harley-Davidson motorcycles to create a popular and profitable new line of clothing and accessories. The company's not really selling motorcycles at all; it's selling lifestyle and attitude.

The dramatic turnaround of Disney Corporation between 1985–87 owed much to a different kind of value potential: A more aggressive and intelligent exploitation of that company's strategic but underutilized landholdings, movie-studio infrastructure, voluminous film library and the goodwill attached to the Disney name.

Sometimes the hidden value potential lies in financial alchemy. European based companies such as British Petroleum and Asea Brown Boveri have transformed their once sleepy (and costly) treasury functions into dynamic profit centers. BP Finance currently creates a $50 million-a-year profit out of raising capital for the firm's mainstream business projects. And if the financial excesses of the 1980s accomplished little else, Michael Milken and others demonstrated that hundreds of millions of dollars in latent value potential can be liberated by skillfully reworking companies' capital structures. Many companies have substantial untapped balance sheet potential, such as the strategic real estate holdings of companies like Santa Fe Railroad in the U.S.A. Santa Fe's core railroad business was apparently so far removed from real-estate development that the true value potential of its underlying railway rights-of-way went unrecognized for decades.

A number of large, knowledge-based companies have recently recognized that the expertise they gained solving their own information technology problems has both relevance and commercial value to outsiders. (In the case of declining companies such as DEC and IBM, this is also one of the few significant weapons with which they can begin to reverse a decade of corporate degeneration and decay.) Similarly, modern scanning technologies in retailing have allowed companies such as Britain's Marks & Spencer to amass, update and provide real-time access to reams of information about consumer purchasing patterns. Some of the more prescient of the retailers, such as Levi Strauss, are even repackaging this information and selling it to outside marketing and public opinion research firms.

In this chapter, we will examine a variety of creative and successful efforts to uncover and leverage hidden value potential. While the sources of that hidden value vary as widely as the companies' industry sectors and geographic locales, the examples all have one thing in common: Each required a genuine flash of insight and creativity initially to recognize the value potential, and then a considerable amount of good, old-fashioned hard slogging to exploit it.

## Swords Into Plowshares: Reinventing California's Defense Industry

They say that nothing concentrates the mind like the prospect of being hanged the next morning. In a similar vein, nothing concentrated the minds of the deep thinkers in California's defense industry like the end of the Cold War in the late 1980s. Although American defense department budgets had been under modest pressure for several years, nothing had prepared major defense contractors for the radical shift in both public opinion and the budgets of their customers after the abrupt implosion of "the Soviet threat," circa 1989.

Like AT&T in its previous incarnation as a monopoly, large defense companies had grown fat and sassy feasting off specialized, high-margin, sole-source contracts with the defense department for such pricey military hardware as Stealth fighters and Trident missiles. The defense contractors had become de facto public utilities, operating in a noncompetitive environment with publicly guaranteed rates of return. Their ability to navigate the Byzantine and highly politicized defense department procurement labyrinth was at least as critical to their commercial success as any technical excellence they might have had. The competitive and strategic thinking I've discussed in earlier chapters was largely superfluous.

Trouble was, the market for highly specialized military hardware and the supporting expertise in public-sector-procurement procedures disappeared, almost overnight. The Pentagon was downsizing faster than IBM. Not all defense contractors would be able to respond to this radical upheaval in their business environment. The corporate one-trick ponies would have to either learn new tricks or head for the glue factory. New sources of value and competitiveness would need to be found—or else. No defense contractor found it easy to reinvent its entire corporate culture to operate in this new, civilian industrial context. Massive layoffs were the norm, and "restructuring" continues to this day. However, two companies, Lockheed and Raytheon, did better than most. Each was able to identify and leverage new sources of previously hidden value potential in their core competencies and technology skill bases.

Lockheed, for example, set up a new Information Management Services division, to leverage the company's core competence in the computer manipulation of massive amounts of data. Designing and manufacturing Trident missiles and then monitoring their in-flight performance requires highly sophisticated software, capable of processing literally billions of bits of information and data. Lockheed is now deploying this same skill set and Star Wars artificial intelligence technology for the somewhat more prosaic purposes of monitoring and tracking unpaid parking tickets in Boston, delinquent child support payments in Los Angeles, and so on. The new division already has over 130 state and municipal customers, and is poised to grab even more as American governments privatize public sector services. In its overall corporate context, where most of Lockheed's traditional defense business is either static or in decline, the new Information Management Services Group is currently generating double-digit growth.

Another of Lockheed's recent efforts to liberate new value from its data technology skill base is its work on "smart highways." Lockheed is developing a system whereby motorists can pay highway tolls without even slowing down, by using dashboard-mounted transponders, roadside computers and debit cards. Quite apart from its potential impact on the motorists' productivity (and Lockheed's bottom line), this new initiative also promises environmental benefits. By reducing the amount of time drivers spend languishing at toll booths with their motors idling, the smart highway initiative should strike at least a small blow for air quality. In states like California, every little bit helps. Thank God for the peace dividend.

Raytheon has enjoyed similar success in turning technological swords into plowshares. Some of the same remote tracking technology that made the Patriot missile the star of the Gulf War is now used in Motorola's emerging global personal communications system, as well as in air traffic control systems in developing countries' airports. In another civilian application of its defense technology, Raytheon has teamed up with superstar heart surgeon Michael DeBakey to develop a remote diagnostics system. The interactive video system will allow specialists in one location to examine, diagnose and even treat patients in faraway sites. The potential for both cost savings and dramatic improvements in the quality of healthcare in remote locations is enormous.

Both Raytheon and Lockheed have succeeded in leveraging entirely new value from resource bases that were originally conceived and developed for other purposes altogether. Not only were the applications of their original core competencies radically different from their innovations, but their innovations had to be generated within an entirely new cultural context. This is the essence of their achievement. It is one thing to develop new products and services in a corporate culture that has always been competitive and client-driven. It is another matter entirely to transcend a decades-long tradition of serving a single, captive customer with essentially no financial constraints. Raytheon and Lockheed are by no means out of the woods yet, but the early prognosis seems favorable. It seems that you can teach an old dog new tricks, after all!

## *Thermo Electron: The Perpetual Idea Machine*

New England-based Thermo Electron is another science-based company with a history of leveraging new value from a central core of assets. In Thermo Electron's case, however, it isn't simply a matter of leveraging new products and services out of core scientific competencies—as important as these are. As we shall see, Thermo Electron's innovation and value creation owed at least as much to *organizational* innovation and leverage as to pure scientific excellence.

Thermo Electron was and remains the creation of George Hatsopoulos, an entrepreneurial scientist who parlayed $50,000 and a Ph.D. in mechanical engineering from MIT into a billion-dollar company employing over six thousand people. While the process took over thirty years, today Thermo Electron is one of those exceptional corporations capable of combining the resources of a big company with the agility and "feel" of a ten-person start-up. In a very real sense, Thermo Electron was built on leveraging hidden value potential. The original concept of the company was to create a core competence in thermodynamics, and then to leverage it into a multitude of different business applications. While any single application might be high risk by itself, the sheer volume of new business ideas leveraged off the core technology meant the risks could be amply hedged. When you have that many "at bats," you don't need to hit .400 to get your fair share of base hits.

The strategy has clearly worked. Labeled a "perpetual idea machine" by one Wall Street analyst,[1] Thermo Electron has leveraged its core competence in thermodynamics into such diverse fields as cogeneration, biomass and other alternative energy, instrumentation, the manufacturing of process equipment such as paper recycling equipment and biomedical equipment. As impressive as this performance is, Thermo Electron is by no means the first science-based company to leverage a basic core competence into multiple applications. What really makes Thermo unique is its creation of an innovative organizational structure that, in essence, leverages the leverage created by the basic science.

Since founding the company in 1956, Hatsopoulos has been obsessed with two overriding imperatives: maintaining the entrepreneurial fervor of his start-up days, and keeping a strongly commercial orientation and discipline in the group's pursuit of science. With a single, clever organizational device, Hatsopoulos solved both problems simultaneously. His solution: spinning off substantial portions of each of his businesses to the public. By separating Thermo Electron into a number of discrete, publicly traded companies, Hatsopoulos was able to give each of his management teams a slice of the company's equity, as well as introduce the sobering market discipline of public stockholders. The equity stake kept the managers thinking and behaving like owner/entrepreneurs, while the presence of public shareholders helped ensure the companies' hefty R&D expenditures were tightly focused on commercial payoffs. And while many large corporations have spun off peripheral business-es, Thermo Electron was one of the first to take its *core* business public. In fact, in July 1991, Hatsopoulos committed the ultimate corporate heresy: He spun off the group's R&D unit. The R&D arm was *the* major source of Thermo Electron's intellectual capital, but Hatsopoulos reckoned that a healthy dose of market discipline and reality therapy would do nothing but good for it too. To paraphrase the cliché about acquiring new in-laws, George wasn't really losing an R&D unit, he was gaining new capital, stakeholders and an ongoing window onto commercial reality.

While keenly interested in creating a series of independently-minded, entrepreneurial companies, Hatsopoulos was also well aware of the need for each operation to reinforce the others and maximize the technical, financial and managerial synergies among them. Once again, Thermo Electron's inno-vative organizational structure proved a useful instrument. The stock options used to reward and motivate senior executives in each company are usually divided as follows: 40 percent in the spinoff itself, 40 percent in the parent company, and 20 percent in sister spin-offs. This ensured that Hatsopoulos's senior managers were forced to adopt a broader outlook and maximize value for the Thermo group as a whole.

Now here's where Thermo's leverage of its organizational value potential really gets interesting. Conglomerateurs like GE's Jack Welch have often complained that stock markets routinely penalize his companies for their diversity. Stock analysts can't get a clear and unambiguous bead on any sin-gle business unit, and so the diversified company is often valued at the level of the lowest common denominator. Thermo Electron has effectively elimi-nated this problem: Each of its spin-off businesses is evaluated as a separate "pure play," and receives a premium valuation accordingly. Of course, in classic Hatsopoulos fashion, Thermo gets the best of both worlds: While the stock market treats each of his companies as essentially free-standing entities, internally George is free to leverage core resources—such as the central trea-sury function—to borrow money for the spin-offs at far more attractive rates than any of them could possibly command on their own. And, in the ultimate triumph of Thermo's strategy of value leverage, the price of the parent company's stock has been consistently buoyed by the strength of the subsidiaries' performance. A rising tide, it seems, lifts all boats at Thermo.

By any measure, Thermo Electron is a successful company. What makes it both an exceptional one and an exemplar of value leverage is its ability to multiply both scientific knowledge-value and its organizational/balance sheet potential.

### *Marks & Spencer: Leveraging Integrity*

While almost every company in the world aspires to generate customer loyalty, few have done a better job than Britain's Marks & Spencer. But what makes M&S really remarkable is its ability to generate new and innovative kinds of value potential from that loyalty and trust, once it has earned it.

Marks & Spencer is currently Britain's most admired company,[2] a fact that is absolutely central to its entire competitive strategy. Almost everything M&S does is designed to either strengthen that loyalty or to leverage new value out of it. The company has come a long way from its humble origins as a market stall in Leeds, northern England and a string of Marks & Spencer "penny bazaars" in Manchester in the 1880s.

Today, those "pennies" have added up to some US$11 billion in revenues (1994) encompassing 354 stores and employing 62,000 people.[3] But one of the firm's most important assets—which does not appear anywhere on its balance sheet— is the reputation for integrity and trust it has fostered with both suppliers and customers. Explains Chairman Sir Richard Greenbury: "If I were asked the two qualities that mean most to me, I would say integrity and fair dealing were number one. Number two is courage, not physical courage, but courage to make decisions and get on with things."[4] The firm has consistently made customer loyalty a top priority ever since its "everything for a penny" days, and has successfully leveraged this solid reputation for integrity.

Life as a Marks & Spencer supplier is no cakewalk. The company has stringent quality standards enforced by regular visits by company technicians, and it uses its power as a large buyer to force suppliers to keep prices low. Why do suppliers accept this? Because Marks & Spencer is legendary for developing tight, long-term relationships, giving its suppliers long-term contracts, including, on occasion, some leeway if the supplier is in a tight financial situation. The company also pays its suppliers much more quickly than the industry average: within ten days for food suppliers and twenty days for the rest. The firm also collaborates closely with its suppliers in new product development. By treating its suppliers firmly but fairly, Marks & Spencer can keep its fixed costs down and operate much like a manufacturer without factories, basically coordinating the delivery of products from dozens of suppliers to its millions of customers. Even its delivery trucks, though bearing the Marks & Spencer name, are owned and operated by a third party. In this respect, M&S has become a bit of a "virtual" corporation, not unlike Italy's Benetton in fashion and Silicon Valley's Sun Microsystems in computers. M&S concentrates on doing only those things it does best, and one of those things happens to be managing large networks of outside suppliers.

Recent advances in information technology have allowed M&S's already close supplier-customer relationships to become even tighter. For example, when Marks & Spencer stores close each Saturday, sales are added up and a computerized ordering system automatically sends details of each store's needs to its suppliers, which they receive first thing Monday morning. Suppliers can see which of their products are selling best, and Marks & Spencer can receive deliveries within days, almost on a just-in-time basis. This minimizes inventory carrying costs, reduces the spoilage and waste of food produce, and most important of all, allows M&S to respond almost instantaneously to the changing tastes and requirements of its 14 million weekly customers, the real source of M&S's value potential.

Nowhere has that value potential been leveraged more effectively than in the area of financial services, where a reputation for integrity is of particularly great value. It all began simply enough, with the Marks & Spencer credit card, launched in the mid-1980s and still the only credit card accepted in the company's stores. In an age of increasing competition for consumer credit, holders of the Marks & Spencer card now number upwards of 3.5 million. The card generates fee and interest revenues for the company, and increases the firm's brand recognition and loyalty. But that's only the beginning. The credit card also generates an extensive point-of-sale database on the credit card holders. And the company has leveraged this important asset well. For example, in March 1992, half a million people who had recently bought cut flowers at Marks & Spencer received a direct mailing offering them a home-delivery flower service. Within months, the firm had captured fully 10 percent of the national home-delivery flower market. The credit card allows the firm to develop a "living database," including constantly updated profiles on each customer. That this is far superior to the standard mass-market tool of "average customer profiles" scarcely needs to be pointed out.

Nor do the benefits of obtaining customer information end there. Marks & Spencer has leveraged the data from its credit cards to design a growing range of financial products, including personal loans (it now handles 10 percent of the general purpose loans in Britain), unit trusts (mutual funds), personal equity plans and more recently, life insurance and pensions. Financial products sales representatives are paid on a salary basis, not commission, to maintain their objectivity. The results have been excellent, with profits for the financial services up 40 percent in 1994 to US$70 million on revenues of US$207 million.

From a single market stall in Leeds to an international retail giant and a growing force in financial services. Not bad. And none of this would have been feasible without the strength and integrity of the Marks & Spencer name, leveraged by information technology.

## Canada's Syncrude: Leveraging Native Talent

Human resources are at once the most obvious and the most difficult source of corporate value potential to recognize and leverage. Company sloganeers are wont to pontificate that "our people are our most precious resource," but very few are capable of translating that bromide into action. Fewer still are capable of turning it into a meaningful competitive weapon. Syncrude Canada is one of those rare exceptions.

Syncrude is a major player on the northern frontiers of Canada's oil patch. It is currently the world's largest producer of synthetic crude oil, which it extracts and upgrades from oil and tar sands. The Athabaska deposit near Fort McMurray, where Syncrude's operations are located, is the largest single petroleum deposit in the world. Using highly sophisticated technologies, over 300 billion barrels of high-quality light crude are potentially recoverable from Syncrude's properties. To put it in perspective, this means Syncrude is sitting on roughly one-third of the world's total known reserves of oil—approximately the same level of reserves as Saudi Arabia.

That's the good news. The bad news is that it is both infinitely more difficult and more costly for Syncrude to get *at* its oil than it is for King Fahd in Saudi Arabia to get at his. This is where the human-resource dimension comes in. If ever there was an underutilized human resource, it is Canada's northern aboriginal population. The story of Canada's Native population is, in the main, a profoundly tragic one. Ghettoized and kept on remote, impoverished reserves for decades, the Native population in general enjoys only a fraction of the educational, health, housing or employment levels of the mainstream population. Incidence of alcoholism, suicide and substance abuse are all exponentially greater than among the white population. Caught in an economic no-man's land between their vanishing traditional livelihoods of hunting and fishing and the often unattainable demands of high-tech society, Canada's Native people are not a resource in which Canadian companies are often rushing to invest.

It is not altogether unusual, however, for resource companies in the Canadian north to make at least perfunctory overtures to the Native community. After all, in many cases the Natives actually have at least nominal legal control over the natural resources. On more than one occasion, Native protests over major proposed resource development projects in northern Canada have been sufficient to actually kill projects, flushing millions of dollars of effort—and billions of dollars of potential profit—down the drain. So a certain level of at least putative deference to the Native community has always been politically expedient in Canadian business politics. But Syncrude's commitment goes far beyond that: As a conscious business strategy, Syncrude identified the Native population as a grossly underutilized human resource, and set about trying to harness and leverage it.

What is perhaps the most impressive part of Syncrude's approach is that it was flexible, iterative and adjusted as it went along. In its first incarnation, as little more than a glorified affirmative-action hiring plan, their approach was a disaster. The problem was that as fast as Syncrude hired Native workers, it lost them to attrition. The cultural gulf separating the aboriginal people from the demands of a state-of-the-art industrial complex was simply too wide. So Syncrude changed course dramatically, recognizing that the business they really needed to be in was not just hiring Native people, but developing their talents. There could be no quick fix.

Syncrude set about the task in earnest. They hired a community development specialist, Jim Carberry, to work full time in the eleven different Native communities surrounding the plant. Carberry's mission was not unlike that of a baseball scout: To spot high-potential prospects and make sure they received the necessary education and training to play in the big leagues. This meant creating customized, training, apprenticeship and community-college programs, and providing the necessary support to ensure that they could be used to their full potential. At the same time, as part of a multipronged effort to build more positive images of the Native community, Syncrude sponsored an exhibition of aboriginal art, which toured widely throughout Canada and Japan.

Meanwhile, Syncrude recognized that they also had serious work to do with their non-Native employees, giving them crosscultural training to minimize the conflicts and misunderstandings arising from the interaction of two profoundly different world views.

Syncrude's executives also discovered something very interesting and, to them, unexpected: The aboriginal people had an enormous amount to teach *them* about business, and proved to be a genuine source of competitive advantage. This was particularly true in the area of team building. Aboriginal cultures are intrinsically far more collaborative than the mainstream Canadian culture. In an era when companies are spending hundreds of thousands of dollars on outside "teamwork gurus," all Syncrude had to do was look at its own Oil Containment and Recovery Crew in Fort Chipewyan. With the best performance, attendance and safety records in the entire company, this predominantly Native unit was a working example of the sort of mutual support and teamwork so often eulogized in annual reports, but so seldom seen in practice.

Syncrude has also been proactive in launching and nurturing new Aboriginal businesses. The company identifies high-potential Native entrepreneurs, helps them develop strong business plans, and often steps up to the plate as their first customer. Sometimes the new ventures are spin-offs from Syncrude, where Native entrepreneurs start out as employees and then privatize themselves, creating new companies to bid on and win contracts for work being outsourced. One such example is Clearwater Welding, which now has over one hundred qualified Native tradespeople. Today Syncrude purchases over $20 million in goods and services from Native businesses, and CEO Eric Newell fully expects this figure to top $30 million within two years. Newell is not afraid to subject his performance in this area to independent review and measurement. He has contracted an outside agency, the Athabasca Native Development Corporation, to develop and monitor a computerized inventory of educational- and business-attainment levels among the region's Native community. And Syncrude even publishes the equivalent of a specialized annual report, *Aboriginal Review*, which reports on the progress of its ongoing partnerships with the Native community.

Newell is quite clear, direct and unsentimental in explaining his extraordinary efforts in leveraging a previously hidden resource: "There's a very good business reason for training and developing our Native employees: They are the source of thousands of small and large ideas that together add up to the significant productivity gains that will enable us to stay competitive."[5]

Enough said.

## IMES: Japan's Over-the-Hill Gang

While it is a gross and unfair overgeneralization, the perception persists that Japan is not exactly a hotbed of entrepreneurial innovation. Fabulous engineering talent, work ethic and the ability to add big-time value to others' innovations—sure. But the Japanese culture is often thought to be far too homogeneous and conformist to be much of an incubator for entrepreneurs.

Why, Japan doesn't even have a proper business school! So goes the conventional wisdom "confirming" the West's superiority in entrepreneurship.

Well, don't try that one on Tokio Mizukami. Like Syncrude's Eric Newell in the Canadian tundra thousands of miles away, Mr. Mizukami discovered a gold mine of value potential in underutilized human resources. In Mizukami's case, the resource lay in retired computer engineers rather than young aboriginals. But the result is the same: dynamic new businesses and wealth created essentially out of thin air.

The unexploited anomaly that launched Mizukami into orbit was the curious fact that IBM Japan allows employees to retire at age fifty on full pensions. (There's good ol' IBM again: What an eye for creating and capturing value!) Given that most crackerjack computer engineers still have a few weeks of useful professional life ahead of them even at the ripe old age of fifty, Mizukami reckoned he'd stumbled upon a major opportunity. He would recruit the cream of the retiring crop (maybe even nudging one or two into retirement a bit earlier than they'd planned), and get them to work with him. Even if he paid them half their IBM salaries, on top of their full pensions, they'd be earning a very nice living indeed, thank you very much. And even more importantly, they'd be doing what they loved and were good at rather than being put out to pasture.

Mizukami called his company the International Manufacturing and Engineering Services Company, or IMES. IMES' stock in trade was the development and manufacture of computer peripherals such as CD-ROM drives and lighting systems for liquid crystal displays. Started in 1990 with just fifteen IBM alumni and US$100,000, IMES now boasts 270 professionals, with an average age of fifty-three. Over half are veterans of IBM, like Mizukami himself. In its first four years of operation, IMES' revenues grew by a factor of twenty, with 1995 sales projected to exceed $10 billion yen. Perhaps most encouraging of all, IMES now makes over half its sales to companies other than IBM, so its dependence on a single customer is decreasing.

Mizukami ends up with top talent, both highly motivated and highly experienced, and only pays them about half the going rate. It's pretty hard not to make money under those circumstances! IMES is able to combine the experience and brainpower of an IBM with the agility and nimbleness of a small entrepreneurial company. In a business like computer peripherals, where product life expectancies are measured in months, the ability to stop on a dime, change direction and accelerate after new opportunities is indispensable. The way I see it, Mizukami isn't in the computer peripherals business at all. He's in the business of leveraging hidden value potential.

## *The Wuhan Match Factory: Shock Therapy, Chinese-Style*

When is a match factory not a match factory? These days, apparently, only weeks after it is privatized by the local government of Wuhan City in the People's Republic of China. All innovation must be judged relative to its histori-cal and cultural context. Although the metamorphosis of the Wuhan Match Factory into a residential and mixed-use land development project might be of only passing interest in Toronto, in the context of the P.R.C., it stands as a striking example of innovation, entrepreneurship and value leverage.

The Wuhan Match Factory, at ninety-eight years of age, was a perfect metaphor for the industrial and economic decline of Wuhan City, once one of the four most important financial centers in China (along with Shanghai, Beijing and Tianjin). Both the factory and the city itself had seen much better days, and Wuhan's continued decline was made all the more conspic-uous by the recent economic renaissance of the other three cities. In order to reverse the decline, the Wuhan municipal government decided to privatize at least forty state-owned factories, with the full concurrence of Deng Xiaoping's central government in Beijing.

The Wuhan Match Factory was duly sold to a new company called Wuhan Dadi, for an "incentivized" price of almost US$5 million. The com-pany's chairman, Li Yuan, was already a successful entrepreneur, having grad-uated from selling calculators on the street to building a successful comput-er company.

One of the first things Li Yuan noticed about his new company was that fewer than 40 percent of the 1,800 workers on his payroll were actually work-ing. The rest had literally retired but continued to draw full salaries. Of the remainder, Li Yuan reckoned that only one hundred or so were up to the job. So he promptly fired 94 percent of his workforce (with the approval of the authorities), and then went on a recruiting drive to hire the three hundred or so new workers he needed. Now, it's one thing for "neutron" Jack Welch to sack 90 percent of his employees after a new acquisition or restructuring in the United States; in the historico-cultural context of China, it is quite another matter.

The mass layoffs were themselves unprecedented, but Li Yuan wasn't done yet. He created a generous, Western-style "severance" package for the dis-placed workers that amounted to roughly half the total acquisition price. Next, after concluding that making matches might not be the high-tech wave of the future, he dismantled and sold the factory's machinery to small entrepreneurs in Wuhan. At present, Li Yuan is demolishing the old factory and redeveloping the site into a large, new complex including housing and an electronics factory. First-year profits from the new development are pro-jected to be US$2–3 million, roughly equal to the annual losses previously piled up by the match factory.

Li Yuan's initiative leveraged at least two kinds of hidden value potential. On a purely physical level, by identifying and redeveloping a centrally locat-ed but grossly underutilized, undervalued parcel of urban land, Li was able to liberate one major source of latent value. (Think of him as the Donald Trump of the Wuhan real estate market.) On a more subtle but perhaps more important level, Li was also—quite consciously—applying techniques already familiar in the West for wringing new value out of undermanaged companies. In this respect, he was a pioneer in China. Skeptics might counter that calling Wuhan Match Factory an undermanaged company is a bit like calling World War II a minor quarrel among friends. Perhaps. And in the West (or even Central Europe), Li Yuan's intervention might well have been unremarkable. But innovation is all relative to its context, and in the context of Wuhan in the mid-1990s, Li's ability to discern and unlock hid-den value in an obsolescent match factory was little short of remarkable. He completely reinvented both the company's mission and its workforce, with-in a cultural ethos that provided little precedent for either.

## Leveraging Hidden Value in Latin America

Of all our examples of leveraging hidden value potential, none is more ambi-tious, impressive or ingenious than two cases from Latin America's "infor-mal" sector. In both instances, local reformers identified a latent resource and developed innovative mechanisms to harness it on a large scale. In one case, the hidden value potential lay in underutilized land; in the other, it was the latent financial power of the urban poor.

In Peru, economist Hernando De Soto had become an international lit-erary superstar with the 1989 publication of his blockbuster, *The Other Path*. Aimed squarely at the Maoist terrorist group Shining Path, the book argued that what ailed the Peruvian economy was not too much capitalism, but too little. More specifically, De Soto had argued that Peru's marginalized peasant class and urban "informals" had to be empowered to participate directly in the mainstream economy. This meant giving them access to credit and other key instruments of economic development, so that the enormous energy and resources of the underground economy could be liberated.

Following the publication of his book, De Soto decided to put his propo-sitions into practice. His target? Land reform. De Soto saw that only 20 per-cent of Peruvian land was covered by legal title; the vast majority was simply occupied and worked by squatters, sometimes for generations. But without legal title to their properties, the Peruvian informals were unable to sell them, mortgage them or otherwise capture any of the real value of years of sweat equity. Here was hidden value potential on an epic scale. If the peasants could somehow be given legal title to their property, they could use it as collateral for loans from mainstream financial institutions.

So De Soto and his colleagues at the Institute for Liberty and Democracy in Lima set to work. In a little over two years, they and their supporters in the liberal Fujimori government created legal title for over 150,000 Peruvian families, at an average administrative cost of roughly $12 per parcel. Now that's empowerment. Buoyed by his success in Peru, De Soto then convinced President Alfredo Cristiani of El Salvador to launch a similar initiative in 1992. In less than a year, 40,000 new property titles were created for Salvadorean informals, bringing the world of commercial credit within their reach for the first time. De Soto is discussing similar initiatives with the new government of Bolivia, and India and Russia have also shown interest.

One word of warning to those who may be tempted to emulate De Soto's ingenious value-creation model: Try and find a test site well away from the strongholds of any Maoist terrorist groups. While De Soto's work has attracted many admirers, the Shining Path guerrillas are not among them. In July 1992, they detonated eight hundred pounds of dynamite at his institute's Lima offices. Fortunately, De Soto is none the worse for wear, and most corporate reformers and innovators can reasonably expect a considerably less hostile reaction.

In Peru, the hidden value potential lay in the conversion of informal land to legally recognized property rights that could then be converted into borrowing power. In Colombia, an innovative bank saw a similar opportunity to unlock the economic power of the urban poor. In this case, they eliminated the intervening step and provided the credit directly.

The fundamental insight driving the Caja Social de Ahorros (roughly, Social Savings and Loan) was the fact that poor people are actually extraordinarily good credit risks, provided the amounts involved are small and manageable. Armed with this simple, counter-intuitive insight, the Caja Social has proceeded to blend social development and profitability into a seamless web. Caja Social is currently the only bank servicing a Bogota slum of over a million people. After only four years of operation, the Caja has over ten thousand accounts, most of them held by small shopkeepers, street peddlers and housewives. Roughly three thousand of them visit the Caja's Ciudad Bolivar branch every day, and the average transaction size is about five dollars. The typical savings account has roughly two hundred dollars in it, and the average loan is under three thousand dollars.

Now, none of those sums is likely to make the pinstriped, conventional banking fraternity at the Chase Manhattan Bank headquarters salivate. However, the Caja's default rate is virtually zero, a feat I can't recall Chase or its competitors ever coming close to pulling off. What's more, the Caja was recently ranked by the trade magazine *America Economica* as Latin America's most profitable bank.[6] With a return on equity of 143 percent and profits of $38 million against revenues of $344 million, the Caja should be conducting clinics for the Chase Manhattans and J. P. Morgans of the world.

The Caja Social didn't actually invent "micro-lending" to the poor; that distinction arguably goes to Bangladesh's celebrated Grameen Bank. What the Caja did do, however, was recognize the latent commercial power of the urban underclass in its own country, and build an institution capable of bridging what are so frequently and unnecessarily two solitudes: social progress and empowerment on the one hand, and profitability on the other.

All it takes is the paradigm shift that allows apparently contradictory impulses to be integrated and reconciled. That, plus the creative vision to uncover hidden value potential in the first place and the discipline, fortitude and persistence to stay the course long enough to harvest it.

---

# CONCLUSION

---

Leveraging hidden value potential is unquestionably one of the toughest of the 11 Commandments to follow. Along with strategic reframing and organizational learning, it requires the greatest creativity and innovation. It takes real intellectual effort (not to mention ability) to survey one's organizational resources and environment with enough ingenuity and strategic insight to uncover new sources of value.

In cases such as Canada's Syncrude and Japan's IMES, the hidden value potential exists in the form of unrecognized or underutilized human resources. In others, like Raytheon and Lockheed, it lies in core organizational competencies that need to be recognized, reconfigured and applied to new areas and opportunities. In still others, like Marks and Spencer, the potential lies in leveraging and transferring the power of a "brand" or reputation for integrity earned in one area—retailing —to another where it has power and resonance—financial services.

Those cases involve identifying and leveraging resources that lie, at least potentially, *within* the organization. But enormous hidden value potential also exists in the company's *external* environment. The two Latin American cases provide powerful illustrations of this external kind of value potential.

The Caja Social recognized hidden value in the considerable but unexploited borrowing and economic power of the urban poor. Hernando De Soto and his colleagues were likewise able to create economic value for Peruvian peasants essentially out of thin air, by the simple expedient of providing legal title to their informal landholdings.

Whether the hidden value potential lies within the organization or outside it, the fundamental point is that there is lots of it. The reason hidden value is only rarely identified and exploited is because it is so difficult for most CEOs to transcend their conventional frames of reference. The tyranny of conventional industry wisdom and the weight of "expert" opinion are enormously difficult to escape, especially when many CEOs toil under the daily scrutiny of relatively myopic financial analysts and shareholders. But the experience of the innovators in this chapter demonstrates that it *is* possible to find and exploit new value—lots of it—in previously undiscovered places.

Make no mistake. Tomorrow's leading CEOs will spend much less of their time controlling and managing existing operations, and much more of it dreaming up entirely new ways to create value. The ones who hang onto their jobs the longest will be the ones who learn how to do it the fastest and best.

# THE QUICK AND THE DEAD
## COMPETING ON SPEED

*"I'd rather be roughly right and fast than exactly right and slow."*
PERCY BARNIVIK CEO/ ASEA BEOWN BOVERI

When you get right down to it, there are really only three viable strategies for coping with the accelerated pace of change: Continuous innovation, learning and speed. That's what our 11 Commandments boil down to. Innovation and continuous learning are dealt with in other chapters, though they're really different faces of the same coin. The imperative for the third corporate virtue, speed, is self-evident—or at least it ought to be. Confronted with a constantly shifting kaleidoscope of customers, competitors, strategic alliances and capital market volatility, the only hope for survival lies in developing the ability to move and change at least as rapidly as your competitive environment. Since it's become exceedingly difficult to see more than a few months into the future in most industries, you've really only got two alternatives to bankruptcy: Either achieve a commanding enough position to dictate the changing rules of the game yourself, or develop the ability to react *immediately* to those who do. Either way, you either get quick—and quickly—or you get dead.

Few industries illustrate this accelerating velocity of change better than the computer industry. In the period between 1976 and 1992, the effective cost of 100 megabytes of computing power was reduced by a factor of over one hundred, while the physical space required to house it was reduced by over seven hundred times.[1] Here's a sobering bit of trivia: The new generation of Sega videogames that your six-year-old plays with contains as much computing power as the Cray supercomputers of the mid-70s. At that time,

Crays were the exclusive preserve of elite physicists. With breathtaking price/performance acceleration like that, either you develop the capacity to perform at that pace too—like Intel—or you go belly-up.

But what we're talking about here is not defensive, keep-up-with-the-Joneses type speed. We're talking about *proactive* speed, the kind that companies like Toyota, CNN and Sun Microsystems use as offensive, preemptive, competitive weapons. We're talking about creating a climate and a culture of speed—speed of decision making, speed of execution, speed of performance feedback and speed of making compensatory adjustments. You know: *speed.* If you can't move fast enough, you're going to get run over. It's that simple.

Of course, one of the greatest threats to developing this kind of organizational quick-strike capability is the age-old syndrome of "paralysis by analysis." Corporate Pollyannas would have us believe that the widespread vaporization of several layers of middle management in the early 1990s greatly speeded up the process of corporate decision making and analysis. On the whole, however, it hasn't. All it's really accomplished in most companies is to dump the same volume of analysis on fewer and more senior desks, thereby creating even more bottlenecks than before.

In response, I've created my own 80-20 rule: You can generally get 80 percent of the information and analysis you need for virtually any decision within the first week. By the time you get the remaining 20 percent six months or more later, the opportunity will likely be irrevocably lost and at least one of your competitors will be laughing all the way to the bank.

Much of what passes for rigorous business analysis suffers from the same problem confronting the contemporary astronomer: Light from a distant star takes so long to reach the astronomer's eyes that the star may in fact have vanished 200,000 years ago. The same is often true of the business universe our captains of industry survey from their Olympian heights, and think they understand. There's actually a better than even chance that their "real world" doesn't even exist anymore. Remember when the hard-headed "realists" in the Detroit auto industry refused to believe that anybody could possibly buy those funny little Japanese compact cars made by upstarts like Toyota and Honda? It took them five years to realize their picture of reality was badly outdated and another five years to do anything much about it.

Conventional private sector mythology holds it to be self-evident that the public sector has a monopoly on ponderous, cumbersome decision making. In their sector, however, men are really men, decisions are unerringly quick, strategic and, well, *decisive.* Ha! When was the last time *you* tried to force a multibillion dollar company to think about a new business opportunity quickly, even when it could make them hundreds of millions of dollars if they acted fast enough? If the opportunity lies so much as one micron outside of the company's current core focus, good luck to you! Even if you were trying to sell life preservers on the deck of the corporate Titanic, by the time your idea had been studied by the Recreational and Flotation Devices Committee, referred to New Acquisitions, Legal, Finance and then on to the Executive Committee, the corporate boat would be pushing up seaweed from the bottom of the Atlantic.

No, the only sane response to an increasingly complex, fast-changing world is not more and more analysis. It is building companies that can move almost as quickly as the changing business realities around them. Just as action is ultimately a far more precious commodity in business than pure analysis, speed will beat perfection every time in the emerging world of 21st century competition. I'd much rather be 80 percent right and first to market than 100 percent right and six months late. Try something, test it, learn from it and try it again—quickly. Companies like Sun Microsystems, Toyota and CNN have all turned a bias for action, experimentation and speed into the cornerstone of extremely successful competitive strategies.

## THE DIVIDENDS OF SPEED

Let's be clear about what's at stake here. For those who really can do things faster than their competitors, the rewards can be extraordinary:

- The ability to set *de facto* industry standards by being the first to market with innovative offerings.
- The ability to stay on the leading edge of innovation by incorporating technological advances in products and services faster than competitors.
- The ability to respond more quickly to market opportunities by reducing product development cycle time.
- The ability to reduce business risk dramatically by introducing new offerings closer to the time when the opportunities are first identified.
- The ability to extract premium prices based on first-mover advantage.
- The ability to attract and lock up the most attractive and strategic distribution channels through a preemptive first strike.
- Productivity improvements and cost reductions through lower inventory carrying costs.
- Dramatically higher staff morale and commitment, as problems get resolved faster and individual contributions get translated more quickly into concrete results.
- Confused and off-balance competitors, bewildered and put on the defensive by your constant, quick-paced innovations.

Not a bad harvest to reap, if you can manage to overcome the frequently overwhelming power of organizational inertia. Each of the companies profiled in this chapter has done this. Actually, to be strictly accurate, in the cases of CNN and Sun Microsystems, it was less a question of conquering the inertia of an existing organization than a matter of building the capacity for speed into a new one, right from the outset. As the following real-life examples demonstrate, there are myriad different specific techniques for harnessing the competitive power of speed. The particulars don't even matter that much. What is essential, however, is to do what all these companies have done: Recognize the competitive power of speed and turn the pursuit of speed into a central organizing and cultural principle in your company. Let's look at some companies who've done it superbly.

## Toyota: They Wrote the Book on It

If Toyota didn't flat-out invent speed-based competition, they've sure as hell raised it to the level of an art form. Ironically, however, becoming the fastest in the world can take some time. Toyota has been continuously improving its time-based operations since developing its much-copied Toyota Production System (TPS) in the 1970s.

The basic theory underpinning the TPS is disarmingly simple: The smaller the operation, the faster it can move. As we have seen in so many cases profiled in this book, small companies are often more competitive because they can respond most quickly to market imperatives. And large companies like Silicon Graphics, which owe so much of their success to the nimbleness of their original small size, go to heroic lengths to keep that small feeling as they grow and become increasingly complex. Big companies like Hewlett-Packard divide their operations into smaller units to compete in the fast lane.

But in the '70s, the Big Three of American car manufacturers reigned supreme and the theory that big was beautiful prevailed. Size gave you muscle to steamroller the competition. It also slowed you down. Factories operated on inflexible manufacturing schedules. Lot sizes were huge and, as in the Soviet Union, sales were based more on what was produced than on what the customer wanted. The spirit of Henry Ford's famous line about the Model T, "You can have any color you want, as long as it's black," still lingered. But Toyota—not Ford—had a better idea.

The keys to Toyota's revolutionary, speed-based strategy were threefold: First, drive flexibility throughout its entire manufacturing schedule; second, create small, autonomous teams to manage all aspects of product development; and third, use parallel rather than linear processes for design and manufacturing. Suppliers were included at the earliest possible stage, so that all participants in the development chain knew what would be needed ahead of time to preclude unnecessary delays. Manufacturing lot sizes were reduced by up to 95 percent, so that inventory holdings could be maintained at lower, as-needed levels. When inventory arrived, it was used; it didn't sit around taking up time and space. Factories were reorganized and retooled to create flexible cells that could respond quickly to emerging sales patterns. The overall result of this strategy was a dramatic reduction in manufacturing time: The period from the arrival of raw materials at a factory to the rolling out of a finished vehicle was reduced from fifteen days to one. By the late 1970s, Toyota had achieved almost a fivefold productivity advantage over its Big Three American competitors, which allowed Toyota to weather the effects of the global recession much better than its rivals.

Toyota's revolutionary approach later came to be known in the West as the Just in Time manufacturing system. All the key elements of JIT—simultaneous, parallel manufacturing, early supplier participation in process and product design, and inventory minimization—remain powerful, state-of-the-art concepts to this day. Indeed, the JIT ethos has now expanded beyond manufacturing to embrace the service sector. It requires a bit of an effort of will to remind ourselves that, when Toyota pioneered JIT in the 1970s, it was absolutely unheard of. In that sense, Toyota can truly be considered the "father of time-based competition" in the modern era.

Having successfully reinvented the manufacturing side of its operation, Toyota then set about reinventing its sales and distribution systems to keep pace with these incredible gains. First, Toyota Motor Sales was merged with Toyota Motor Manufacturing, to remove any organizational impediments to spreading the JIT gospel from the manufacturing to the sales side. Next, everyone went on line. Sales staff were linked directly to the factories, so that manufacturing schedules could respond immediately to match customer orders. Suppliers were also computer networked to receive up-to-the-minute plant schedules; only precisely specified inventory was delivered, at the precise point in the process it was required.

The most valuable byproduct of this speedy communications network was greater corporate responsiveness. Toyota could now respond much more quickly to customer demands for new product design, options packages and model availability. Henry Ford had been turned on his head: Now you *could* have any color you wanted, and you could have it faster than you could possibly get it from the competition—two-thirds faster in fact.

Toyota's remarkable and fundamental restructuring left it extraordinarily well positioned for the "post-lean" manufacturing years of the 1990s. While other companies have convulsively slashed thousands from their work forces in a reflex attempt (misguided, in my view) to bring costs under control, Toyota's cost base is already at hypercompetitive levels. Over the past two decades, Toyota has lowered costs consistently, but relatively painlessly, by ruthlessly cutting time and waste out of its design, production and manufacturing processes.

As a result, Toyota is now in a position to remain profitable, despite the growing strength of the yen in international currency markets. (Since 1990, the yen has appreciated by nearly 70 percent against the U.S. dollar.) Today, Toyota's cost base is so lean and mean that President Tatsuro Toyoda believes the company can stay competitive with an exchange rate as low as a once unthinkable 90 yen to the dollar.[2]

As with any truly world class innovator, however, this gazelle among international manufacturing giants is never satisfied with the status quo. Toyota is embarking on one of the most revolutionary manufacturing changes in its history, perhaps in anyone's history since the Industrial Revolution. In what may come to be known as a "postmodern industrial revolution," Toyota is actually replacing machines with man! Yes, you read correctly. In Toyota City, Japan, Toyota is currently producing its new four-wheel-drive RAV4 using 66 percent *less* automation than in its normal assembly line. De-automation circa 1995 may strike the casual observer as a latter-day equivalent of the Luddites smashing machinery in the 1800s in a futile attempt to halt the march of industrial progress. Nothing could be further from the truth. Indeed, it is a perfect illustration of Toyota's organizational humility and constant willingness to push the limits of orthodoxy in search of continuous improvement.

A few years ago, Toyota invested a lot of money in Japan and elsewhere betting that more, not less, automation was the way to go. This proved to be false economy. What it saved on assembly line workers it ended up spending on equipment maintenance. It also lost opportunities for continuous improvement because manufacturing teams consisted almost solely of maintenance engineers for the robots, a rather lean source of intellectual capital and knowledge transfer.

Although the final verdict on the new operation is not yet in—if indeed, one can ever have a final verdict on a company dedicated to continuous improvement—early indications suggest that Toyota has once again set new records for speed. The RAV4 took less than four years to design and produce. Many of its parts have already been used successfully in existing models, which saves time and money in design, production and maintenance. The re-use of previously designed parts is a practice Toyota intends to rely on increasingly in future. Productivity on the new "humanomated" line has apparently risen by 20 percent, and defects have actually dropped to only 12 percent of their previous, automated levels. Company-wide, this new round of value engineering is already estimated to have saved US$500 million.[3]

So there you have it. Just when the rest of its competitors have finally begun to figure out and duplicate its last major set of innovations (arguably ten to fifteen years too late), Toyota is off and running with the next one. And what's really scaring the hell out of the American automakers is the following thought: Toyota's latest spectacular productivity gains were specifically created to permit its Japanese factories to overcome adverse currency conditions to stay competitive in foreign export markets. So what would happen if Toyota now transferred the same ultra-lean production techniques to their factories in America, where there would be no exchange-rate problems to inhibit them? It will come as scant comfort for Detroit to learn that Milio Kitano, the man responsible for the RAV4 line in Japan, has just been transferred to Kentucky to run the Toyota plant there. Speed kills!

## CNN: *Where Speed Is Job One*

No company on earth better demonstrates the importance of speed-based competitive advantage than CNN. Everything about the company, its original business promise, its day-to-day operations, and its core technologies, is predicated on speed. As we have argued, in the new 21st century business paradigm, the race will be won by the swift—by the person who recognizes where the crowd is going *before* the crowd knows it, and is there to greet everyone when they get there. And no one understands this better than Ted Turner, captain of industry, sportsman, environmentalist and creator of CNN.

We may look back now and say "Twenty-four-hour news on demand? Wasn't it always done this way?" And who can blame us for our amnesia? We live in a world where a potato is baked in ten minutes in a microwave when it used to take an hour in a conventional oven, and our letters take seconds to send by fax or E-mail when they took a week or more by post (and still do most of the time). So why would we accept waiting hours until six o'clock to get the news when we want it now? When Turner first recognized the explosive potential of the rapidly converging fields of satellite and cable technologies in 1980, the idea of instantaneous news transmission around the globe was unprecedented. His launch of CNN that year stemmed from recognizing a latent customer demand for news that was genuinely current, not canned and reprocessed like the prevailing offerings. Turner says: "I came up with the concept for a news channel even before my Superstation was up on the satellite. Business is like a chess game and you have to look several moves ahead. Most people don't. They think one move at a time. Any chess player knows when you're playing against a one-move opponent you'll beat him every time."[4]

Turner's revolutionary insight was twofold: First, that there could be a substantial public appetite for an all-news TV channel; and second, that the new communications technologies could be leveraged to ensure that the new channel's coverage could be both global and instantaneous. CNN utilizes technologies that aren't just fast, they're instant—and you can't get much faster than that.

Before CNN, network affiliates were obliged by their networks to buy glossy, highly produced news shows that mainly reported events from earlier that day or even the day before. Turner liked the idea that he could buy news from a vast, licence-free array of live remotes, which no network could afford to match. During major news events, such as the now famous coverage of Operation Desert Storm, CNN's audience share went off the graph. Not only did CNN's Gulf War coverage attract 50 million viewers in the United States alone, but it featured the delicious spectacle of NBC's Tom Brokaw being reduced to interviewing CNN reporter Bernard Shaw to get details on a key story.

Since the Gulf War, CNN has continued to develop and expand its international credentials. Despite increasing competition from regional competitors such as Euronews, CNN was available in over 140 countries by early 1994 and is firmly established as the "international gold standard" in its industry, precisely because of the speed and timeliness of its news coverage. As was abundantly clear during the Gulf War, at times not even the Pentagon was able to match CNN's ability to get first-hand information quickly. As a result of this extraordinary role reversal between the makers and the reporters of news, arch-enemies George Bush and Saddam Hussein acquired at least one common trait: They both relied as much on CNN as on their senior staffers for accurate updates on the war's developments. CNN has become the premier global information source because viewers believe it will always have the most current information. And they're right.

It should come as no surprise that CNN manages its operations differently from the news programs at the older, more conventional networks. Every aspect of CNN's system is geared toward maximizing the network's capability for speed. The day's programming is loosely set out in a hasty thirty-minute early morning meeting. But this initial schedule is by no means sacrosanct. After all, natural disasters, accidents and wars don't happen according to CNN's timetable. Stories are constantly updated as they are broadcast. Some are dropped and others are added. Decisions are made on the run and in a matter of seconds. Committees are almost nonexistent and highly informal.

News teams are pared to the bare minimum, often consisting of a reporter and a single camera person, unheard of at the other networks. Although the big policy decisions are taken by a few people at CNN headquarters in Atlanta, staff in the field are encouraged to take the initiative in decisions about news events as they happen. This decentralization of responsibility and decision making also contribute mightily to speed. If video journalists on location had to relay questions to Atlanta and wait for answers before they could broadcast, the delay might only be a matter of minutes—but in the news business, that could be enough to lose the story advantage. (UN peace-keeping operations, among others, could learn a valuable lesson from CNN about the virtues of decentralized, field-level decision making.) Events happen so fast that, on average, every broadcast hour contains twenty-two fresh minutes of coverage. Compare this to the major networks, which broadcast the news two or at most three times a day, often using video footage and reporting produced twelve or more hours earlier.

CNN was the first, and remains the best in the world at harnessing state-of-the-art technology with a speed-based organizational structure to feed the growing international appetite for instantaneous information and analysis. Others may well succeed in closing the gap one day, but by then you can bet Ted Turner will have jacked up the competitive ante even higher, with some other innovative breakthrough. Right now, and for the foreseeable future, he gets to set the rules of the game which he essentially invented. All that, plus Jane Fonda and the Atlanta Braves.

## Sun Microsystems: Do It Fast or Don't Do It at All

December 5, 1995 marked a defining moment in the history of the computer industry. That was the day that Microsoft finally capitulated and joined the growing stampede of first-tier information technology companies rushing to embrace Java—Sun Microsystem's dazzling new computer language for the Internet. On the strength of Microsoft's move, Sun's stock rose nearly $340 million *in a single day*. There is a certain irony in this; it is entirely possible that Java's success will ultimately prove the undoing of both Microsoft's entire computing paradigm—and its long-standing corporate hegemony. For Java has the potential to liberate literally millions of computer users from the tyranny of Microsoft's proprietary operating system. In the words of one outside analyst: "Jave doesn't have to actually make money for Sun, just help them break Microsoft's business model."[5]

For Sun and its ultra-iconoclastic CEO Scott McNealy, Java is only the latest in a series of coporate triumphs. In the fourteen years since its founding in 1982, Sun has built a company generating $6 billion in annual sales by raising rapid-fire innovation and execution to the level of an art form.

In an industry (high-performance engineering workstations) where competitors' product life-cycles were typically three to five years, Sun set itself the formidable task of doubling the performance of its workstations every twelve *months*. It issued the challenge to both employees and competitors publicly, in its annual reports.[6] Like other innovators profiled in this book, Sun is quite prepared to bring out new products at price and performance levels that savage their existing lines. Their reasoning? Far better to render your own products obsolete than have someone else do it for you. Sun was one of the first to articulate and harvest the virtues of "auto-cannibalism." When you're in the speed business, annihilating your own products is simply an inescapable occupational hazard. The advantage of doing it yourself is that at least you can dictate the timing and circumstances.

But Sun was not the only computer firm in Silicon Valley to recognize the competitive importance of speed. What made, and continues to make, Sun exceptional is its ability to translate that insight into action and *execution*. And that ability is, in turn, due to the single insight that lies at the core of Sun's competitive strategy: In a fast-paced, interdisciplinary field like computing, no one can possibly be on the leading edge of all the relevant technology. In the words of Sun cofounder Bill Joy: "Sun's strength is the recognition of a central truth: Technological change in the computer industry is continually accelerating. No single company can possibly be at the forefront of every important breakthrough, and those that try doing it all themselves inevitably fall behind."[7] So Sun focused instead on doing what it did best—designing the hardware and software for high-performance workstations—and ruthlessly farmed out virtually everything else to specialists who are the best in the world at what they do. Sun manufactures almost nothing itself; its integrated circuits, disk drives, memory chips, monitors, keyboards and the computer boxes themselves are purchased from outside suppliers. Even the final assembly of the components is farmed out. One happy result of this fanatical concentration on a few core competencies is extraordinary productivity. Sun's thirteen thousand employees generate almost $300,000 in sales per employee, nearly twice the output of IBM.

Sun's detractors carp that by using essentially off-the-shelf components, Sun leaves itself vulnerable to low-cost, copycat clone makers. Sun's response: Once again, a reliance on superior speed. Executive VP Bernard La Croute makes the point succinctly: "Copying something that moves faster than you can copy it isn't a very good business to be in."[8]

Sun employs another interesting technique to strengthen its capacity for rapid-fire innovation: It licenses its technologies to others as quickly as it develops them itself. This counter-intuitive strategy has at least three major benefits. First, by licensing the technologies to muscular partners like Toshiba and Digital, Sun disseminates its technologies widely and rapidly, thereby increasing the odds of creating de facto industry standards. Second, the licensees then enhance the technologies even further, and Sun reaps both technical and financial benefits. And third, most important, Sun uses its licensing strategy to pressure itself into coming up with the next innovation.

The knowledge that competitors will soon share their latest technologies provides a powerful motivation for Sun employees to concentrate on staying ahead, by innovating even faster.

Sun can hardly afford to stand pat. Growth in its traditional stronghold, the workstation market, is beginning to slow. Sun's own individual market share is being squeezed: at the top end, by cheaper, high-performance machines from the likes of Hewlett-Packard and Silicon Graphics, and by Pentium-powered PCs from below. So Sun CEO Scott McNealy is beginning to attack what he views as computing's next battleground: networked PCs. McNealy reckons that a major opportunity beckons at the crossroads of two countervailing industry trends: downsizing and upscaling. On the one hand, many large companies are downsizing off multimillion dollar mainframes onto cheaper, more flexible networks of smaller machines. At the same time, branch offices and small departments are moving in the opposite direction: upscaling from lightweight PC systems. McNealy plans to be waiting in the middle with solutions for both groups: cheaper workstations and midsize "servers" to run entire networks of PCs.

No one, least of all Scott McNealy, should underestimate the magnitude of Sun's latest challenge. For one thing, the new strategy will require quantum improvements in customer support and service, which have never been Sun's forte. Even for a company with Sun's demonstrated agility, reinventing a major component of its corporate culture will be no trivial matter. On the other hand, Sun has at least four potent attributes working in its favor. One is a still healthy 37 percent share of the $10 billion workstation market. Not a bad financial base to start with. Second is McNealy's resolute iconoclasm. As he puts it, "I *want* Sun to be controversial. If *everybody* believed in your strategy, you'd have zero chance of profit."[9] Third is the timely emergence of the Internet as the dominant coputing medium of the decade. Sun was *made* for the Internet, and vice versa. Ever since the early 1980s, Sun machines were predicated on and designed for the sorts of network-friendly technology platforms of which the Internet is only now emerging to the apotheosis. Fourth, and perhaps most importantly, there is no sign that Silicon Valley's fastest company is slowing down at all.

## *Chiron: Making Haste Slowly in Biotech*

You might well ask why on earth a biotechnology company would be included in a chapter on speed as a critical factor in competitiveness. After all, don't products in this field take ten years or longer to bring to market?

Well yes, and that's the bad news. The good news, however, is that all the competition is operating on the same, level playing field, and all that really matters is who ultimately wins the race. As Albert Einstein rather convincingly demonstrated, speed is a relative concept. And he should know. For thirty years he competed with some of the greatest scientific minds of the 20th century in the race to articulate a compelling theory of relativity. Can anybody remember the names of those other men and women? No? But we all know the name of Einstein, the guy who crossed the finish line first. And that is really the essence of speed as competitive advantage: Whether the development cycle in your particular industry is thirty years, ten years, or one to two years (as in the computer industry), the spoils go to whomever wins the race. Period.

This is especially true in the biotech business, where companies are generally also playing with roughly the same level of talent (everyone's a genius) and face the same imperative to produce before the seed money runs out. So, despite the relatively lengthy product cycle times in the biotech industry, or perhaps because of them, speed becomes not just one of the most essential components of success, but the very basis of survival. One of the very few companies to have not only survived but thrived in that merciless competitive environment is Chiron Corporation, based near San Francisco. Of the more than four hundred entrants in the genetic engineering sweepstakes over the past two decades, only two have remained solidly profitable. Chiron, the former start-up with a current market capitalization of over $1.5 billion, is one of them.

Cofounder and CEO Ed Penhoet understands the make-or-break importance of speed as well as anyone, and better than most. As he puts it: "The winners in the biotech industry will be the ones who can produce the inventions the fastest . . . if our history has taught us anything, it is that you have to focus on speed as the key element in building any organization." [10]

So far, Chiron has been a conspicuous winner in an enormously demanding industry that has produced more than its share of losers and bankrupts. Started in 1981 at the labs of the University of California at San Francisco, by 1986 Chiron had brought a blockbuster vaccine for the scourge of hepatitis B to market faster than any competitor. The company is currently doing clinical trial testing (normally the last lap in an eight- to-ten year marathon) for vaccines against a number of other deadly diseases, including malaria, hepatitis C and AIDS. Chiron has parlayed these discoveries and distribution agreements with the likes of Merck, Ciba-Geigy, and Johnson and Johnson into one of the very few consistently profitable, major biotech companies in the world. (A sad and somewhat surprising fact, given the amount of hype that pervades the biotech field.)

So if everyone in the biotech biz is very, very smart, and they all have to scramble for the same development money, how do they go about doing things faster in a field where slowness is endemic? Penhoet, a Ph.D. in bio-chemistry, believes the answer is simple. First, you personalize the challenge, and then you flat-out work harder than everyone else. Sixteen-hour days, seven days a week is not an unusual schedule in this business. So what's really needed in the biotech world is the speed of a world-class sprinter plus the stamina of a marathoner.

Several factors contribute to an employee's willingness to take on such a punishing schedule. In the first place, most of Chiron's scientists come from the type of academic background that breeds an entrepreneurial mindset. This may come as a surprise to nonacademics who stereotype all of academe as an ivory tower of leisure and unreality. Not true. The world of university scientific research is intensely competitive and entrepreneurial. Its denizens live the dictum "publish or perish." But you can't publish if you don't have original research to report, and you can't do original research without grant money, of which there is always too little to go around. And in the academic world, one is competing against a lot of other very smart people for the same scarce funds. So every scientific researcher either becomes a successful intellectual entrepreneur or they end up driving a cab. Penhoet has made it his business to get more than his share of workaholic, entrepreneurial scientists and very few cab drivers. And once he finds them, he gives them a personal financial stake in the outcome of their work, by distributing equity in the company.

Another incentive built into Chiron's ethos of speed is keeping the competition personal. The company keeps close tabs on what the competition is doing and usually knows the particular people within those companies who are doing it. It's a variant on the notion of "know thine enemy." So competition becomes a matter of personal pride. And that encourages speed.

Penhoet uses organizational structures as a conscious weapon in his ongoing quest for speed. Every time the company threatens to get too big and impersonal, Penhoet breaks it into smaller units of two hundred or fewer to keep the personal, make-every-minute-count, entrepreneurial spirit and urgency alive. Penhoet is something of a fanatic on the subject; he sees the creation of a culture of immediacy and urgency as his number one job as CEO. Given the company's growth from fifteen employees to five thousand, this is no small task.

Of course, for the winners, the biotech industry enjoys enormous financial rewards. But there is another incentive that has no dollar value, but is an even more powerful motivator for the true biological scientist: Their work can save lives. There are very few business people who can go home at the end of the day and say, "I had a good day today. I made a million dollars —and I may just have saved a million lives." Many of the folks at Chiron can do just that.

## Black & Decker: The Tortoise and the Hare

Black & Decker's early success was built on a single innovation: the handheld power drill, which turned everyone into a home carpenter (with the conspicuous exception of this author). However, by 1984, this once trusted name in electric hand tools and small appliances found itself losing money for the first time since it was established in 1910. A new emphasis on marketing and finance had eroded Black & Decker's concentration on its traditional core competency in manufacturing. Equally important, the manufacturing environment had changed dramatically, but Black & Decker hadn't changed with it.

Huge retailers such as Wal-Mart were now demanding much shorter delivery periods to keep their own inventories low and to remain responsive to customer demand. If a supplier could not keep up with orders, the orders went elsewhere. Simply put, Black & Decker could not keep up. Its manufacturing cycle was as long as three months, and delivery times were a week or more. If Black & Decker were to survive, it would have to modernize every aspect of its operations: product development, manufacturing, marketing, the delivery cycle—the works. And it did. And the modernization continues to this day.

Black & Decker borrowed aspects of a number of new manufacturing approaches such as "agile manufacturing," just-in-time and synchronous manufacturing and added a few twists of its own. The bottom-line objectives were clear: Black & Decker had to become a flexible, quick-response manufacturer or throw in the towel. The old formulas simply wouldn't cut it any more. Many of the changes were enabled by state-of-the-art computer technology. A computerized database containing information on the company's entire operation was constructed. This provided, for the first time, a comprehensive, integrated and accessible picture of the company's entire operation. Once specific areas of weakness were identified, multifunctional teams were set up to explore and implement solutions. Most importantly, the teams were chaired by employees with direct, hands-on exposure to the problem, not by potentially remote senior executives. This left the ultimate responsibility for executing the working groups' final decisions with the same people who had made them in the first place. This strategy encouraged a faster acceptance of change by the employees and, concomitantly, a quicker implementation of the new processes.

Computers also allowed Black & Decker to simulate proposed new manufacturing processes, to test their viability before large amounts of time and money were invested and possibly wasted. Black & Decker's CEO Nolan Archibald, who led the modernization drive, swears he would never build another facility without first running a computer simulation.[11] Black & Decker also introduced a computerized design system that helped reduce its new product design cycle, in some cases, from over two years to less than twelve months.

Computers are also being used to facilitate a just-in-time, Toyota-like approach to materials and logistics management. Parts are now ordered and moved on an as-needed basis. Computers link company operations worldwide. Each factory runs on daily computerized schedules that can be changed in minutes in response to sudden problems. Mechanization was also computerized to keep up with the new short, flexible scheduling and production runs. For instance, under the old system, readjustment of machinery to a different function used to take several days. With computer-controlled lathes, this investment of time is greatly reduced and Black & Decker can respond much more quickly to changing orders and customer requirements.

This newly acquired, hard won corporate culture of speed and responsiveness is now beginning to permeate the entire company. The original—and narrow—objective of Black & Decker's focus on speed related to manufacturing logistics, but the benefits have clearly spilled over into the equally, if not even more, critical area of new product innovation. By the mid-1980s, the company's record for bringing new products to market was abysmal. Almost all the company's revenues were generated by products three years old or more. As Black & Decker's "speed revolution" began to really take hold in 1990, the company was able to bring out as many as forty new products a year, an unthinkable feat only five years previously.

The ultimate objective of Black & Decker's speed-based modernization effort is to develop the capacity to manufacture custom orders, instantaneously. For now, they'll have to content themselves with an over 30 percent market share in the worldwide power tool market, a growth rate of over twice the industry average, increased annual sales of some $5 billion, and a blizzard of innovative products leveraging new value from Black & Decker's core competencies and the rejuvenated market power of its name. Black & Decker may be a venerable senior citizen among American companies, but it is changing and growing more like a youngster.

---

# CONCLUSION

---

Most people find change, particularly rapid and unpredictable change, frightening and upsetting. The bad news part of this book's message is that CEOs and executives had better get used to it and lay in a generous supply of Maalox. Turbulence and change not only aren't going away, they're likely to get even more pronounced. The good news is that, while we can't slow down the velocity of the external business environment, there's lots we can do internally to speed up our own companies to try to keep pace.

A telling study by McKinsey and Co. reveals just how crucial speed can be. In the area of new product introduction, companies that met their time targets outperformed those that were six months late by fully eight times. So important were timeliness and speed that this outperformance persisted even when the speed was purchased at the cost of going as much as 50 percent over budget.[12]

The only effective response to rapidly changing market conditions is to develop the capacity to move at ultra-high speed oneself. While no company on earth can realistically expect to move as rapidly as the constantly changing competitive kaleidoscope around it, those who can come closest will be best positioned to survive.

The best alternative of all is to be the one who's driving most of the industry changes in the first place (see Chapter 1). But not everybody can be the next Bill Gates, Ted Turner or Steve Jobs. So it becomes incumbent on the rest of us mortals to do the next best thing: Develop super-fast organizations that can react quickly, turn on a dime, and make near instantaneous adjustments to the turbulence of the marketplace. There is simply no alternative. It's the only way to avoid becoming the Gutenberg press to your competitors' laser-based desktop publishing.

So how do we build super-fast organizations? As we've seen throughout this chapter, some speed-based techniques relate to creating new organizational structures, such as smaller, empowered, multidisciplinary teams. Many involve concerted efforts to push both resources and decision-making power "down" the organization and closer to the front-line troops. Still others relate to overall corporate strategy, such as Sun Microsystem's decision to focus ruthlessly on a few core competencies and farm out everything else. Almost all involve leveraging the power of the new information technologies to move information into the right hands at the right time. But all of them, if they're going to fulfill their potential, need to do one thing: Create and maintain a corporate culture that recognizes the supreme importance of *urgency* and *speed*, by placing them at the center—not the periphery—of their competitive strategies.

### CHAPTER SIX

# GET ENTREPRENEURIAL
# AND EXPERIMENTAL

*"Everything is experimental."*
RICHARD BRANSON CEO/ THE VIRGIN GROUP

There was a time when being the biggest, most experienced corporate kid on the block was a guarantee of commercial success and even dominance. Those days are long gone. Size and experience do confer some potential advantages. But in the absence of a thoroughgoing commitment to and capacity for leveraging them strategically, it becomes all too easy for those potential virtues to turn into vices.

For many of the faltering Fortune 500 companies, their early success actually became something of a liability. Market dominance came a little too easily, as the sheer gravitational mass of the company attracted new orders and clients with little or no effort. As a rule, the balance of power between buyer and seller heavily favored the seller; there was no particular pressure to please the customer because he or she had relatively few realistic alternatives.

But that was then. This is now. For one thing, competition can now come from almost anywhere, anytime. Technology has empowered smaller, nimbler competitors dramatically. In the banking industry, ten-person boutiques can take on the J. P. Morgans of the world for specialized and prestigious pieces of business—and win. Software engineers from Bangalore, India can and do run rings around their counterparts at larger, more established North American firms. The days of simply sitting back, waiting and depending on corporate size and reputation to attract business by gravitational pull are effectively over.

Global competition has become much too tough, too ubiquitous and too unpredictable. These days, you've got to go out and make things happen proactively.

Let's be clear. The relationship between size and entrepreneurial behavior doesn't have to be an inverse one. People like Bill Gates have already demonstrated convincingly that even huge companies like Microsoft can be as proactive, aggressive and in your face as the most entrepreneurial start-up. In this chapter, we'll see some pretty entrepreneurial behavior out of Bell Atlantic, a $30 billion behemoth, And I've even met dyed-in-the-wool entrepreneurs in such unlikely organizational settings as Her Majesty's Post Office in London Conversely, I've seen some twenty-five person firms in Silicon Valley that made IBM on its worst days look like a gazelle. So it isn't really a matter of size or organizational setting at all. It's more a question of *attitude*.

Entrepreneurial behavior can no longer be the exclusive preserve of twenty-five-year-olds in jeans and sneakers wolfing down junk food at 3:00 A.M. in Silicon Valley start-ups. Everybody has to get into the act. And they are. As we'll see in this chapter, green shoots of entrepreneurship are sprouting in some pretty unexpected places, not least of them "Communist" China and Siberia.

Entrepreneurship is a bit like dieting: Everybody's in favor of it in principle, but only a few have the intestinal fortitude to do what it takes to reap the rewards. In my view, the major source of the problem is cultural and is rooted in our almost pathological fear of failure.

For most Western-trained, macho business executives, failure is worse than a rude insult to one's masculinity. Why, it's downright un-American! And companies like IBM and McKinsey should be eternally grateful that that's the case, for it's this aversion to both failure and criticism that leads otherwise intelligent executives to consistently hire the "safe" providers of corporate goods and services. After all, no executive ever got fired for hiring McKinsey and Co. as strategy consultants and no information technology chief on record ever lost his or her job for buying computer hardware from IBM, though it is arguable that quite a few should have. The "solutions" produced by these major, mainstream suppliers may or may not be the most cost-effective, imaginative or tailored to the client's specific needs. Sadly, trifling considerations of quality and fit are often distinctly secondary to the imperative of avoiding criticism and failure. It is this same paralyzing fear of failure that causes executives to avoid trying new approaches and to ignore or camouflage corporate carcinogens until they have metastasized beyond the point of repair.

What is needed instead is a far more entrepreneurial corporate culture, one where experimentation, risk taking and even failures are not only tolerated, but actually celebrated. After all, the only real alternative to experimentation and risk is decay and decline. The essence of risk is the possibility of failure. Writer Kevin Kelly makes an eloquent case for a more tolerant and opportunistic outlook towards "failures." "Honor your errors. To advance requires a new frame. But the process of going outside the conventional method is indistinguishable from error. Evolution can be thought of as systematic error management."[1]

Scratch a successful entrepreneur, even a little bit, and you'll find a failure or two—or ten. Virgin's Richard Branson has had his share of fiascos along with his high-profile successes. In March 1995, for example, Branson had to admit that his American partnership with Blockbuster Entertainment's Wayne Huizinga was going nowhere. He threw in the towel. What elevates Branson and his ilk above the rest of us is not that they don't experience setbacks, it's that they absolutely refuse to be defeated by them. If anything, they seem to stiffen their resolve to succeed the next time.

The emerging rigors of 21st century hypercompetition leave us little choice. We must experiment, and experimentation inherently carries with it the near certainty of at least occasional failure. In a truly entrepreneurial culture, failure tends to be regarded as a learning opportunity, a necessary precondition to eventual success. Says one senior executive who already got the message: "Around here, we don't shoot people for failing. But we *do* shoot 'em for not even trying." The status quo is simply not a viable option any longer. You can stand still if you like, but your competition certainly won't.

One other crucial point about entrepreneurs. They are, above all else, men and women of action. Not terribly surprising. If your mortage, wife/husband and kids were on the line every day, you'd be a man/woman of action too! When you have to spend 40 percent of your time worrying about meeting payroll and fending off creditors for just a few more weeks, langorous analysis is simply not a luxury you can afford.

As a breed, entrepreneurs are sublimely disinterested in fancy strategic planning exercises, elegant five-year financial projections and consultants' team-building exercises at exclusive resorts. They aren't even terribly interested in proper market surveys of the sort to which the Proctor and Gambles of this world seem so heavily addicted. And why should they be? After all, has anybody ever seen the market surveys taken before the launch of the Sony Walkman, Chrysler minivan or microwave oven? Of course they haven't. The studies didn't exist. No suburban housewives were frantically phoning Lee Iaccoca demanding something bigger than a station wagon and smaller than a truck. Instead, each of those three blockbuster products resulted from entrepreneurs (yes, they do still exist in large companies) creating an attractive new offering *before* there was a clearly articulated market demand for it. Market surveys are fine when you're dealing with old-fashioned, head-to-head competition in stable, well-established markets. But when you're trying to *create* new markets and new competitive space, by definition you're exploring new territory where there are no road maps.

Which is precisely where the true entrepreneur likes to be. Entrepreneurs instinctively understand the importance of real-world experimentation, trial and error and speed. They are fanatical about getting feedback on their business ideas from living, breathing potential customers, not from antiseptic market surveys. Get the new concept out into the real world, test it, refine it and then get the next iteration out—fast. To the entrepreneur, strategy *is* action, not some sort of abstract intellectual exercise that occurs every October at headquarters or an offsite retreat.

Experimentation, feedback, "failure," learning, adjustment, action. That's what successful entrepreneurship is all about. Whereas the corporate motto of a depressing number of companies these days seems to be "ready, aim, aim, aim, aim . . . ," entrepreneurial outfits are quite prepared to fire away, eager to get some real-world feedback, reload and fire again.

Entrepreneurship, like innovation, is a profoundly relative concept. At its core, it implies a willingness to take the risk of challenging conventional wisdom and prevailing approaches. And since conventional wisdom in Silicon Valley may be markedly different from conventional wisdom in Guangdong, People's Republic of China, we must adopt different standards for entrepreneurship in different places. Let's look at some examples.

## *The Virgin Group: Entrepreneurship Writ Large*

No individual on earth better exemplifies the qualities of an entrepreneur than Britain's Richard Branson. A look into the success of his Virgin Group of companies is really an examination of one man's determination to constantly reinvent his business, start up new companies and take risks. The archetypal iconoclast, Branson is an executive who has never let fear of failure—or failure itself—stop him from adopting unconventional corporate structures or attempting the seemingly impossible.

Since entering business twenty-five years ago at the tender age of nineteen, Branson has engaged in an endless series of business start-ups. Despite achieving tremendous success (he is currently ranked as one of the ten wealthiest men in Britain), Branson certainly does not resemble the other members of the billionaires' club. Often clad in jeans, his smiling, bearded face is the essence of boyish enthusiasm. He has actively fostered a reputation as a thrill seeker and has been mentioned in the Guinness Book of World Records for his speedboat and hot-air balloon exploits.

But his greatest achievement to date must surely be the Virgin Group, a mini-empire of companies whose name aptly mirrored Branson's initial beginner status in the business world. Along with its major airline and record companies, the group has handled hotels, music megastores, holiday package dealers, interactive entertainment, publishing, radio, television and investments. Throughout it all, Branson has displayed the classic entrepreneur's disdain for conventional market analysis, preferring instead to rely on his "nose" for successful business ideas. "With many companies we start, we don't even do the figures in advance. We just feel there's room in the market. We try to make the figures work out after the event."[2]

It all began with Virgin Records, which attracted notice in 1973 when its first original record, *Tubular Bells* by Mike Oldfield, became the theme for *The Exorcist* selling five million copies. Branson continued to follow his now famous instinct for the unconventional, and signed such offbeat groups as the Sex Pistols and Boy George, many of whom went on to become household names. To this day, Branson maintains that his tastes are simply those of the masses and trusts his instincts about what people really want, considering himself to be the "ultimate consumer." By the age of twenty-three, he had also become a millionaire.

While working on his record company, Branson traveled constantly and was continuously disappointed by airline service. As he puts it "I thought it should be an entertaining experience."[3] His solution? Build a better airline himself. Why on earth not? In 1984, he created Virgin Atlantic Airways Ltd., which would go on to shake up the stuffy world of transatlantic travel. The original idea was simple: Virgin Atlantic would offer discount fares and target mainly young people who were keen to save money. Soon after its creation, Branson began asking celebrities who were signed to his record label to fly on his airline. The airline rapidly became a touchstone for nonconformist travelers tired of the mediocre service provided by many of its larger competitors. Branson succeeded in applying many of his personal attributes, i.e., youth and vigor, to Virgin Atlantic. He did, however, have the good sense to combine people with "Bransonesque" attributes with more stable employees, including several senior executives with many years of airline experience. He also avoided pilots with his own penchant for risk taking (how would *you* like to hear that your pilot had recently set the world record for speed-boat racing?). Branson later went on to segment his market further and developed "upper-class" service, costing roughly the same as business class but providing services such as in-flight massage and manicures, tailors and even gambling. More recent innovations have included "mid-class," offering amenities somewhere between economy and business class for passengers paying full economy fares. Branson recognized early on that such innovations were the only way such a small airline could compete with the big players; Freddie Laker's earlier and spectacular failure had proven that deep pockets win the price war game every time. By most measures, Virgin has succeeded. In 1993 it claimed 22 percent of passengers on the London-New York corridor.[4]

Typical of his personal style, Branson becomes actively involved in the flights he takes, setting an example for customer service that his staff rapidly picks up. Branson takes advantage of his time in the air by talking to passengers, finding out what they want and even helping serve drinks. "Every time I fly, I come back with new ideas," says Branson, who jots notes to himself on napkins or even on his hand.[5] Virgin Atlantic has overcome some of the disadvantages of smallness through a new strategic alliance with Delta Airlines, which is block-booking a third of the seats of Virgin flights between seven American cities and Heathrow and also agreeing to "codeshare" and pool air miles.

Branson adopted the motto "small is beautiful" from a 1973 book of the same title by E. F. Schumacher and has consistently applied this principle to the Virgin Group. He explains "The smaller you make your company, the better. The only advantage to large is muscle, but you lose motivation."[6] Branson splits up his companies when they grow too large. "Once people start not knowing the people in the building and it starts to get impersonal, it's time to break up a company. I'd say that the number is around 50 or 60 people. By keeping it small, you give more people a chance. A company operates at its peak when people are able to know each other's strengths and weaknesses. I don't want people to get lost in the corridors of power."[7] Branson believes that by creating a series of smaller companies, they each maintain a better balance between creativity and order. He certainly makes an effort to ensure Virgin remains personal. Each of his six thousand employees has his home phone number and calls him "Richard."

The decentralized structure has other advantages too. Because each company is run by a director, on whom Branson places few constraints, there are many positions available for advancement within the Virgin Group itself. This is borne out by statistics that showed that in 1992, 85 percent of the new vacancies at Virgin were filled internally. By creating this internal promotion market, Virgin can offer a combination of both job security and career variety that many companies can't or won't match. As Branson explains "Too many Western companies offer no stability. They're always hiring and firing. A last resort for any company should be firing. If your children misbehave, you don't shut them out. People feel secure here. In 20 years with Virgin Records, we have never lost a major artist. And all of my managing directors are still with me."[8]

His personal style also helps attract new employees. Several studies in recent years have revealed that British schoolboys, asked to name who they would most like to be when they grow up, cited Mr. Branson more than any other U.K. personality.[9]

With the airline doing well, and having sold the Virgin Music Group to Thorn EMI in 1992 for $980 million (the biggest sale of an independent label in the history of the music industry), Branson turned his attention to new frontiers. He is capitalizing on the Virgin name's widespread aura and recognition value to expand into snack food and "leisure products." For example, Branson recently launched a line of consumer products under the "Virgin Retail Brands" umbrella, including Virgin Vodka, Virgin Spring mineral water and Virgin Cola (produced by Canadian cola manufacturer Cott). With typical in-your-face audacity, Virgin fully expects to knock Coca Cola into the Number 2 spot in the U.K. cola wars. Don't bet against them: Virgin Cola is already earning a million pounds' a week profit and climbing fast.

Branson's latest initiative may be his most creative and ambitious yet: He's selling mutual funds and investment products. And get this: He's also musing about getting into life insurance. Richard Branson as a life insurance salesman? The mere thought boggles the mind. Next thing you know, the Pope will be starting a franchise of birth-control clinics! But Branson's latest idea is nowhere near as crazy as it sounds. He and his team have correctly identified hidden value potential in the form of an entire generation of young Britons who have never participated in the mainstream market for financial products, regarding it as the stuffy preserve of their less with-it elders. Branson reckons that by combining Virgin's hip, iconoclastic image with the necessary level of financial rectitude and investment expertise, he could entice a whole new generation into the market in droves. And he appears to be right. The starting point, as always, is Branson's personal reputation for integrity—no small asset when you're flogging investment products. Branson's name is golden. Indeed, he recently placed fourth in a British survey rating the perceived integrity of public figures. No shame in that; the first three finishers were the Pope, the Archbishop of Canterbury and Mother Teresa. Virgin has leveraged its founder's personal reputation for probity, the company's image as a trendy iconoclast and a partnership with a leading British investment manager into what should prove to be a formidable new competitor in the British financial products industry.

Further down the road, Branson plans to expand his airline into Asia, and is even talking about starting his own private railroad in Britain. British Rail makes a mighty inviting target for the likes of Virgin. As Branson explains: "We're a company that likes to take on the giants. In too many businesses these giants have had things their own way. We're going to have a lot of fun competing with them."[10] What better epitaph could an entrepreneur possibly have? And, if Branson can upgrade the notorious British Rail sandwiches, there could even be a knighthood in it for him!

## Softimage: Canadian Boy Makes Good

The story of Daniel Langlois and Softimage may well become the Canadian, cyberspace equivalent of the American rags-to-riches story of Sam Walton and Wal-Mart. From inauspicious beginnings nine years ago in a single room in a dilapidated warehouse on Montreal's Boulevard St-Laurent, Langlois has built Softimage into a world leader in the exploding new area of computer animation. Today, Softimage's handiwork can be seen in such high-profile films as *Jurassic Park* and *The Mask*, neither of which could have been made without its software.

In classic entrepreneurial tradition, Langlois launched the company at age twenty-nine with $75,000 raised by mortgaging his house, cashing out his pension contributions and maxing out on his credit cards. Talk about incentive to succeed!

In 1994, Bill Gates thought enough of Langlois, his company and the growth potential of merging computing power with artistic creativity that he paid US$130 million for Softimage. What's even more remarkable, Gates transferred some of his best software developers and researchers to work with Langlois in Montreal, rather than reel in his new acquisition to headquarters in Redmond, Washington. Not bad for the son of a chicken farmer from north of Montreal.

A designer and animator by trade, Langlois became intrigued by the possibilities of harnessing the power of high-performance computing and using it to empower the creative artists with whom he worked. After graduating from design school in Montreal, Langlois secured a job at Canada's National Film Board, which has enjoyed an international reputation in the field of film animation for half a century. He seized upon a powerful but neglected computer at the NFB, and eventually taught himself to write code for it, pushing the computer's capacity towards 3D graphics. After struggling with the technology to produce what would now be regarded as crude 3D animation, Langlois recognized the need for more artist-friendly software. Unable to pursuade either the NFB or private firms to take on the task, he founded Softimage in 1986 to do it himself.

In typical entrepreneurial fashion, Langlois took on freelance assignments to help fund the development of the new software. By the end of the first year, those earnings and his savings had almost evaporated. Despite his imperfect English, Langlois put together a "roadshow" and eventually convinced thirty-five private investors in Toronto to part with a total of $350,000. In return, the investors got roughly one third of the company. Fortunately, Langlois had both the prescience and the eloquence to convince them to give him three years of freedom to execute his business plan without interference. Early-stage entrepreneurs are not always this farsighted, persuasive or fortunate.

After four years of operation, Softimage's revenues had grown to US$8.5 million. This allowed Langlois to raise $10 million in an initial stock offering to the public in 1992 and a further $13.6 million the following year. By the time of the Microsoft deal in early 1994, Langlois' one-man band had grown to about two hundred professionals using eighty Silicon Graphics workstations— as we have seen, the product of choice for top computer graphic designers. The one room had expanded to three floors in the warehouse; same warehouse, but now tastefully renovated.

How did he do it? The good old-fashioned way: Risking everything he had to create an innovative, state-of-the-art product in a highly strategic field that was poised for explosive growth. Not unlike what his new boss and business partner Mr. Gates did some years ago. Today, the skills Langlois brings to the Microsoft family leave him extraordinarily well positioned to supply important chunks of the DNA of the next global monster industry: multimedia. Together, Langlois and Gates are hoping to leverage the techniques Softimage pioneered for high-end film and video into a platform for the broader market of interactive computer tools. The first step in that ambitious voyage is likely to be the "Digital Studio." The basic concept is to extend the Softimage magic beyond the relatively narrow field of animation to create a full-service, PC-based postproduction capability. This would allow a whole series of functions currently performed separately—audio effects, titles, two-dimensional graphics, editing and interactive content—to be combined into a simple, integrated creative capacity. In short, a digital studio. Exciting stuff and that's only the beginning.

Like all successful entrepreneurs who succumb to the overtures of a giant partner, Langlois is now at a crossroads. The transition from tapped-out entrepreneur/founder to millionaire employee in somebody else's company is rarely an easy one to make psychologically. (Okay, so the money helps assuage the angst a bit.) What remains to be seen is whether the new partnership can marry Langlois' artistic genius and entrepreneurial gifts with Microsoft's resources and market muscle without stifling the dynamism and creative flair that made Softimage such an attractive acquisition in the first place. The early signs are encouraging.

## Teknekron: The Entrepreneurial Launching Pad

Who says academics make lousy entrepreneurs? Well actually, come to think of it, I guess I did, or at least I strongly implied it in earlier chapters. But there are exceptions to every rule and Teknekron Corp. from Berkeley, California certainly blows that particular generalization of mine right out of the water.

Founded in 1968 by a few Berkeley professors and some disgruntled misfits from large companies, Teknekron Corp. today generates about $250 million a year in sales and has had a consistent annual revenue growth rate of a remarkable 40 percent. Like a lot of innovative companies, Teknekron was formed out of a deep frustration with the status quo. Founder and CEO Harvey Wagner had tired of watching American corporate and university research labs generate brilliant and revolutionary new ideas such as transistors, relational databases, flat panel displays and RISC computing, only to have them commercialized successfully by others—usually Japanese corporate giants or American entrepreneurial start-ups. The main problem, in Wagner's view, was the lack of effective "innovation transfer mechanisms" and incentives that could serve as catalysts for getting new ideas out of company and university research labs and into real-world product and service offerings.

Wagner was determined to build a company that would bring together in a single innovative organizational platform, the three critical success factors for technology commercialization: leading-edge innovation sources; cutting-edge, demanding users; and catalytic entrepreneurs to bridge between the two. Structurally, the new organization would occupy the middle ground between large company and small start-up. And it would renew itself continuously through the constant formation, maturation and divestment of new entrepreneurial companies. Thus was born Teknekron.

Teknekron is a fascinating hybrid, combining elements of both a technology incubator and a virtual venture capital company. Wagner and his cronies are constantly on the lookout for bright young people with a good, information technology concept and some entrepreneurial flair. Teknekron then works with the entrepreneurs to create a start-up, immediately putting them together with leading-edge potential customers, to give their efforts a market focus from the outset. Teknekron also supports the entrepreneurs with capital, and technical and marketing advice. It even hooks them up with leading academics to ensure their concepts stay on the cutting edge, technically and intellectually. In return, the academics get the rights to equity in the company down the road. In two or three years, the start-ups may grow to twenty-five or thirty employees and attain "affiliated company" status, at which point the entrepreneurs are deemed to have earned a significant equity stake in the venture. (Wagner is adamant on this point: ". . . all rewards should follow performance, not precede it.")[11] Accordingly, although large chunks of equity are set aside for the entrepreneur/managers from the outset, individual allocations are never actually handed over until the new venture has proven itself in the marketplace and individual contributions can be better assessed. Once this occurs, Teknekron is quite prepared to spin off the affiliates completely. Wagner calls his organizational paradigm "the open corporation": open to entrepreneurial talent, open to technological innovation and open to market needs. He summarizes Teknekron's corporate mission this way: "Identifying and nurturing entrepreneurs and connecting them to sources and users of innovation are the open corporation's raison d'être and the main driving force of corporate growth."[12]

The intermediate, affiliate stage of corporate development is one of Teknekron's real innovations and contributions to the art and practice of entrepreneurship. It recognizes a simple truth that conventional venture capitalists habitually ignore, to their own detriment and that of their investee companies: Five people and a clever idea do not, in and of themselves, make a real company. You've gotta walk before you can run. Wagner et al. recognized from the outset that an enormous amount of nurturing and experience would be required before their entrepreneurs could fly solo. So the affiliate designation becomes the ideal middle ground. The entrepreneurs are given enough autonomy and distance to keep the entrepreneurial fires stoked, but enough support and guidance from the parent company to ensure they could really achieve sustainable profitability, hire first-rate people, expand their markets, manage their growth strategically and delegate responsibilities intelligently. In short, act like a real company.

Teknekron creates three or four start-ups a year. To date, about a dozen have graduated to full-fledged affiliate status, serving customers ranging from energy utilities to investment banks. Another four have either gone public or been purchased by major technology companies such as TRW and Litton. Another dozen start-ups have yet to progress to the affiliate stage.

Wagner's success rate of roughly 50 percent is fully 400–500 percent greater than the traditional "hit rate" for high-tech start-ups. I believe there are two overriding reasons for this abnormally high success rate. The first is Teknekron's unconventional, open-corporation organizational model. The second is the discipline created by Teknekron's ruthless focus on the *commercial* utility of technology. Wagner's philosophy is clear: No matter how intrinsically interesting or attractive a technology might be, it has no value unless there is a profitable market for it. In Wagner's memorable phrase:

"Building a better mousetrap is valueless if no one has a rodent problem."[13] The place to start, therefore, is with the customer with the rodent problem, *not* the technology or the mousetrap engineer. Teknekron drums into each of its affiliates that they must begin by identifying customer problems and then develop solutions that are both technologically and economically compelling. In my experience, the world's entrepreneurial wannabes could save themselves incalculable grief (and money) by heeding Wagner's simple but powerful message—and example.

## Bell Atlantic: The Nimble Behemoth

Few industries have undergone a more rapid or dramatic transformation than telecommunications. Technological change is rapidly obliterating the formerly neat distinctions among the telephone, computer, wireless communications and even entertainment industries. They are blurring together, into an evolving and indistinct but incredibly dynamic gestalt known as multimedia. Sweeping regulatory changes and, in some countries, outright privatizations have exposed telecommunications companies to both the perils and the opportunities of competition. Some telephone companies have been more successful in adapting to the rigors of their new competitive environment than others. After all, entrepreneurial behavior has rarely been the first instinct of monopolists. One of the more conspicuously successful and entrepreneurial of the formerly stagnant telephone companies is Philadelphia's Bell Atlantic. Its story is most encouraging. If a sluggish, highly centralized, domestically focused monopolist can somehow transform itself into an entrepreneurial innovator with diverse international interests, there's hope for the rest of us.

Formed in 1983 after the court enforced breakup of AT&T, Bell Atlantic is one of the seven so-called Baby Bells. (Some baby: Bell Atlantic's annual revenues are currently roughly US$30 billion.) Its original charter was a straightforward, plain vanilla one: to provide local telephone service to six mid-Atlantic states and Washington D.C. Barely ten years later, Bell Atlantic is now involved in everything from joint ventures with Hollywood mega-mogul Michael Ovitz to mobile cellular phone networks in the Czech Republic. How did it get there?

Like most radical corporate transformation processes, Bell Atlantic's was neither quick nor painless. It started with the realization that the status quo was unsustainable and that nothing less than fundamental change would suffice. Not only was Bell's core business under attack, but the available alternatives seemed limited in the extreme. Bell was being squeezed between the rock of tight regulation and the hard place of new, less fettered competitors. The regulations strictly controlled Bell's rate of return on local telephone service, while simultaneously restricting its ability to branch out into attractive new fields, like cable television. Meanwhile, nimble new competitors such as Sprint and MCI were making serious inroads into Bell's most profitable line of business, long-distance telephone service. Something had to give. The first thing on the agenda was corporate culture.

Before new opportunities could even be identified, much less acted upon, Bell Atlantic had to dismantle the sluggish, monopolistic mindset that had prevailed for decades, and replace it with a new ethos of entrepreneurial dynamism. CEO Raymond Smith uses a nice metaphor to describe the old situation: "The old Bell system was like a great football team with the best athletes and the best equipment. Every Saturday morning we'd run up and down the football field and win 100 to 0 because there was no one on the other side of the line of scrimmage. We were a monopoly."[14] Not only this, but a highly centralized monopoly at that. None of the individual operating companies or divisions had sufficient autonomy to introduce a new product or service on its own. Nor, for that matter, did they have much inclination to do so, in the absence of any real competition.

Smith began by holding extensive, day-long sessions with his top fifty executives, discussing in detail the changed attitudes and behaviors Bell would need to thrive in the new environment. Next, each of the fifty acted as "executives in residence" for larger working groups covering the company's top four hundred managers. The process was repeated until all twenty thousand employees were directly involved in sessions designed to communicate and create "buy-in" for the new "Bell Atlantic Way," which stressed personal initiative and accountability, teamwork, innovation and even—wait for it—constructive dissent. None of these qualities had exactly been conspicuous in the "old" Bell way.

Predictably, these sessions initially elicited a healthy degree of skepticism from employees inured to successive rounds of pious rhetoric from the executive suite. But at least four things proved different this time around. First, Smith was able to make a convincing case that radical change was indeed necessary and that clinging to the old success formulas would be a recipe for disaster, both for individuals and for the company. Second, Smith and his senior lieutenants were determined to actually "walk the talk" and model the behaviors they were advocating to others. They invested many days in the group change sessions and were careful to try to practice what they preached. Unlike the past, loyalty to the overall corporate team was shown to be more important than narrower departmental or divisional loyalties. Third, there was a major new emphasis on communicating company-wide business issues, strategies, priorities and results so that individuals understood, often for the first time, how their individual roles fitted into Bell's overall strategic direction and performance. Fourth and most importantly, Smith and his team acted. Budgets and compensation systems were quickly and substantially changed to better reward the innovation, teamwork and entrepreneurship the executive team was now demanding.

One of the more important and dramatic mechanisms Smith introduced to create the new culture of entrepreneurship was the requirement that staff support groups, such as training, accounting and business research, had to market and charge for their services. For the first time they would actually be subjected to the discipline of the marketplace. Client groups within the company were suddenly freed to shop around for those same services on the open market. Talk about shock therapy! All of a sudden, if you weren't offering superior services at competitive prices, you had nothing to do and no way to justify your salary. While the transformation wasn't instantaneous, it was dramatic. The spectacle of formerly sleepy, introverted departments creating their own marketing brochures, electronic newsletters and trade show exhibits to attract customers *from their own company* provides some indication of the shift to a more entrepreneurial corporate culture.

The centerpiece of Bell Atlantic's entrepreneurial revolution is the Champion program, which provides seed money, training and mentoring for "intrapreneurs" within the company to develop new products and services. Everyone is eligible for the Champion program and when an individual's proposal is accepted, the intrapreneur gets to devote company time to it and run the project him or herself. To inject even more entrepreneurial realism— and incentive—employees can invest a portion of their salaries in the project in return for a share of its revenues. Since the program's inception in 1988, Bell Atlantic has produced over 250 Champions, whose products and services now contribute over $100 million to Bell Atlantic's bottom line. One of the program's stars is Jack Copley, a budget manager in the network services group. Copley developed Thinx, an innovative software graphics program that integrates data and images. The program was sufficiently innovative; it was one of five finalists for *Discover* magazine's award honoring scientists and engineers for technical breakthroughs. As important is the product's reception in the marketplace, which has been enthusiastic since its launch in late 1990.

But the real significance of the Champion program goes far beyond individual triumphs and the $100 million boost to Bell's bottom line. Its true value lies in its contribution to the growth of an ethos of entrepreneurship throughout the entire company. That entrepreneurship culture, totally foreign a decade ago, allowed Bell Atlantic to create new joint ventures with partners as diverse as Sun Microsystems and accountants Deloitte and Touche at home, as well as with Spain's Telefonica, Germany's Siemens and the Korean Telecommunications Authority abroad.

Bell Atlantic's latest entrepreneurial foray could prove to be its most audacious yet. Determined to be a major player in the convergence of communications technologies, Bell Atlantic engineered a blockbuster megamerger with cable company TCI in late 1993. Then, in March 1995, Bell teamed up with two Baby Bell siblings and Hollywood super-agent Michael Ovitz to create a $300 million joint venture in interactive television. The idea is to leverage Bell's state-of-the-art switching capabilities with TCI's cable distribution network, combine them with Ovitz's access to world-class programming, and create what Bell executive Stuart Johnson calls "a new form, almost a new dimension—a fourth dimension of entertainment and programming. It allows you to customize programming to individual needs."[15] Heady stuff indeed for a telephone company, but they just might pull it off. To head up the venture they've hired Howard Stringer, former CEO of the CBS Broadcast Group and one of the most highly respected television programmers in the business. Success is hardly assured, however. Among their likely competitors is a group headed by some fly-by-night outfit called Walt Disney Co. Still, the mere fact that Bell Atlantic could mount a credible entry in the interactive TV sweepstakes is an eloquent testimony to its metamorphosis into a truly entrepreneurial company.

## *Wheeling and Dealing in Guangdong, China*

I believe that entrepreneurship, like innovation itself, is a relative concept heavily dependent on the cultural, historical and organizational context in which we find it. It is, therefore, somewhat surprising to find genuine entrepreneurship in the bosom of an organization that is at once large, governmental and ostensibly Communist. Maybe orthodox Chinese Communism has been getting a bad rap at Chamber of Commerce meetings for the past forty years or so, but it just never springs to mind when you think of entrepreneurship. Collective state farms, sure, even world-class table tennis teams, but not entrepreneurial dynamism. For that reason, Huang Yantian and his colleagues in Guangdong, People's Republic of China, are of considerable interest. They run what is, in all but name, China's first real merchant bank.

For over a decade, two powerful and mutually reinforcing trends have been dramatically reshaping the Chinese economy. The first is a profound decentralization of economic power from Beijing to provincial and local government. At the same time, under Deng Xiaoping's economic reforms, a number of "special economic zones" were created to encourage experiments with capitalism. Nowhere in China have these two trends converged with greater impact than in the southern province of Guangdong, near Hong Kong. In 1994, the Guangdong economy had the fastest growth rates in all of China, at 15 percent. Analysts fully expect growth to be sustained at those rates well into the 21st century. Guangdong is already the single largest focus for both infrastructure spending and foreign industrial investment in China. Indeed, some financiers now refer to Guangdong as "the fifth Asian tiger," putting it in the exalted company of the other Asian economic success stories: Taiwan, Singapore, South Korea and Hong Kong. As its economy becomes fully integrated with Hong Kong's after 1997, Guangdong's vitality can only increase. At the center of this economic web, virtually monopolizing the interface with Western investors, sits Huang Yantian.

The fifty-something Mr. Huang is president of the Guangdong International Trust and Investment Corporation (GITIC), the financial and deal-making arm of the provincial government. Think of him as Communism's answer to Richard Branson and Michael Milken rolled into one, before the latter went to prison for a few, niggling securities violations. GITIC's assets are estimated at some US$5.5 billion and include everything from ten McDonald's restaurant franchises to a patent license for Merck's hepatitis B vaccine. You name it, GITIC does it. They make commercial loans, issue bonds, trade securities, and have served as financial advisors to over a dozen Chinese companies undergoing privatization. And GITIC isn't content to be a mere lender and advisor; it also owns substantial equity stakes in real estate projects, aluminum plants and leasing companies. Huang the entrepreneur is also leveraging GITIC's financial savvy into new wholly owned businesses such as a PC-based stock quotation service.

Most long-time Communist Party stalwarts might be content at this point to simply rest on their $5.5 billion asset base and their quasimonopoly on one of the fastest growing economic regions on the planet. But not Huang. He's already onto his next project. The main focus of his fourteen-hour work days is satisfying Guangdong's insatiable appetite for foreign capital to build its industrial infrastructure: power plants, telecommunications systems, bridges and highways. With Beijing lacking both the credibility and the resources to play that role effectively, Huang has hurled GITIC into the breach. Before the end of 1996, Huang will attempt to create a special Guangdong investment fund in New York to raise money for these major projects. He is also working with joint venture companies in Guangdong to acquire listings on foreign stock exchanges as means of bringing foreign investment capital into the region.

How does Huang do it? Well, he starts with an enviable position as the principal gateway and interlocutor between Western investors and the exploding infrastructure and commercial needs of this burgeoning region. Beyond that, there are three major keys to Huang's success. First, he achieved not only Western-style financial literacy, but outright excellence. Huang is perfectly comfortable discussing hedging strategies and currency-linked borrowing with visiting luminaries from Citibank and Goldman Sachs. This in turn enables the second prong of his strategy: Building long-term alliances with world-class Western industrial and consumer companies such as Merck, McDonald's and Daimler-Benz. And finally, GITIC is determined to be more than a mere financier. It wants to be a direct, value-added principal. It therefore usually acquires an equity stake in the ventures it finances, such as the $100 million Guangdong Float Glass Plant, a recent joint venture with PPG Industries. GITIC's role as a strategic equity investor allows it to participate in companies' long-term growth and profitability, and to share in the considerable added value its participation creates.

Sadly, however, Huang must soldier on without the benefit of an MBA or even so much as an advanced course in entrepreneurship from Wharton or Harvard. Quite the contrary. Like many of his contemporaries, Huang's major at university was Marxist-Leninist-Maoist thought. Go figure.

---

# CONCLUSION

---

The two most defining qualities of an entrepreneur are an appetite for *risk* and a visceral need for *action*. For many years—too many years, in my view—business conditions militated strongly against the entrepreneur. Size, stability and industry experience were the only commodities recognized as having value in the business world; without them you could forget about making an impact.

All that's changing. The 21st century business landscape will be more hospitable to the entrepreneur than any we've seen for a long, long time. The volatility and unpredictability of global hypercompetition have completely devalued most existing corporate currencies and virtues. What good is company size if you're too slow and muscle bound to capitalize on new, fast-moving opportunities? What use is lengthy industry experience if your most ferocious competitor is likely to come at you out of an entirely different sector? What's the point of conducting exhaustive market surveys if the market changes so fast they're obsolete before you've analyzed them? Under these kinds of conditions, what counts most is the willingness and ability to take risks, get real-life feedback and react quickly. In short, the ability to be entre-preneurial. As a commercial organism, the genuine entrepreneur should prove to be ideally adapted to the evolving imperatives of the 21st century competitive environment. Emboldened by its radically different competitive dynamics and liberated by the new information/communications technolo-gies, the entrepreneur's time has finally come.

### CHAPTER SEVEN

# BREAKING BARRIERS

*"Our dream is the boundaryless company—breaking the barriers that separate us from each other on the inside, and from our key constituents on the outside."*
JACK WELCH CEO/ GENERAL ELECTRIC

The fall of the Berlin Wall in 1989 did more than just usher in a new era of geopolitics; it also served as a powerful metaphor for both the necessity and the possibility of breaking barriers that once seemed impregnable. A few years later, South Africa's (relatively) peaceful transition to the multiracial, democratic government of Nelson Mandela provided a similarly compelling reminder.

This entire book is about breaking barriers of one kind or another—most importantly, the psychic shackles of orthodoxy. There is arguably no more potent threat to the vitality and dynamism of the global economy than the apparent inability of so many corporate leaders to transcend the tyranny of yesterday's managerial and strategic approaches. Internal intellectual, cognitive and ideological barriers are by far the most difficult kinds to break, and other chapters of this book attempt to deal with some of the most pervasive. In this chapter, we are primarily concerned with a different kind of barrier: organizational barriers.

A few years ago, in Geneva, I had the rare opportunity to work on a special international project with the CEOs and senior executives from over forty of the largest industrial corporations on earth, from over a dozen different countries. Since the project lay outside the core businesses of all the companies involved, it provided a unique opportunity to interact with the executives in settings where they were largely unconstrained by the formality and artificiality of their normal corporate personas. The results were fascinating. In private discussions, I was forcibly and repeatedly struck by an apparent anomaly. All these men (and they were almost all men) were bright, experienced and talented, some of them brilliant. Yet each of them, to varying degrees, expressed profound feelings of frustration, even impotence, over their acutely limited ability to make their corporate machines *perform* the way they wanted them to.

At the time, this struck me as extraordinary. Here were these supposedly omnipotent titans of global industry, lionized if not deified by the business press, confessing privately to being little more than corporate eunuchs. The more I thought about it, however, the more sense it made. There were a host of insidious, systemic organizational and cultural barriers preventing the effective transmission of leadership, insight and learning throughout large organizations. The bigger, more established and successful the company, the more likely it was that these barriers had become more intractable and, simultaneously, more familiar and therefore less apparent. By contrast, more dynamic companies had learned to break whatever barriers are necessary to move both energy and insight up, down, sideways, in and out. In some cases, they were lucky and farsighted enough to prevent the barriers from growing up in the first place.

But what exactly are these silent killers of corporate dynamism, and how can they be neutralized? For the most part, organizational barriers come in three basic varieties. First, horizontal barriers, which so often prevent collaboration between different departments and functional specialists. Second, vertical, hierarchical barriers, which separate senior executives from rank and file employees at the coal face. And the most intractable of all, the corporate boundary itself, that psychological Great Wall of China that separates the entire company from the other key players in its business ecosystem: customers, suppliers and competitors.

The evils of hierarchical and horizontal barriers have been well canvassed by others. (So well, in fact, that most of us have become so numbed by the rhetorical barrage that the problems have been trivialized almost out of existence.) Globalization has exacerbated the situation. If you thought it was tough before to get Henry down the hall onside for your new initiative, try rallying and sustaining support from Miguel in the new office halfway round the world in Santiago. And technology alone can't save us. The new information technologies have given us the infrastructure and *potential* to democratize information and flatten hierarchies, but the average executive brain remains firmly hardwired in the old patterns. Empowering them with new technology is a bit like giving the keys of a shiny new Lamborghini to a blind crack cocaine addict.

The barriers that have received much less attention, however, are those that insulate the company as a whole from its external environment. This simply has to change. For one thing, the demands of the competitive environment have now become both so extreme and so mercurial that not even the best endowed companies can cope with them alone. As a result, "strategic alliances" have become a way of life for companies, large and small. This represents a fundamental sea change in corporate strategy, one that renders the macho, go-it-alone corporate Lone Ranger model increasingly anachronistic. Britain's moribund, state-owned automaker, Rover, parlayed an alliance with Honda into a sufficiently successful capacity-building exercise that BMW bought a major stake in the venture for a premium priced $1.2 billion. Germany's telecommunications giant Siemens has teamed up with America's Corning to create a successful, fifteen-year-old alliance in the fiber optic cable business. Software leader Oracle recently teamed up with Sun Microsystems, Apple, Hewlett-Packard and Microsoft to develop software applications for its new co-operative-server data base. If successful, the alliance will create a de facto industry standard, and a powerful set of barriers to would-be competitors. Such examples are legion, and their numbers are growing every week.

This shift poses major challenges and problems for an entire generation of CEOs steeped in the business equivalent of Cold War thinking: a linear, black and white, us versus them, zero-sum game mindset. Teaching those old competitive dogs the more subtle new tricks of collaborative advantage and alliance building is no easy feat. For one thing, most of them aren't particularly convinced of the need to learn in the first place. Even those who are convinced soon discover the new game is a lot more complicated and difficult to play than the old one; an entirely different set of negotiating and management skills is required. The traditional boundaries between your own company and those of your collaborators (and even competitors) become blurred and more porous.

The arrival of the Age of Strategic Alliances is not without its problems. It raises a host of both strategic and practical issues. How much proprietary information and know-how is it prudent to share before your company's core competencies get "hollowed out"? More than one "strategic" alliance has ended up a competitive surrender, with one partner extracting so much intellectual capital from the other that the victim was left with no distinctive competence at all. The trick is for alliance partners to share enough skills to create advantage vis-à-vis competitors outside the alliance, while simultaneously guarding against a wholesale transfer of their own core skills. Another key question: How do you motivate, manage, measure and reward people who may now be spending as much as 75 percent of their time in another company's offices? These are by no means straightforward or easy questions.

As we approach the 21st century, "collaborative advantage" will likely become equally, if not more important than traditional competitive advantage. Love 'em or hate 'em, there's no way you can ignore these alliances. By one recent estimate, they have increased 25 percent per year consistently for the past five years.[1] Companies that are particularly adept at creating and managing them will have a distinct advantage over those who can't. Later in this chapter, I'll profile Toshiba as a leading-edge exemplar of a company that is mastering this emerging art of generating collaborative advantage.

Strategic alliances may be pushing the limits of conventional conceptions of business organizations, but the rise of the "virtual corporation" explodes them altogether. If there is an apt organizational metaphor for the mid-to-late 1990s, it must be the virtual corporation, a constellation of people, skills and organizations that coalesces for a particular project or task, then disbands and reconfigures itself for the next one. Virtual corporations usually operate with a central nucleus of anywhere from two to twenty people, surrounded by a constantly shifting kaleidoscope of special-purpose employees, contractors, suppliers and alliance partners. Their earliest antecedents were the major law and consulting firms, which have been assembling and disbanding interdisciplinary, project-specific teams for decades. The major difference is that it used to be done entirely in-house. Today's virtual companies assemble teams from all over the place.

Virtual corporations are the almost inevitable byproduct of two megatrends. They were made *necessary* because the intensity and velocity of hypercompetition requires a wide, constantly changing repertoire of skills that few permanent organizations can muster in their entirety. They were then made *possible* by the new information and communications technologies, which integrate the contributions of virtual team members from all over the world. Professional service firms like Andersen Consulting were, consciously or otherwise, among the first virtual organizations. Project-specific teams are routinely formed, complete their task, and then metamorphose into whatever new configuration is required for the next assignment. Recently, Andersen added a new twist to the virtual corporation: they are now running a thriving business supplying *temporary* CEOs and CFOs to client companies for specified assignments or periods of time. It's the ultimate: "just-in-time" delivery of senior executive talent for the precise moment it's needed, and then "returned." And it's entirely logical. Why shouldn't virtual companies have virtual CEOs? And why shouldn't they be senior Andersen employees, on loan for specific, temporary assignments?

Another classic example is provided, appropriately enough, by futurist John Naisbitt, of *Mega-Trends* fame. Naisbitt is essentially a virtual corporation all by himself and a global one at that. With a full-time staff of precisely three, subcontracting everything possible to a dizzying and constantly changing array of collaborators all over the globe, Naisbitt produces, coordinates and distributes an avalanche of books, speeches, articles and videos. And he presides over this global empire from his "corporate" command center in tiny Telluride, Colorado. It is difficult, if not impossible (not to mention useless), to discern where Naisbitt's own company ends and the rest of his complex business ecosystem begins. Naisbitt has seen the future and he's it. Even large companies like Sears, IBM and Kodak will start to look a lot more like Naisbitt Inc. and a lot less like their former, bloated selves.

A quick word about two other kinds of barriers that need surmounting by 21st century companies. An obvious but relatively underappreciated one is geography. As the realities of globalized competition work their way through the corporate food chain, the imperatives—and the difficulties—of managing across borders, time zones and cultures will become even more pronounced. As many a North American CEO has discovered to his or her considerable sorrow, you simply cannot run an international company the same way as a purely domestic one. Everything has to change: marketing and distribution strategies, manufacturing and production, strategic alliances, government relations and, most important of all, strategies for acquiring and disseminating knowledge-value throughout the organization.

The final and most difficult barrier is not really organizational per se, but creates a whole series of organizational pathologies in its wake. It is the barrier of ideology and mindset. Later in this chapter, I'll profile two organizations that are attempting to overcome one of the most formidable barriers any business entity could confront: a legacy of Marxist ideology and state communist monopolies. But the barriers don't need to be that extreme to be debilitating. Within the OECD countries, it is far more common to encounter such pernicious psychological barriers as the famous "not-invented-here" syndrome or the organizational sluggishness caused by a highly regulated quasimonopoly. Whatever their historical or cultural genesis, psychological barriers are both the most insidious and the most difficult to eradicate.

Barriers to innovation can and do come in all shapes and sizes. The principal focus of this chapter will be on the barriers of organizational orthodoxy: problems created by outmoded conceptions of everything from internal organizational structure to the outer boundaries of the company itself. Let's take a look at some companies that have successfully transcended those barriers.

## BREAKING INTERNAL BARRIERS

### *Denmark's Oticon*

Although managers routinely pay lip service to tearing down *internal* corporate barriers to communication, action and learning, in practice very few have pushed these ideas as far as Oticon, a $100 million producer of hearing aids located on the outskirts of Copenhagen, Denmark.

The world leader in hearing aids throughout the 1970s and early 1980s, Oticon's position began to deteriorate in the mid 1980s when a weaker U.S. dollar exposed its competitive shortcomings. The situation deteriorated rapidly. Oticon's market share plummeted from 15 percent to 7 percent, and the fall in revenues caused the company to tumble from first to third place internationally, in a field of competitors that included such behemoths as Siemens and Philips. By the late 1980s, it was clear to the board that radical changes would be needed if Oticon were going to survive. In a company that had seen little change over its first eight decades of existence, the board appointed industry outsider Lars Kolind to the CEO's job in 1988.

Kolind's first task was not unusual: cut costs. But after laying off some 15 percent of head office staff, Kolind began to realize the company would never be able to starve itself back into industry leadership. More profound changes and creative alternatives to corporate anorexia were clearly required.

Like many companies, Oticon had a "functional" organizational structure, with separate, clearly defined departments handling marketing and sales, finance, manufacturing and operations. Each department had a director who oversaw his or her department and sat on the top management group, which made all the strategic decisions. Kolind's revolutionary idea was to replace all the specialized functions with a company consisting of just one team—all 150 headquarters employees—who would become a flexible, creative and continuously developed workforce. Oticon employees would be multiskilled and would routinely take on several different tasks within the organization. Not only would the new organization respond well to change, it would actually *seek it out.* After an extensive period of communication and staff involvement, Kolind implemented his innovative ideas for new processes and organizational structures.

When Oticon staff members returned from their summer holidays in August 1991, the new building they entered was radically different from their previous headquarters. Employees no longer had offices. Instead, each floor consisted of a large open space with desks, each equipped with a computer, telephone and supplies. Also notably absent were the name plates; every desk was now available for anyone to use. An employee's personal effects and work were now contained in a mobile caddie, a small filing cabinet on wheels that he or she can wheel over to an available desk and begin work. The wheels are used frequently; rather than settling into one particular work area, employees sit with other members of the project group with whom they happen to be working on their current project.

The two major benefits of this radical change are speed and enhanced organizational learning. No more project team meetings need to be convened to discuss issues: If you need information from someone, just walk over and ask. Advertising people can see and hear what the marketing crew is doing beside them and each can overhear the production specialists. Secretaries can learn the background for the letters they type.

Coffee bars are scattered throughout the office with a view to encouraging informal information exchange and discussion and even the elevators were replaced with a large, centrally located spiral staircase for the same reason. The open concept encourages the free flow of communication needed to foster creativity and fast responses to the market.

As many large companies have long recognized, paper has a knack of slowing processes down. Kolind has a strong personal belief that paper is inefficient and that talking about solving problems is much faster than writing about them. Paper is virtually banned in the new Oticon.[2] Today, all incoming mail to Oticon is scanned into the computer and promptly shredded (with the important exception of legal documents!). As proof, all shredded paper flows through a large transparent chute in the dining area throughout the day. In a highly visible demonstration of the new regime, employees can now watch the morning mail literally disappear. Everyone's mail can now be accessed through the computer system.

But perhaps the most radical aspect of the new Oticon is its organizational structure. Strictly speaking, there really isn't one. Rather than organizing the company along various stages of a conventional "value chain," Kolind created a "spaghetti structure," a flexible system in which project groups create value in cooperation with customers.[3]

This new organization includes no job descriptions or titles; business cards no longer specify any particular position. Along with the walls, employees realized that August day that their former jobs had likewise disappeared. So they create new ones. Employees are free to apply their diverse skills on a variety of projects to make better use of their full range of capabilities. In fact, employees are encouraged to be able to perform at least three different "jobs."

A management committee remains in place to look after company-wide strategic issues, but the real work occurs at the project level. For example, an employee with an idea for a new project begins by recruiting a project leader, who in turn takes responsibility for building a project team from available employees and for acquiring the necessary resources. To help determine who is available, the company developed a sophisticated computer system that provides an indication of each employee's current commitments. Everyone's schedule, including Kolind's, is easily accessible. A project leader can simply look down the list and select people to approach. Such a system has the additional virtue of being a sort of self-regulating, performance-appraisal system, since it became evident within a few months just who were the most effective or ineffective project leaders and participants.

Creating a multiskilled workforce in an industry characterized by rapid technological advances means Oticon cannot afford to overlook employee training. To guard against the possibility that the project-oriented structure would neglect employees' skill development needs, several "skill coordinators" were appointed. These coordinators have budgets of their own and are able to finance training above and beyond that required for immediate project needs. Training decisions are not left up to the coordinators, however; Oticon employees are empowered to make their own decisions regarding their training needs and they generally do so.

Has Oticon's bold experiment worked? Well, pre-tax profits in 1993 have increased to five times the 1991 level, sales are up 23 percent, productivity is up 30 percent,[4] and the company achieved an industry record 30 percent return on sales.[5] Oticon's radical "spaghetti structure" might not work for every company, but it certainly suggests the competitive power that can be unleashed by breaking internal barriers.

The Oticon case illustrates clearly both the importance and the potential dividends of breaking down the internal barriers within a company. But that's only the beginning. In the 21st century—indeed, right now—it will be even more important to break down the external barriers that isolate most companies from their competitive environments. New relationships need to be created with outside suppliers, customers and even competitors. This is fundamental stuff, calling into question our traditional notions of just what a company is, and where it begins and ends.

## Chiat/Day: The Virtual Entrepreneur

From the day Jay Chiat first opened his ad agency in Los Angeles in 1968, he has consistently broken barriers. At Chiat/Day (C/D), the roles of employees, clients, consumers, bosses and even office space have all been turned on their heads. Obeisance to the traditions of old-style, monolithic ad agencies was anathema; creativity, experimentation and risk taking became business as usual. In the process, Chiat/Day created some of the most memorable and provocative ads of the last twenty years, and garnered a client list to die for, including the likes of Apple, Nike, Nissan, American Express, Reebok, MTV and Eveready Energizer (who can forget that relentless pink bunny?). Worldwide billings for 1994 were over $1 billion.

Jay Chiat's greatest genius as an entrepreneur is his ability to break down barriers: barriers among fellow employees, between agency and client, between agency and consumer and, most importantly, barriers to experimentation, risk taking and creativity. In many ways, Chiat/Day was the testing ground for a sea change in management style that has since been emulated by many of Silicon Valley's most innovative and successful companies, including Intel.

At Chiat/Day, individual staff don't have job descriptions; nor do their business cards bear any hierarchical or descriptive titles. It is understood that whatever skill an employee might have originally been hired for, there are to be no impediments to creative participation beyond that. If secretaries have creative ideas and want to assume different or challenging work, they can and do. In fact, flexibility to contribute widely is an unwritten job descriptor. Account management staff are expected to have a totally different concept of their role than account people in traditional ad agencies. They have a responsibility to act as *advocates* for the creative staff in meetings with clients; to encourage, cajole, push and sell the more leading-edge, creative, risky ad campaigns that clients might initially reject. That the job also be considered fun is almost mandatory.

That requirement is made easier by the innovative "cocreator" relationship Chiat/Day insists on between creative staff and client. Chiat/Day has been known to refuse accounts, including *Vogue* magazine, when a client would not accept such an arrangement. In addition to their creative contribution, there is a sound business reason for including clients in the creative process from the beginning: They become much less risk averse. When a client participates in the development of bold advertising ideas, there is a higher comfort level bred from familiarity, and a personal commitment that results in greater support for the risk taking and entrepreneurial style that have always been Chiat/Day's trademarks. From its iconoclastic campaign to launch Apple's Macintosh computer during the 1985 Super Bowl (the ad portrayed zombie-like IBMers marching over a cliff) to the Nike murals it painted on Los Angeles buildings during the 1984 Olympics, Chiat/Day's strength is its willingness to take artistic, and therefore business risks. Jay Chiat's risks and experiments haven't always panned out: Chiat/Day lost some pretty impressive clients along with the ones it won and kept. The c/d style isn't for everyone. But they've won way more than they've lost.

The ultimate clients, though, are the consumers who will decide to plunk down their cash on the strength of c/d advertisements. Old-style ad agencies traditionally relied on consumer and market profiles compiled by companies specializing in this information. Instead, Chiat/Day makes *direct* contact with consumers. Employees talk to them about the product before creating advertising, and then go back to them with the completed ad campaign to test its effectiveness before the actual launch. This is now standard industry practice, but Chiat/Day pioneered the entire concept of direct, consumer-driven research in North America in the 1970s.

One particularly daring experiment Jay Chiat introduced to his company was the "no barriers between staff" concept. By 1980, there were no separate offices at c/d, only open, uniform-sized cubicles. (Chiat shares his with his secretary and makes his own coffee.) This kind of free-flow work space suited to perfection the Chiat/Day company culture of no job descriptions, little hierarchy and an emphasis on flexibility and fun. But Jay Chiat is an avowed iconoclast who is not satisfied unless he is actively pushing the envelope. In 1993, he introduced one of his most daring experiments: the virtual ad agency.

Reminiscent of the Honda-style working arrangement for executives, Chiat devised the concept of a common space where teams work together on projects. If an employee is not working on a particular account, there is no reason for him or her to be there—at all. They don't need private space in a building to sit and store paper. They can go home and communicate by E-mail between meetings. Information needed by other employees can be stored in a CD-ROM library. Among its other virtues, the experiment also cut down on c/d's space requirements and real estate costs.

When the virtual agency concept was new, it was met with considerable skepticism. Today, only a few years later, Jay Chiat is hailed as an entrepreneurial visionary who pioneered the marriage of ad-agency creativity with the electronic infrastructure of the information highway.[6]

The final vindication has been provided by the marketplace itself, as is so often the case in business. In 1995, the giant agency holding company Omnicon Group Inc. bought Chiat/Day for a reported $60 million, a handsome sum for an acquisition made during the depths of the worst ad industry recession in half a century. Omnicon will be merging its new acquisition with TBWA International, the agency that brought you the high-profile creative campaigns for both Absolut vodka and Evian mineral water. This merger is no different than most; it is a symbiosis that provides something for everybody. TBWA needed the stronger presence on the American west coast that Los Angeles-based C/D can give it. At the same time, Chiat/Day acquires the global presence that previously eluded it.

As with all such mergers, the danger exists that the entrepreneurial culture of the smaller partner, Chiat/Day, will be stifled and swallowed up in the bureaucratic mindset of the larger one. It would not be the first such occurrence in the turbulent history of advertising and public relations companies. But based on Jay Chiat's track record as an innovator and a barrier-breaker, my bet is that, like the Eveready Energizer bunny, his company will just keep on going.

## BREAKING EXTERNAL BARRIERS

One of the most successful paradigms for breaking the outer barriers of a company is incubating, then spinning off new companies built around ideas that are compelling, but fall outside the core company's business strategy. By assisting its own "intrapreneurs" to develop and launch their business ideas, a company can retain financial and organizational links with outstanding employees who would otherwise be lost to the company. This approach also serves as a powerful motivator and stimulus to innovation for all employees. Few companies have played the intrapreneuring game more assiduously or successfully than Xerox.

### *Xerox Technology Ventures: Breaking Barriers to Liberate Value*

We have observed repeatedly that the odds of business success are immeasurably enhanced by an ability to learn from mistakes and move on, preferably as quickly as possible. This is generally both easier—and more essential—for small, nimble, start-up companies. Unfortunately, until recently, precisely the opposite has been true of larger companies. They have had the luxury (and the capital) to make bigger mistakes and to perpetuate them longer.

Xerox was a classic case in point. How many times have you heard people say they have to "xerox" a copy, when in reality they probably went down the hall and used a Canon copier? The sad fact is that other companies got rich capitalizing on the brilliant research coming out of Xerox's cauldron of technology at its Palo Alto Research Center in California, while Xerox lumbered along playing catch-up on its own ideas. Indeed, Xerox has long had a reputation for having created more value through innovation—for other people

—than any other company on earth. The list of Xerox innovations successfully commercialized by others reads like a who's who of the computing industry: object-oriented programming language, the graphical user interface, the mouse, local area network computing architecture and on and on. All leading-edge innovations, all commercialized by somebody else. Innovations generated at Xerox have subsequently generated tens of billions of dollars in revenues for companies such as Apple, Hewlett-Packard, Sun Microsystems, Adobe and MicroSoft. Xerox finally decided that this reputation for "fumbling the future" had to come to an end.[7]

Xerox launched a frontal and multifaceted assault on the problem, spending at least as much time on organizational innovation as on purely technological and product innovation. One of the most interesting of the organizational innovations was the creation of Xerox Technology Ventures (xTV) in 1989. In the words of chairman Paul Allaire: "xTV was a hedge against repeating the mistakes of the past. This new organization will provide the right entrepreneurial business climate for ideas to develop and prosper." Veteran Xerox executive Robert Adams, the man who pioneered what is now the multibillion dollar laser printing industry and ran Xerox's $2.6 billion systems business, was chosen to head up the new venture. No hidebound corporate bureaucrat, Adams was abundantly clear about his mandate and his entrepreneurial approach to fulfilling it: "We need a system to prevent technology from leaking out of the company . . . Most large corporations are unable to recreate the energy that propelled them when they were smaller. I believe xTV may be one way to regenerate this energy flow."[8]

xTV's mission is an ambitious one: To identify, harvest and leverage the most commercially promising ideas bubbling up out of Xerox's $500 million per year R&D budget, even though they don't fit neatly into the company's mainstream strategies.

xTV is essentially run as a venture capital fund, with an initial capitalization from Xerox of $30 million. Outside investors are welcome in the individual spin-offs, but Xerox retains a majority of shares, which it can then sell when a successful venture goes public—the ultimate aim of the operation. The spin-offs each have their own boards and management teams and if one of these spin-off companies fails—so far, only two have—the participants don't get a second chance. Unlike many intrapreneuring programs in other companies, there is no guaranteed safe haven awaiting them elsewhere within the company. On the other hand, if the venture succeeds, the prime innovators get 20 percent of the shares in the newly profitable company. That's a risk/reward equation that's calculated to concentrate the mind.

In its first four years of operation, xTV funded a dozen start-ups in fields such as electronic imaging, document processing, encryption and software.

Eight of the ventures are already profitable and three are early candidates for going public. In 1994, the XTV stable of companies was generating $100 million in combined sales. Only two of the twelve have gone belly-up, a track record that compares favorably to that of even the best venture capital specialists.

XTV is designed to strike an optimal balance between the effective leverage of the enormous resources of the corporate parent, and the maximization of the entrepreneurial dynamism of the small spin-offs. Needless to say, the spin-offs' links with Xerox confer a number of priceless advantages:

- Legitimacy and credibility, flowing from their status as Xerox companies or associate companies, depending on the level of the parent's shareholding.

- Access to leading edge, "lighthouse" customers such as Boeing, who would normally avoid early start-up suppliers like the plague.

- Access to technical expertise: patent counsel, quality control, marketing, etc.

- Access to additional capital. XTV is instrumental in helping its spin-off entrepreneurs raise additional venture capital from outside sources.

- Access to experienced managerial talent. Xerox's networks are of great assistance in recruiting top-flight management to strengthen the spin-offs. As a matter of strategy, XTV often prefers to look outside the Xerox family, in order to promote a greater cross-fertilization of ideas.

The benefits to the parent are substantial too, and the financial returns are only the beginning. XTV keeps the rest of Xerox employees both motivated and ever vigilant for the next opportunity to innovate. In the words of Xerox's Palo Alto Research Center director John Seely Brown: "We hope to turn company size, so often seen as an obstacle to innovation, into an advantage—a rich seedbed of fresh insights about technology and new work practices." [9]

The risks are high, but for entrepreneurially minded employees, the payoff from a successful venture can make it well worth their while. Just ask Tony Donit, the president of Advanced Workstation Products Inc. This company was the first success story to come out of XTV. In fact, it almost succeeded a little *too* well. Advanced Workstation developed a circuit board that could be used with an IBM personal computer, thereby eliminating the need for consumers to pay $10,000 for a Xerox office workstation. This was one time Xerox moved quickly. It bought the fledgling company outright and now sells the product itself. The technology's developers made a tidy $2 million in the deal. This time, nobody beat Xerox to the marketplace with a Xerox idea.

The XTV model of breaking corporate barriers is a variant of the spin-off approach we have already seen at Teknekron. The major difference lies in the original sources of the innovations. Teknekron identifies talent externally and brings it inside, XTV starts with internal resources and then spins them out. But the results are the same: A largely successful effort to balance the support and resources of the parent with the appropriate level of risk taking and entrepreneurship by the spin-off. Other large companies, notably Apple, 3M, Hewlett-Packard, Alcan and AT&T, have followed variants of the XTV model, but few have made it work more effectively than Xerox.

## STRATEGIC ALLIANCES: BUILDING COLLABORATIVE ADVANTAGE

A second prevalent and powerful manifestation of the "new physics of business" is the growth of strategic alliances between companies that were formerly completely free-standing and autonomous, sometimes even competitors. Constructing, maintaining and leveraging value from strategic alliances—developing "collaborative advantage"—will be as important to the next decade as competitive advantage was to the last one. Let's look at one of the real masters.

### Toshiba: The Master Builder

Breaking down barriers between competitors through strategic alliances is nothing new to this venerable Japanese consumer electronics firm. Founded in 1875, it has enjoyed a lucrative partnership (interrupted only by World War II) with North America's GE since the turn of this century. Toshiba first entered the American television market by allying itself with Sears, who agreed to sell Toshiba televisions under its own label. These were manufacturing and distribution agreements, advantageous to both parties and as uncomplicated as the relatively uncomplicated times.

But there is nothing uncomplicated about today's business environment, and just wait till you see tomorrow's. The rate of new product development and the exponentially increasing sophistication and cost of new products, require R&D expenditures that are becoming prohibitively expensive for even the largest and most successful companies. This is particularly true in Toshiba's field of digital electronics. With the rapid convergence of telecommunications, computing, consumer electronics and entertainment, there is a diminished capacity for any one company to do everything and do it well.

The key building blocks of the new digital age—high-speed microprocessors, mega-capacity memory chips and data storage and the software to drive them—are becoming too expensive for even the industry giants to master. Toshiba CEO Fumio Sato puts the case well: "It is no longer an era in which a single company can dominate any technology or business by itself. The technology has become so advanced and the markets so complex, that you simply can't expect to be the best at the whole process any longer."[10]

Recognizing these changes to the competitive landscape, Toshiba has devoted an extraordinary effort to creating strategic and sustainable partnerships with an impressive array of outsiders, some of them former competitors. It has broken through the psychological barriers that previously viewed companies as totally independent, free-standing entities. This mindset was especially common in Japan, where the strength and breadth of the *keiretsu* (industrial "family") was so enormous that external allies were regarded as entirely superfluous.[11] This isolationist thinking was particularly entrenched in the Japanese electronics industry, where giants such as Hitachi and Matsushita were historically dominant. Toshiba took a radically different approach.

One of the necessary incentives for overcoming barriers to collaboration is the belief that someone else has something you need. Toshiba had strategically identified both its core competencies *and* its limitations. Toshiba had reached the 1990s as a leading manufacturer of laptop computers. With the flat-panel screen market heating up, Toshiba's expertise in active-matrix liquid crystal display technology (the LCD market is worth about $7 billion) was becoming an enormously valuable commodity. Enter arch-competitor IBM, with chip design skills essential to the production of the new color LCDs and money for R&D, but lacking the LCD and manufacturing skills of Toshiba. It was a marriage made in heaven. With IBM's help, Toshiba came from out of nowhere to become the world's Number 2 supplier of color flat-panel displays for PCs, in the space of only three years.

A similar design and manufacturing alliance with Motorola led to Toshiba's world dominance in the production of dynamic random access memory chips (DRAMS). Although this success gave Toshiba a temporary head start, it will not be enough to stay there, nor to overcome the projected cost of $1 billion to develop the next generation of DRAMS. Toshiba is now collaborating with both IBM and Siemens to produce this new generation of chips, the DNA of the next phase of the computer age.

Toshiba's list of strategic alliances goes on and on. Through partnerships with Apple Computer, Sun Microsystems, Siemens, Alcatel, Time Warner, Samsung and dozens of others, Toshiba is making a bid to enter the rapidly converging markets for interactive media, digital communications, micro-processor workstations and telecommunications. Toshiba is also engaged in other alliances involving everything from nuclear power generating equipment to fax machines.

Combining core competencies and R&D budgets to make huge pots of money is the upside of Toshiba's talent for beaking down the barriers to strategic collaboration. However, the downside is the constant danger that the company's core competencies will be hollowed out by its partners, leaving it with short-term gain but long-term pain. To date, Toshiba and its partners have managed to avoid this pitfall, primarily through detailed agreements that the outset defining the roles, responsibilities and limits of each partner. Toshiba is well aware, however, that legalese can only take you so far and it places great emphasis on involving its senior executives personally in nurturing its key alliances. GE's CEO Jack Welch, not a notoriously easy guy to satisfy, gives Toshiba high marks in this area: "I've dealt with Toshiba for 15 years and it's always been a very easy relationship. When things go awry, a call to Sato-san will take care of the problem in 24 hours."[12]

Toshiba's skill and experience at managing such strategic alliances give it a new and increasingly valuable form of competitive advantage: *collaborative* advantage. It is not a talent that comes easily to large companies, particularly Japanese ones. But as we enter the 21st century, it will become an increasingly essential corporate survival skill.

## *WorldTel: The Mother of All Strategic Alliances*

The idea of a farmer in India checking his or her voice mail and ordering fertilizer by cell phone might sound humorous, but it is no laughing matter to the world's largest aid and development agencies. The lack of a telecommunications infrastructure is arguably one of the greatest barriers to economic development in the Third World. Neglecting the growing telecommunications needs of developing countries will only *widen* the gap between rich and poor. Says a recent McKinsey report on the subject: "While the First World races into the information age on the information superhighways it is rapidly building, nearly 4 billion of the world's 5 billion people still lack the most basic access to simple telecommunications."[13] To help knock down some of these North-South barriers, the Geneva-based International Telecommunication Union (ITU) launched WorldTel, one of the most ambitious and farsighted strategic alliances in recent history. Its potential impact could be awesome, empowering some developing countries' economies to leapfrog directly into the 21st century after only barely entering the 20th. In terms of its conceptual, geographic and organizational reach, WorldTel might justifiably be seen as the Mother of All Strategic Alliances.

The United Nations has confirmed that, despite one hundred years of telecommunications progress in the industrialized countries, 80 percent of the world's five billion people still lack access to even rudimentary telephone services and are thus denied the "basic right to communicate."[14] This lack of progress is largely due to the vicious circle in which many developing countries find themselves: They desperately need foreign capital to invest in a modern telecommunications infrastructure, but they cannot attract foreign investment without having that very infrastructure already in place.

The traditional approach of developing countries to this problem has been to ask for foreign aid, which they then pay to local monopolies and external equipment vendors to install wire telephone lines. This old paradigm" method has led to some new phones being hooked up, but progress is painfully slow. According to one official interviewed for WorldTel's feasibility study: "The World Bank takes years to evaluate a project and imposes countless conditions on things beyond the control of individual companies or even our Ministry."[15] The level of funding is also woefully inadequate. In 1992, development banks made only $2.4 billion available for telecommunications worldwide, less than 2 percent of their overall budgets. Compare this to the estimated $12 to $30 billion needed each year until the year 2000 to provide even the most basic telecommunications services to the developing world.[16]

The blame for this shortfall does not rest solely with development agencies. Both the World Bank and the European Community have stated that the main constraint to increased investment is not a lack of available funds per se, but rather the poor quality of the proposals coming from developing countries. Also, the very real risks and costs involved in many parts of the developing world cause telecommunication companies to use higher than normal hurdle rates while making investment decisions. As a result, nine times out of ten, they don't invest at all.

How can these seemingly insuperable problems be overcome? WorldTel essentially changed the rules and created a whole new game, whereby countries ready to play by commercial rules can more fully benefit from recent advances in both technology and economic liberalization. It does so against the backdrop of a changing political and economic context, where the private sector is taking over many roles from the less than dynamic public sector in providing international development capital. The basic idea is for WorldTel to identify potentially profitable telecommunications investment opportunities in the Third World and then assemble the necessary alliances among financiers, governments and telecommunications companies to plan and execute them successfully. In essence, WorldTel will use its muscle, credibility and geographic reach to create a functioning market where only inchoate demand previously existed.

Although the basic concept of WorldTel dates back to 1984, its original incarnation as a multilateral development organization did not even reach the business plan stage. Through the late 1980s and early 1990s, the idea slowly became more commercially focused and in 1992 an international advisory council of private and public sector leaders in telecommunications was established to refine the concept. The council developed a feasibility study with the help of such world-class companies as AT&T, Cable & Wireless (U.K.), NEC (Japan), Nokia (Finland), Sprint (U.S.), Teleglobe (Canada) and McKinsey & Company. In early 1995, the ITU (affiliated with the UN) approved WorldTel's business plan and the venture was officially launched.

WorldTel will play two different but complementary roles in developing countries, depending on their stage of economic development:

- *High value-added venture capitalist.* In countries with strong skills in project implementation and good financial track records, WorldTel assembles packages of debt/equity for telecommunications projects using its base of private investment, and provides information, expertise and access to needed capabilities.

- *Developmental operator/solutions provider.* In countries with lower telecommunications skill bases but a strong desire for business partnerships, WorldTel functions as a joint venture partner and provides venture capital. It assembles consortia on a Build-Operate-Transfer (BOT) or Build-Own-Operate (BOO) concession basis between local partners and international operators. Private investors benefit from large, newly created markets and diversified portfolios. According to Pekka Johannes Tarjanne, secretary-general of the ITU: "These joint ventures permit the private sector to have full control of its investment and allow clear accountability of management and timely responsiveness to market conditions."[17]

WorldTel is run separately from the ITU to ensure its operations are both independent and businesslike, though it benefits politically from the UN's imprimatur. In terms of structure, WorldTel investors elect a board of directors from the private sector to run the company, which accepts input from an assembly of governors, including representatives from the client countries. Governments, equipment vendors and telecommunications operators may participate at the individual project level, but they cannot invest directly in WorldTel. As one potential investor put it: "WorldTel will lose its commercial discipline if governments are involved as owners."[18] Investors are more likely to be "visionary" investors, such as infrastructure investment funds, institutional investors and private placements.

With WorldTel, developing countries gain the benefit of vast, rapid improvements in access to investment capital for their telecommunications infrastructure, with the accompanying benefit of accelerated socioeconomic development. The industrialized world gains the creation of huge new markets for the most cost-effective equipment, plus the ability to access that market with much lower risk. WorldTel will serve as a commercially oriented bridge to narrow the global communications gap. It is, in essence, a massive strategic alliance between North and South, and public and private sectors, as well as among its Northern investment partners. In the words of ITU chief Pekka Tarjanne: World Tel is a win-win situation for investors, developing counties, industrialized nations, operators and the telecommunications industry."[19]

WorldTel also breaks down another key barrier to investment in some developing countries: the often substantial political obstacles that have prevented large multinational firms from contributing their expertise and financial resources to telecom development in the Third World. The nonpartisan nature of the ITU largely takes care of that problem. As one developing country communications minister says: "It is politically impossible for me to let a multinational company operate part of our network; but partnership with a neutral entity like WorldTel is a different story."[20]

So what does this new WorldTel system look like? Picture this: Each village has a wireless telephone, operated by a local agent and connected to a radio tower, which communicates with a switch. The switch is connected by wireline to the national and international networks. Each household head in the village buys a prepaid "Smartcard," including a telephone number and voice mail box, from his or her local agent. The Smartcard could then be inserted into a shared terminal, which conveniently displays the cost of each call and value remaining on the card. The agent supplies on-the-spot assistance and training to new users of the technology. In return, the agent receives a commission on each prepaid Smartcard, and purchases additional terminals using these funds. The Smartcard eliminates receivables risk and minimizes fraud.

The cost advantages are significant. At current costs (which will only go down), access can be provided for US$100 to $200 per head of household compared to US$450 to $2,500 or more for a similarly shared wireline network. On the revenue side, a study of community telecommunications in the poor homelands of South Africa suggests it is possible to achieve average annual revenues per terminal of nearly US$5,000, and it was estimated that revenue per terminal of $400 would be more than sufficient for commercial viability.[21]

Even in its early stages, WorldTel has already demonstrated how, with a little ingenuity, even North-South barriers can be broken down effectively by carefully crafted strategic alliances.

WorldTel is as conceptually and organizationally ambitious a strategic alliance as any I've seen. If we're fortunate, it will represent the wave of the future: public/private sector collaborations among partners from different industries, regions and developmental stages. Another important part of that wave—an extension of the same logic that drives strategic alliances in the first place—is the emergence of the so called virtual corporation. And who better to demonstrate its virtues than the master business strategist himself: Mick Jagger.

## The Rolling Stones' Voodoo Lounge Tour: Prototype for the Virtual Corporations of Tomorrow

I know what you're thinking. The only barrier British rocker Mick Jagger ever broke is the sound barrier. That and perhaps the barriers of common sense and propriety that normally inhibit geriatrics from prancing around a stage half naked in front of sixty thousand adoring fans. But the Rolling Stones' latest worldwide tour, which ended in August, 1995, is the prototype of the virtual corporation of the late 1990s.

The Voodoo Lounge Tour brought together all the elements of a company operating internationally, with gross revenues of £250 million. Architects, stagehands, lighting and sound technicians, longhaul drivers, pilots, camera crews, merchandisers and security personnel, among others, were brought together to work for the "corporation" and to ensure the tour was a financial success. The tour employs over 250 permanent road people and numerous temporary employees in the cities booked for the shows. All in the interests of leveraging new value from one of the best brand names in the world: the Rolling Stones.

While there is absolutely nothing new about touring productions, the sheer scale and complexity of the Stones' tour puts it in a class by itself and creates management challenges on an unprecedented level. There are three different stages, each weighing over 170 tons. They are transported using fifty-six semitrailers and three jumbo cargo planes. The stages are used in rotation; while one is being used, the second is being dismantled in another location, and the third is being erected. Talk about just-in-time delivery!

Even Toyota could learn a thing or two from this logistical tour de force. One admiring journalist said: "It's like IBM moving its corporate headquarters every two days."[22]

The mastermind of this mammoth operation is Toronto entrepreneur Michael Cohl. Cohl basically invented the genre, and the business plan, of the stadium mega-tour in the late 1980s. It is an enormously costly, high-stakes game, that very few bands and empressarios can pull off. The P. T. Barnum of rock, Cohl is basically the chief operating officer of the Stones' virtual corporation. Cohl travels with the tour and, like Raychem's Paul Cook, communicates incessantly by cell phone, fax and laptop to keep the business running smoothly. He has entered into an agreement with what could be viewed as a family firm, with the family producing the sellable product. Mick Jagger is the de facto CEO, with drummer Charlie Watts and guitarists Keith Richards and Ron Wood joining him on the virtual board of directors. (To my knowledge, Richards is the only successful, high-profile board member who wears both an earring and a ruby surgically implanted in one tooth.) Cohl promotes and directs the show, and they all take advice from Prince Rupert Loewenstein, the Stones' financial advisor and virtual chairman of the board.

What's so "virtual" about this corporation? For one thing, the Voodoo Lounge Tour doesn't intend to be in business for much more than a year—thirteen months to be precise. The whole operation is a massive exercise in the just-in-time assembly and delivery of a wide variety of specialized skills and talent for a particular and temporary purpose. Little if anything is superfluous, wasted or permanent.

Another virtual aspect of the Stones' moveable rock feast is its lack of—well, structure. There is no bricks-and-mortar headquarters for this organization; HQ is whatever hotel room or limo Cohl happens to be in with his cell phone. Hierarchy is essentially irrelevant; ditto with organization charts. If something needs to be done, you do it yourself.

The third virtual aspect of the tour is its extensive use of specialist sub-contractors, orbiting around a remarkably small central core. Like a small-scale Sun Microsystems, "Stones, Inc." contracts out almost all the noncore functions, essentially keeping only artistic and financial control and marketing strategy to itself. Lighting, sound, tickets, merchandising and logistics are contracted out.

But make no mistake. For all its virtuality, the Stones' tour is a real corporation, and an extremely efficient and profitable one. It is also a fascinating glimpse into the organizational future. With or without ruby dental implants, 21st century companies will look a lot more like rock tours than they will look like, say, IBM circa 1985. Or at least they had better.

## Breaking the Barriers of Ideology

Of all of the barriers to innovation discussed in this book, none is more powerful or difficult to surmount than the entrenched mindset. And nothing has the power to entrench a mindset like ideology. This is precisely what makes the following two examples from Russia and Vietnam so remarkable. In both cases, the barriers to corporate innovation were nothing less than a decades-long domination of state communism, not normally an ideology that breeds entrepreneurial innovation.

## *Breaking Barriers in Ho Chi Minh City*

I have stressed repeatedly that innovation is a relative concept wholly dependent on its historical and cultural context. Nowhere is this more the case than in Ho Chi Minh City in Vietnam, where officials are busy making heroic efforts to shake off twenty-five years of inertia and building a modern economy. Their initiatives to reform the system might not be judged remarkable in New York City, but in the Vietnam of mid-1995 they represent an heroic achievement.

This chapter is all about breaking barriers. We have already seen how difficult it is to overcome barriers of hierarchy, disciplinary outlook and corporate boundaries. The companies profiled in this chapter have all done this and their achievement is considerable. But the most difficult barriers of all to break are mental and conceptual models. Imagine, then, what is required to overcome a lifetime of training in Marxist ideology and collectivist thought to try to build competitive businesses and a liberalized, Western-style economy.

In 1986, the Vietnamese Communist Party Congress adopted a series of radical reforms designed to reinvigorate and liberalize an economy that had remained virtually comatose since the Vietnam War. For the first time, foreign investors were allowed to own 100 percent of a Vietnamese operation, and to repatriate their profits. The two major drivers for this initiative were the deteriorating economic conditions in Vietnam and the spectacular growth rates enjoyed by the liberalized economies in neighboring Southeast Asian countries. Ho Chi Minh City, with its previous capitalist history as Saigon, seemed to be the most promising laboratory for reform.

But we're not exactly talking about a Silicon Valley-style hotbed of entrepreneurial dynamism. In the early 1990s, creating a new business in Ho Chi Minh City required some fifty-four separate approvals and signatures. Perhaps more importantly, the supply of talented business leaders and managers is extremely thin. The vast majority of the prewar business elite either fled or were pushed out long ago. Most senior managers of Ho Chi Minh City's public enterprises had previously distinguished themselves as guerrilla fighters, Marxist theorists or both. While the former experience is arguably a great training ground for the business world, orthodox Marxist thought is somewhat less so.

Despite the absence of a business culture, accounting systems and a tradition of personally accountable decision making, business innovation is indeed coming to Ho Chi Minh City. The focal point for reform is the city's People's Committee (I cannot entirely banish from my mind the image of its hypothetical Western counterpart: Jack Welch and the General Electric People's Committee.) The People's Committee is, however, the GE of Vietnam. In a city that contributes a third of the country's total industrial production and attracts 40 percent of its foreign investment, the Ho Chi Minh City's People's Committee owns and runs roughly one hundred companies. One of the largest (and one of the few that appears profitable) is Saigon-tourist, which already owns nearly one hundred hotels and restaurants and is currently negotiating a number of major joint ventures with foreign investors. Another jewel in the People's Committee crown is Legamex, a garment manufacturer. Formerly a purveyor of cheap products to Eastern Europe, Legamex has reinvented itself over the past five years to become a highly successful exporter of high-quality shoes and clothing to Western Europe.

In the hope of creating more success stories, the People's Committee recently launched a major restructuring effort. Recognizing the incompatibility of its traditional consensus model with modern-day business imperatives, the committee is reducing its own size and attempting to streamline its decision-making process. It is also reducing the hodge-podge of businesses under its control, rationalizing them into coherent groups of logically related companies. The idea is to create both critical mass and the foundation for large industrial conglomerates and trading companies modeled on the highly successful Korean *chaebols*.

This is much easier said than done. One of the first new groups, Satra (Saigon Trade Group), amply illustrates the difficulties. For starters, there are nowhere near enough capable managers to run even a drastically reduced number of companies. Second, unlike the Chinese situation, there is nothing approaching a social or political consensus in Vietnam that would permit laying off redundant workers. While failing businesses have indeed closed, their workers are unfailingly slotted into previously successful ones. The result can be guessed at. And finally, given these problems at the individual firm level, any attempt to articulate and execute a coherent group strategy will be difficult in the extreme. The *chaebols* can probably rest easy for the moment.

None of this is meant to minimize the impressive gains the People's Committee has already achieved. Cossetted managers in the West, with infinitely easier challenges to confront, should demonstrate as much progress and initiative.

## Business Perestroika: Russia's LUKoil

Until very recently, western Siberia was not exactly a Mecca for students of corporate innovation and entrepreneurial behavior. But Siberia is definitely worth a second look. Of particular interest is the formerly slumbering Russian oil industry and in particular LUKoil, its largest oil company. LUKoil will never be confused with a Silicon Valley start-up, but judged within it its own cultural and historic context, its development over the past three years has been little short of astonishing.

Created in 1990 by former deputy oil minister Vagit Alekperov as part of perestroika's privatization drive, LUKoil has embarked on a growth and development strategy that would intimidate even the most aggressive oil patch CEO in the West.

In order to consolidate and expand its long-term oil reserves, LUKoil launched a takeover of three other Russian oil companies: Permneft, Nizhnevolzhskneft and Kaliningradmorneftegaz. While the new names may be tricky to print on corporate T-shirts, ball caps and coffee mugs, the acquisitions leave LUKoil positioned as one of the world's largest oil companies in terms of proven reserves. LUKoil's estimated 15.7 billion barrels of proven reserves in Russia compares to Exxon's global total of 13.6 billion and Royal Dutch/Shell's 17.5 billion.

Actually developing those reserves, however, will be another matter altogether. It will take enormous financial resources—resources far beyond LUKoil's existing capacity. Current estimates place the price tag for developing its reserves and modernizing itself at around US$5 billion.[23] Hence the second prong of the company's new strategy: attracting substantial investment capital from the West. For a formerly state-owned company operating in the political and economic chaos of Boris Yeltsin's Russia circa 1995, this represents no small challenge. Everything from LUKoil's corporate structure to its accounting practices must be reinvented to make the company comprehensible—and more desirable—to flinty-eyed Western investors. Three of LUKoil's companies were fused into one, under the direction of Alekperov, the dynamic, hard-driving CEO. Western advisors such as McKinsey and KPMG Peat Marwick were brought in to translate LUKoil's accounting systems into something more meaningful and credible to Wall Street and the

City of London. Then there was the small matter of digesting the three major acquisitions at once. All this is just a prologue to the real action: raising US$6–7 billion in Western financial markets in return for a 15 percent stake in the company. As this book goes to press, LUKoil is raising the new money and the jury must remain out for at least a year. But only a fool would bet against the enterprising Mr. Alekperov. He has already signaled to potential Western investors his willingness to trim his 65,000-strong labor force by up to 20,000 over three years. This, of course, is music to the ears of the coldblooded Western money lenders, and suggests Mr. Alekperov has learned his capitalist lessons quickly and well.

Which brings us to the third prong of LUKoil's renaissance strategy. Taking a page out of state-of-the-art entrepreneurial thinking, the newly privatized LUKoil is taking pains to give its senior managers equity stakes in the company. The managers were granted a 5 percent stake in LUKoil, giving them an unprecedented incentive to preserve and build long-term value for the company. It also gave them wealth that is considerable even by Western standards; management's collective stake is currently worth some $2 billion (at least, on paper). Russia's new oil millionaires will definitely bear watching as they seek to consolidate and leverage the incredible progress they've made in only three short years.

While the cultural and organizational obstacles confronting Alekperov and company are enormous, it would be rash to bet against them. They have already demonstrated an ability to break barriers which would make them the envy of many a CEO in the West.

# CONCLUSION

Companies are all about creating value—or at least they ought to be. With the advent of the 21st century, more and more of that value will be *knowledge-value*, and less and less of it will be based on materials, commodities and other tangible assets. Companies will need to pay far greater attention to their intellectual capital base and how to leverage it.

That fundamental insight leads immediately to another: If what's really valuable about companies is their ability to generate, leverage and disseminate innovation and knowledge, then most companies are currently wasting the vast majority of their most precious assets. Why? Because most of the organizational architecture we have inherited from two hundred years of industrial development is manifestly inadequate to cope with the imperatives of innovation-driven, knowledge-based global competition. Far from developing mechanisms for leveraging knowledge, most companies have unconsciously erected barriers to it. Those organizational impediments come in all shapes and sizes: horizontal interdisciplinary and interdepartmental barriers within the company; vertical barriers imposed by 19th century conceptions of hierarchy and status; barriers between the company itself and potentially valuable outside resources, such as customers, suppliers, alliance partners and even competitors; and barriers of ideology and orthodoxy, which are often the most difficult to break. All these barriers prevent organizations from even *identifying* their full value-potential, never mind leveraging it.

The corporate success stories of the 21st century, like the companies profiled in this chapter, will be master barrier breakers. They will have no choice: As knowledge and innovation become the key ingredients of competitive advantage, any barrier to their mobilization becomes a serious—and potentially fatal—competitive liability.

### CHAPTER EIGHT

# EMPOWERMENT

## BUILDING

## THE POSTHIERARCHICAL COMPANY

*"The organization that figures out how to harness the collective genius of its people is going to blow the competition away."*
WALTER WRISTON/ FORMER CEO CITIBANK

Empowerment is one of those progressive management concepts that gets talked about a great deal, but is actually practiced very little. This is largely because, at bottom, empowerment is a concept that is potentially both explosively powerful and profoundly destabilizing, even threatening to the status quo. Its objective is disarmingly simple: To tap the creative and intellectual energy of everybody in the company, not just those in the executive suite. The idea is to provide everyone with the responsibility *and* the resources to display real leadership within their own individual spheres of competence, while at the same time contributing to meeting overall company-wide challenges.

Sounds like a bit of a no-brainer, doesn't it? Why *wouldn't* you want to harness every possible neuron in your company, particularly in these hyper-competitive times? Well, two reasons, actually. The first is that it takes real energy, effort and dedication—commodities in lamentably short supply in today's typical company. The second, and even more compelling reason is that, for the insecure executive, empowerment can represent a significant threat to his or her previous monopoly on power, information and stature. For those reasons, support for empowerment is usually far more rhetorical than real.

In the faddish rush to be seen to be embracing empowerment, the resources half of the equation is far too often overlooked. "Empowering" front-line employees to solve problems that they have neither the training, financial resources nor real-life authority to rectify is not only morally and intellectually fraudulent, it is a recipe for corporate self-immolation. Let's say you're going to "empower" me to fight Mike Tyson. If that's empowerment, then you can keep it unless you're also prepared to equip me with nuclear weapons.

So empowerment needs to be regarded as something like organizational plutonium: Properly harnessed and used for peaceful purposes, it can be a terrific tool; but if it falls into the hands of amateurs, look out. Harley-Davidson CEO Rich Teerlink makes the point about the downsides of empowerment with all the subtlety and understatement you'd expect from the preeminent purveyor of hardware to the world's toughest bikers: "If you empower dummies, all you get are bad decisions faster."[1] But, it's rarely the lack of ability of front-line workers that frustrates empowerment initiatives, it's the lack of resources and genuine support from the corner office.

The unusually frank comments by Hitachi Executive Managing Director Takeo Miura to a senior American business audience nicely capture the magnitude of the empowerment challenge facing North American CEOs:

> *We are going to win and the industrial West is going to lose out; there's nothing much you can do about it, because the reasons for your failure are within yourselves. Your firms are built on the Taylor model (the father of "scientific management"); even worse, so are your heads. With your bosses doing the deep thinking while the workers wield the screwdrivers, you're convinced deep down that this is the right way to run a business. For you, the essence of management is getting the ideas out of the heads of the bosses and into the hands of labor.*

> *We are beyond the Taylor model: Business, we know, is now so complex and difficult, the survival for firms so hazardous in an environment increasingly unpredictable, competitive and fraught with danger, that their continued existence depends on the day-to-day mobilization of every ounce of intelligence. Only by drawing on the combined brain power of all its employees can a firm face up to the turbulence and constraints of today's environment.*[2]

His analysis is spot on, even if his uncharacteristically acerbic obituary for Western companies may be just a trifle premature. Most CEOs' minds are indeed hardwired into hierarchically based patterns and the empowerment ethos is at best a difficult fit and at worst utterly threatening. But as Mr. Miura points out, very few companies have so much intellectual firepower to spare that they can afford to blithely squander half of it. Empowerment is no longer a luxury; it's rapidly becoming a competitive necessity.

For one thing, there simply isn't enough time anymore for the old ways of doing business. Whether you're debating giving a customer refund at an Iowa Wal-Mart or bidding on a new oil license in Siberia, you'd better be quick or you'll lose the customer or opportunity to a competitor who is. Speed requires empowerment. If the people closest to the action don't have the financial and decision-making wherewithal to jump on opportunities—and solve problems—quickly, you can be sure that someone else, somewhere in the world, will.

Like all good things, however, empowerment can be overdone. British merchant bank Barings learned this in a big way in March 1995, when a lone trader in its Singapore office bankrupted the company in the space of a few short weeks with some trading judgments which didn't quite pan out. Any time a twenty-eight-year-old kid is in a position to lose over a billion dollars of a company's money plus a centuries old international reputation, one is entitled to question whether he mightn't have been just a little bit *too* empowered.

Nonetheless, episodes like Barings are hardly a convincing argument against empowerment. Instead, they simply demonstrate that, in order to work, empowerment must occur within a framework and context of adequate controls and support. Those controls must include a corporate culture strong and unambiguous enough to provide employees with meaningful, if unspoken, guidance as they make their on-the-spot judgement calls. And as we have already noted, empowered employees also need the training and skill levels to discharge their new-found mandates with competence and confidence.

Two closely related megatrends are likely to propel the empowerment phenomenon forward even further and faster, particularly within the OECD countries: The continued delayering of corporate hierarchies, and the accelerating diffusion of the new information technologies. Taken together, they promise to create a qualitatively new kind of corporate organization: A "wired" company where workers enjoy unprecedented electronic (and personal) access to senior executives, and where they have both the mandate and the information required to take the necessary decisions on the spot. Companies without these qualities will simply be incapable of responding adequately to the constantly changing, rapid-fire kaleidoscope of 21st century business competition.

Let's look at some companies that have moved beyond lip service and turned worker-empowerment strategies into genuine sources of both knowledge-value and competitive advantage.

## Semco: The Brazilian Iconoclast

Social historians tell us the 20th century was the century of the workers' revolution. It was the century of empowerment of the worker; not workers as individuals, but workers as part of a larger, organized collective that could negotiate, threaten and withdraw its collective might from the means of production—and leave management and shareholders twisting in the wind. Twentieth century labor relations were (and, for the most part, still are) predicated on a union versus owner/management, us against them, confrontational zero-sum game. (The 1994–95 major league baseball strike in North America, while arguably the most infamous, was far from the only recent example.) There are indications that the 21st century will also be a century of worker revolution, but this time the revolution appears to be coming from the top down, with management empowering the workers as individuals.

Perhaps the most famous and successful example of this trend is Semco s/A, based in Sao Paulo, Brazil. Semco is a Brazilian company that develops and produces for international sale everything from dishwashers to cookie factories, rocket fuel propellant mixers for satellites to environmental consulting services. Over the last fifteen years it has increased its profits by 500 percent, and done so within one of the most chaotic and volatile economies in the world. Capital goods output in Brazil has fallen to 1977 levels, 30 percent of manufacturers of capital goods have gone out of business since the 1990s began, and inflation has been known to run in the thousands of percent. When I was in Brazil recently, most retail shops didn't bother putting price stickers on items. There was no point; yesterday's price was sure to have changed by tomorrow.

Staying in business at all in Brazil, let alone creating competitive advantage, is enough to put a company in the textbooks. Yet these remarkable feats are the least of Semco's achievements. Thanks to owner Ricardo Semler, Semco has come to be synonomous with the world standard in employee empowerment. In fact, Semler literally wrote the book on it. It's called *Maverick*, an international business best seller in fourteen languages.[3] The book details Semco's fascinating and often perilous journey from a family-owned, hierarchical, autocratically run company to a family-owned, employee-run, democratic company where the workers control the means of production—at Semler's insistence. If only Karl Marx could have lived to see this.

In Semler's own massively understated words: "Semco has long been a laboratory for unusual employment and management practices."[4] Several key values underpin the sweeping changes Semler introduced to his company. The first of these core values placed worker participation at the very epicenter of the company's strategy and operations. Twelve levels of management hierarchy were quickly reduced to three. To Semler, this made perfect sense. As he says: "Structure creates hierarchy, and hierarchy creates constraint. We have not utterly abandoned all control, but the old pyramidal hierarchy is simply unable to make leaps of insight, technology and innovation. Within their own industries, pyramidal hierarchies can generate only incremental change."[5]

Just how much control has been devolved down the ranks at Semco? Consider this: The workers decide their own hours, pay levels and travel budgets, and they have the power to evaluate and, if necessary, fire their "bosses."

At Semco, the workers assume responsibility for nearly everything: setting production quotas, developing marketing plans and redesigning both products and processes. Unlike many empowerment wannabe's, Semler understands that you can't meaningfully empower employees without also equipping them with the skills and knowledge to exercise their power responsibly and effectively. Accordingly, workers at Semco receive intensive training in pricing, cost control, inventory management and other key business skills. Everyone, including cleaning staff and messenger boys, is taught to read balance sheets and cash flow statements.

Responsibility for the company's success is shared by everyone. As Semler puts it: "I just own the capital, not the company."[6] Major decisions, such as acquisitions, are decided by a majority vote of all employees, with Semler getting the same single vote as the janitor. Six executives rotate the CEO's job every six months. Employees set their own salaries. As Semler says: "There's no one person to blame if the company goes down the drain. When financial performance is one person's problem, then everyone else can relax. In our system, no one can relax."[7]

Employees can even choose to take a decrease in salary and become an entrepreneur, or "satellite" as they're called at Semco. Working under the protection of Semco, on Semco premises, using Semco equipment and know-how and sometimes even competing against Semco, these entrepreneurs bet their foregone salary against a belief in their ability to create new, profitable ventures. What Semco gets in return is a lower payout in salaries and a piece of the successful satellite's venture. Does it work? Semco is so pleased with the system that it is aiming to "satellite" the entire company. Now *that's* vintage Semler: creating the company-less company! By 1994, 50 percent of manufacturing previously done by salaried employees was contracted out to satellites. In the next few years, this could grow to 70 percent. So far only one satellite venture has failed.

A second core value for empowering employees at Semco is profit sharing. Employees' share of the company's profits is normally set at about 24 percent. But it has risen to almost 39 percent during tough economic times, when workers agreed to take 30 percent pay cuts to avoid massive layoffs. This sharing of the wealth has created a company of workers fiercely loyal to Semco and dedicated to their jobs. In the fifteen years since Ricardo Semler took over the family company, sales per employee have risen from $10,800 to $135,000—four times that of most of Semco's competitors.

The third of Semler's fundamental guiding principles is the absolute neccessity of sharing company information—all of it—with everyone in the firm. Employees know who is working on what, what everyone earns, what are the company's costs and profits and details of R&D and potential contracts. The theory is that creativity and productivity can only emerge in an atmosphere of full disclosure. Some critics fear this kind of open management system will jeopardize the secrecy of new product development. Semler believes that, in today's fast-paced business environment, by the time a competitor can steal an idea, it should be in the marketplace for everyone to see anyway, and his people ought to be on to the next one.

Semler's three core principles of management are worker participation, profit sharing and information transparency. As Semler says: "Participation gives people control of their work, profit sharing gives them a reason to do it better, and information tells them what's working and what isn't."[8]

Semler's true genius is his conviction that, just as you cannot be a little bit pregnant, true empowerment is an either/or proposition. There can be no half-measures. Once unleashed, it must take on a life of its own. A vision cannot be mandated from on high. An owner cannot empower his or her employees only as long as their decisions concur with what he or she would have done. Semler's overall objective is the quintessence of empowerment: "to create an environment in which others make decisions. Success means not making them myself."[9] Perhaps, Semler's success is really the result of equal parts genius and an ego that is firmly and refreshingly under control.

Whatever the cause, Semco provides a textbook, world-class illustration of both the human and competitive power of empowerment. And, while Semler's semi-utopian brand of worker empowerment couldn't possibly work for everyone, it does provide a powerful, real-world demonstration of its possibilities. And Semler has carried out his managerial revolution in spite of one of the most unspeakable handicaps imaginable in his line of work: The man actually has a Harvard MBA!

## Levi Strauss: Empowering a $6 Billion Behemoth

Empowerment, like businesses (and blue jeans) comes in all shapes and sizes. It is decidedly not a one-size-fits-all concept. At Semco, empowerment is shaped primarily from "below," by those being empowered. At Levi Strauss, on the other hand, its overall design is still top down, driven by those doing the empowering. What these two companies have in common are owners who are committed to the empowerment of their employees because they believe it is an indispensable tool for competitive advantage. They also happen to believe it's simply the right thing to do.

Levi's owner, chairman and CEO Robert Haas puts the case for empowerment this way: "We are not doing this because it makes us feel good—although it does. We are not doing this because it is politically correct. We are doing this because we believe in the interconnection between liberating the talents of our people and business success."[10] Why? Because, in the emerging new world of global hypercompetition, as Haas says: "If companies are going to react quickly to changes in the marketplace, they have to put more and more accountability, authority and Information into the hands of the people who are closest to the products and the customers."[11] All that is especially true in Haas's chosen field of apparel: The fashion business is notoriously fickle, and its volatility has been further exacerbated by the advent of both technological change and foreign competition. Speed, flexibility and responsiveness are not just virtues, they've become competitive necessities.

For Haas, empowerment is part of a broader, deeply held conception of the firm as an ethical, values-driven entity as well as a commercial one. Since its founding in 1850, Levi Strauss has been famous for combining social and community commitment with profitability. Haas comes by his attachment to the company's values honestly; he is the great-great-grandnephew of Levi's founder, and his grandfather, father and uncle all ran the company before him. Today, values at Levi Strauss are more important than ever. With the eclipse of the hierarchical, "command-and-control" organization, core values have become the only glue capable of holding a diverse company together and providing coherent direction.

Haas is so committed to the principle of empowerment he has enshrined it in the "Aspirations Statement," the company's landmark statement of the core values that are meant to underpin virtually everything it does. The Aspirations Statement, which is taken far more seriously at Levi's than your garden-variety corporate mission statement, says this about empowerment: "By actively pushing responsibility, trust, and recognition into the organization, we can harness and release the capabilities of all of our people." About as good a definition of empowerment as you'll find.

Empowerment is a serious and highly structured business concept at Levi Strauss. Managers must attend training sessions from a core curriculum. These assist managers to manage "aspirationally." Manufacturing staff receive training in how to get along in the new multidisciplinary teams being introduced in many of the factories.

Open communications between management and staff regarding goals and performance are also sacrosanct at Levi Strauss. Like Honda in Japan, Levi Strauss works hard to create a climate where "constructive contention" can prevail, and workers' insights and opinions can be shared freely, even when they challenge the views of more senior officials. All employees, including management, are reviewed using a 360° process in which their subordinates, peers and superiors all have the opportunity to submit an evaluation. Like Semco, the company rewards creativity and innovation with financial incentives. In fact, sewing-machine operators were encouraged to take the initiative in improving the operations of a plant in Georgia. They now run the entire operation. Employees who work as a team to identify and implement cost-cutting measures share in the savings achieved. Managers are judged on their ability to manage "aspirationally," and one third of their raises and bonuses is based on this ability.

Levi's massive reengineering effort provides another good illustration of empowerment in action. Historically, individual staff members had not received either the opportunity or the kind of strategic information necessary to give meaningful input on corporate-level decisions. But in the early 1990s, Levi was losing millions of dollars in revenues to competitors who were quicker in producing new product lines and in replenishing retailers' inventory. Haas decided to systematically tap over 6,000 of his 36,000 employees for their views on how the company's entire operations could be improved. He recognized that both factory workers and front-line sales staff had a wealth of knowledge to contribute; after all, they were the ones in daily contact with customers, buyers, suppliers and all other key components of the Levi value chain. Their input is having an unprecedented impact on the massive, $500 million reinvention of the company's manufacturing, marketing and distribution systems currently underway. Haas reckons that a diverse, empowered and "constructively contentious" workforce is a far richer source of innovation and commitment than a thousand market surveys and focus groups. This may stop somewhat short of Semco's "one person, one vote" system of corporate governance, but then again, Levi has about 35,000 more employees to accommodate. Scale does make a difference in the empowerment business.

As part of its empowerment initiative, Levi Strauss is also working hard to increase the diversity of its workforce and to help minorities and women break through the "glass ceiling." Committees representing a broad cross section of Levi employees set agendas for company policy on such issues as support for working mothers and benefits to partners of gay employees. Critics of these empowering principles are quick to point out that, after many years of espousing these values, of the eight people sitting on Levi's executive management committee, only one is a woman and all are middle aged and white. Nonetheless, women now make up over half of management staff and 36 percent of managers are from minority groups, double the percentage since the inception of the statement of aspirations.

Levi has had some disappointing results during the past few years, but it would be simplistic and misguided to blame them on Haas's preoccupation with values-based management and empowerment. The company also enjoyed record-breaking profits for almost ten years during the implementation of Haas's company values. In the long run, its commitment to empowerment is likely to leave the company more, rather than less able to cope with the volatility of its changing marketplace.

Perhaps most encouraging of all, Bob Haas is the first to admit that Levi's corporate voyage toward the nirvana of empowerment is only just beginning: "We are only a few steps along in our journey. We are far from perfect. We are far from where we want to be. But the goal is out there, and it's worth striving for."[12]

With that kind of impetus for self-questioning and continuous improvement behind it, Levi is almost certain to regain its leadership position in financial as well as human development terms.

## Chrysler: Detroit's Unlikely Empowerer

Empowerment is not a word that springs readily to mind when one thinks of the Detroit auto industry. And of all Detroit automakers, the names of Chrysler and its imperious ex-chairman Lee Iacocca are even less likely to be uttered in the same breath as "empowerment." But Iacocca is gone, Chrysler is back from the abyss one more time, and a good deal of its new-found success is due to an ethos of empowerment at Chrysler that would have been unthinkable even five years ago.

Chrysler Corporation has ridden a roller coaster ride of booms and busts over the past forty years, with the company lurching back and forth from near bankruptcy to taking in cash so quickly it literally didn't know what to do with it. Using a combination of government lobbying and patriotic appeals to consumers in the early 1980s, Lee Iacocca's well-publicized efforts brought the company back from the precipice. As usual, however, its recovery proved short lived. By the late 1980s, profits had again begun to decline steadily.

The company was still depending on its minivans and on the Jeeps it had inherited from its takeover of American Motors in 1987 for its very survival. Chrysler's core market segment was middle-American Iacocca-worshippers who had responded to his patriotic appeals by dutifully buying his cars. But there weren't enough of them. Even Iacocca referred to them as "between fifty-five and dead." Less diplomatic industry observers referred to Chrysler buyers as PODS: poor old dumb shits![13] The only question was which would die first, these loyal customers or the company.

After spending most of its profits from the 1980s on a variety of futile efforts to diversify (it attempted unsuccessfully to become an aerospace and technology conglomerate) and globalize through merger (it failed to woo Fiat), Chrysler was again in serious difficulty. In 1990, the company embarked on a plan to cut a third of its capacity and the same proportion of its white-collar workforce. After losing $538 million in 1991, Chrysler was once again being written off as a serious competitor in the world automobile industry.

Despite speculation about a last-minute change of heart, Iacocca did indeed resign from his position as chairman at the end of 1992. In his later years at Chrysler, Iacocca's management style had become increasingly regal and autocratic. He frequently reminded people that his mentor was former boss Henry Ford II, an old-style corporate autocrat who delighted in the arbitrary use of power. In his place the board hired Robert Eaton, who took over on January 1, 1993. Eaton, in his early fifties, had run GM Europe from 1988 to 1992, a company literally thousands of miles away far from the made-in-Detroit mentality.

It didn't take Chrysler employees long to realize they now had a very different type of manager at the helm. Eaton is resolutely accessible, often answering his own phone and dropping by for informal chats with Chrysler employees. His goal is to create a company where teamwork and empowerment are more than just fancy buzzwords, and he is viewed by his people as a coach and a listener who favors consensus building. As Eaton puts it: "I don't think I'll have any less impact on Chrysler than Lee Iacocca did. It'll just be dramatically different because I'll come at it from an inside, teamwork standpoint as opposed to the approach he had."[14]

To dramatize his plans to senior management, Eaton gathered a large group of executives to announce Chrysler's second-quarter earnings in July 1993, the best since 1984. After patting his troops on the back, he read a series of press accounts hailing Chrysler's turnaround. Then came the kicker: The accolades had been written in 1956, 1965, 1976 and 1983. At least once a decade, Chrysler had sprung from its deathbed to a miraculous recovery. "I've got a better idea. Let's stop getting sick in the first place," said Eaton. "My personal ambition is to be the first chairman never to lead a Chrysler comeback."[15]

When he took over Chrysler, Eaton realized that the first stirrings of a major change were already underway, deep down in the organization. Back in the last 1980s, three middle managers, François Castaing, Glenn Gardner and Bob Marcell, had begun implementing innovative ideas concerning teams. The early signs were good. Eaton's successful strategy was to understand what was going on in his organization, and then to give his midmanagement people the tools and authority to leverage and carry it forward.

To support his middle managers' efforts, Eaton created two new vice-president positions: one for customer satisfaction, and one for continuous improvement. He launched a production systems team in which a small group of middle managers traveled the globe studying ways to improve manufacturing. He implemented a "Senior Management Behavior Team," designed to teach his senior officers to be more approachable, to encourage subordinates to speak up, to listen when they did, and even to—God forbid —make eye contact with their people.

The new support from the top allowed middle managers to accelerate their change efforts considerably. One major innovation was empowered "platform teams," a new concept for Motown, though a similar cross-functional team approach had existed in Japan for many years. The technique consisted of bringing everyone from marketing to manufacturing together, eliminating potential design snags, speeding up product development and sharply reducing costs. As François Castaing explains: "Each team is made up of all of the people and skills needed to bring a vehicle from concept to market: designers, engineers, manufacturers, procurement and supply specialists, marketers, finance people and suppliers. This team approach forced a change in the way we developed vehicles."[16]

It certainly contrasted sharply with the old system, where designers would design the vehicle and then "throw it over the wall" to the engineers, who would in turn throw it over to procurement, who would then buy the parts and throw it over to manufacturing. After much time and costly rework, the vehicle would finally be pushed out the door to marketing and to dealers, who would then try to sell it to the customer.

Castaing continues: "In the platform approach, we have simultaneous vehicle development. Each team is run like a small car company or a Formula One team, very lean and informal. Within teams, everyone focuses on not just pieces of the car, but on the total vehicle. Communication flows are simultaneous and two-way, not sequential and one-way. Our platform team leaders and members are empowered to make the decisions required to develop a vehicle and are held accountable for their program objectives."[17]

One of the first tangible outputs of these newly empowered teams has been the Chrysler Neon. In its early development stages, team leaders enlisted aid from such nontraditional allies as suppliers and the United Auto Workers Union. Line workers contributed over four thousand proposed changes to the project. The results surpassed all expectations, with the Neon challenging the Japanese on their own small car turf.

The Japanese have begun to sit up and take notice. Toyota recently completed one of the most rigorous examinations it has ever carried out of a competitor's car, with a *tanji kai*, or complete dismantling, of Chrysler's Neon. Hundreds of company engineers and suppliers took the car apart, bit by bit to analyze its low-cost construction. Such a major pull-apart exercise has not been undertaken by Toyota since it dismantled Mercedes models ten years ago while preparing to launch the Japanese firm's first luxury model, the Lexus. A leaked copy of Toyota's analysis shows the Japanese marveling at the clever manufacturing tricks Chrysler used, saying that Neon incorporated "designed-in cost savings unprecedented in an American car.[18] Yoshifumi Tsuji, the president of Nissan, was more precise, telling *Automotive News* that "where we would have five parts to make up a component, the Neon has three. Where we would use five bolts, the Neon body-side was designed so well it needs only three bolts." High praise indeed, coming from the Japanese.

Financially, the reorganized and newly empowered Chrysler Corporation has been successful, so far. In 1993, the group achieved record pre-tax profits of $3.8 billion, four times higher than in 1992, and profits for 1994 are expected to be in the same range as 1993.

The trick now is to keep the momentum going. And this time, it's likely to be a team effort, not a one-man show. Chrysler President Robert Lutz nicely captures the new ethos of empowerment at Chrysler: "We need to keep erasing that line between the people who *innovate* and the people who *implement*. We need to make *everybody* feel that they have the freedom to innovate and invent."[19]

## Chaparral Steel: Small, Nimble and Empowered

When Chaparral Steel began operating in Texas in the early 1970s in Midlothian (pop. 5,141), few people noticed. "Big Steel" was still raking in huge profits with its enormous, integrated steel mills in the east, and most effort in the steel industry was being devoted to building ever *larger* plants. But together with some other steel company refugees, British Columbia native Gordon Forward left his job at the Lake Ontario Steel Company to help create a steel company like no other. It stemmed from what must have seemed like a philosophy more akin to "flower children" than the grit of a steel mill: that human beings are inherently good, energetic, creative, trustworthy and capable of achieving great and wonderful things.[20] More specifically, Forward focused on creating a classless company—in the best sense of the term—where universal education and freedom to act could become the cornerstones of corporate strategy.

Like Nucor, Chaparral Steel operates as a minimill, taking cheap scrap steel and using electric furnaces to produce medium-sized steel products (such as reinforcing bars, beams and angles), for the construction, automotive, railroad, mobile home, defense and appliance industries. As the minimill segments of the steel industry grew throughout the 1980s, they displaced much of the market share of the large, integrated companies, and today account for some 40 percent of all steel produced in the United States. Chaparral Steel has ridden these changing industry dynamics to grow from an annual production capacity in 1975 of 220,000 tons, to over 1.5 million tons today, and is currently ranked as the nation's thirteenth largest steelmaker.

Forward decided to combine the best attributes of American entrepreneurialism with Japanese-style worker commitment. He tried to create a collegial atmosphere in which virtually everyone in the company has equal power to contribute to the bottom line. Chaparral's three-part strategy is to be on the cutting edge of technology; to be the easiest steel company with which to do business; and to develop the human side of the enterprise.

Administration VP Douglas Beach summarizes the corporate philosophy this way: "We manage by adultery. We treat everyone like an adult." There are no time clocks at Chaparral. Explains Forward: "When I am ill, I get a day off. Why shouldn't everyone else? Chaparral's management system was designed for the 97 percent who are conscientious people who want to put in a full day's work. The 3 percent who abused the system were let go."[21] Forward's approach emphasizes trust, in the belief that if a worker has to be away for whatever reason, the worker should decide that for himself. The daily absence rate is less than 1 percent.

To reinforce the idea of equal treatment, Chaparral's executive offices and human resources department are located in the same area as the steel workers' lockers. This leads to a great deal of informal discussion among all staff, but production and maintenance employees do more than chat about sports over the water cooler. Everybody participates with supervisors and management in establishing well-defined, challenging goals and objectives. They are not, however, told *how* to achieve them. This allows individuals and work teams to develop their own solutions for reaching their goals, including determining which materials and equipment are necessary to accomplish the task. Because all development projects are led by employees, the company has produced a group of experienced project leaders, as well as many more who know how to make effective contributions as team members.

The compensation system emphasizes the growth of individual competencies for each person at Chaparral. Employees are paid based on their knowledge and performance. No two people receive the same pay. In part this is because salary adjustments are issued on the employee's anniversary date of employment (as opposed to a common date), but much of the pay is determined by the annual best-to-worst rankings supervisors perform on their employees, based on overall performance and job knowledge. The performance ranking is not measured against job requirements or a job description (Chaparral has neither), but against the employee's own goals and objectives. Supervisors make salary adjustments when funds are available for adjustment.

Chaparral's most valuable competitive asset may well be its empowered workforce. CEO Gordon Forward claims that he can take competitors on tours through the plant and show them everything, but give nothing away because "they can't take it home with them."[22] Anyone can sack workers and cut costs, but not everyone can create teams of truly motivated, empowered workers. According to Forward: "We figured that if we could tap the egos of everyone in the company, we could move mountains."[23]

Empowered worker teams help both in solving problems and in exploring new opportunities for Chaparral Steel. When a problem occurs, no inspector needs to be called out by the quality control department to investigate; the operators on the line usually take care of things themselves. As a Chaparral foreman explains: "Probably 90 percent of the problems never even make it to the morning meetings, held among everyone on the shift to discuss problems. They are fixed in the field."[24]

When some cooling hoses burst near a piece of new equipment, a senior operator described what happened: "When something like that comes up, you go see what the problem is. You don't say, 'That's not my area,' or 'I don't know that much about it.' You just show up." In this case, a group of operators, a welder, some foremen and a buyer spontaneously gathered to discuss the problem and scattered to seek solutions. "Everybody telephoned somebody they thought might know how to fix the problem, and within three to four hours we worked the problem out," continued the operator. "If it had been just one foreman, and everyone else walked out, it would have taken him ten times longer to find a solution."

In developing new opportunities, the rule at Chaparral Steel is this: If you have an idea, try it out—now! Line managers have the ability to authorize tens of thousands of dollars for experiments without higher authority. According to production manager Paul Wilson: "In other companies, the word is: Don't rock the boat. Here we rock the hell out of the boat. We don't know the factory's limits. We want it to change, to evolve." And it is not just line workers who investigate new ideas. Every employee from CEO to receptionist has a business card to use with customers, and they use them.

When rising demand led the company to buy a second specialized lathe, the machinist who operated the lathe was given the authority and responsibility of finding one. The task included traveling to Japan and to other American installations to see what they were doing. He finally selected a used lathe from another company, saving Chaparral approximately $300,000 in the process.[25]

Of course, all these empowered workers have to keep *learning* to stay effective. To ensure this happens, each employee has his or her own education matrix, including knowledge and cognitive skill areas targeted for development within specific time frames. At any given time, at least 80 percent of the company's one thousand employees are in some form of education enhancement, ranging from psychology workshops at university to metallurgy courses, with each employee spending an average of 120 hours each year in the classroom. Workers are also encouraged to take full-time sabbaticals (with pay), and spend their time in learning environments ranging from universities to customer sites.

Employees also receive regular cross-training by more experienced employees on the job. In Chaparral's customer service center, for example, sales, billing, credit and shipping personnel all sit under one roof, with all workers trained to handle one another's jobs. If a customer calls the sales department with a credit question, chances are the salesperson will know the answer, saving time for both employee and customer.

To maintain the inflow of state-of-the-art information, Chaparral also sends people regularly to participate in the worldwide learning network the company has developed, which includes top experts from both industry and academe. Another junket restricted to top management? Hardly. More often than not, they're front-line employees. Explains Forward: "We send the people who can best tell us what's going on—whoever they are. They are a source of information for the company as a whole." He continues: "We want them to come back with new ideas about how to make improvements or new ways to understand the problem." When Chaparral's itinerant learners return home, they are expected to share the fruits of their new knowledge with colleagues.

The steel industry notices Chaparral Steel now. The company produces steel with a record low 1.6 hours of labor per ton, versus 2.4 hours for other mini-mills and 4.9 hours for integrated producers.[26] With the high levels of worker satisfaction, learning and empowerment the company is developing, these costs could fall even further. Chaparral's annual job turnover rate is less than 2 percent (half of which is voluntary), and a recent attempt to unionize the workers failed. Who needs unions when you've got genuine empowerment?

Chaparral employees have also demonstrated their faith in the company with their wallets. Two-thirds of the employees own stock in the company, and 62 percent buy more each year through payroll deductions. Eight percent of gross proWts are paid as proWt sharing to all employees.[27] As long as Forward's brand of empowerment stays in place, I'm betting Chaparral will have plenty of proWts to share for a long time to come.

---

## Conclusion

---

Each company profiled in this chapter has found a different way to harness and leverage the energy and ingenuity of its workforce to give it a competitive edge. Each did so in its own style, and none of the approaches should be transposed literally or mindlessly into a different corporate context.

In the years to come, empowerment strategies will become even more critical to competitiveness, as the combined forces of economic and technological change both compel and enable it. Empowerment is *not* a corporate panacea; it is a necessary but not sufficient condition of competitive success. If your newly empowered workers are going to come anywhere close to realizing their full potential, at least five additional ingredients will also be required:

- A coherent corporate strategy or vision, to provide the framework of guidance so necessary to newly empowered employees.

- Supportive top management, with an appetite for risk and a tolerance for "constructive failure."

- The necessary training and skills for workers to discharge the increased responsibilities effectively.

- A new compensation and measurement system that better reflects and encourages the ethos of empowerment.

- Conscious mechanisms to harvest, disseminate and leverage the new learning that will inevitably result.

If those five ingredients can become integral components of a company's empowerment strategy, you'll see some real action.

# GLOBALIZE OR PERISH

*"We are witnessing the emergence of a mutually interrelational and integral
world. The world's economy is becoming a single organism."*
MIKHAIL GORBACHEV

Most executives remain astonishingly provincial and insular in their outlook, training and experience. This is particularly true for North
American CEOs, even in such ostensible hotbeds of business innovation
and creativity as Silicon Valley. I am constantly amazed by the number of
otherwise brilliant Silicon Valley executives whose world view barely reaches
to the other side of the San Andreas fault line. (On a really good day, it might
extend as far east as the Hudson River.)

At one time, it was possible to excuse such corporate solipsism on the
grounds that the size of the domestic North American market was so vast, there
is no real need to export. But the simple fact of the matter is that today, 95 percent of the world's population and a growing proportion of its consumers are
*not* North Americans. What is more, the fastest growing economies in
the world are outside the rather smug boundaries of the OECD altogether.

Only ten years ago, the world's "free" market economies embraced a total
population of barely one billion people. Today, in the wake of tectonic political,
economic and technological changes, another two to three billion new consumers are climbing on board what U.S. Treasury Under Secretary Lawrence
Summers has called "a rapid escalator to modernity."[1] Formerly closed
economies such as China, India, Brazil and Central and Eastern Europe have
thrown their doors open for business, with many offering opportunities greater
than those available in traditional OECD markets. The near universal triumph

of liberal economic ideology has created, for the first time in modern history, the very real prospect of truly global consumer markets.[2] Gucci-toting yuppies driving BMWs in Buenos Aires and Beverly Hills now have more in common with each other than with the huddled underclasses of their own countries, just a few miles beyond the doors of their condos.

At the same time that globalization wired the international business world more closely together, there has been a massive realignment of the world's balance of economic power.

The volatile economies of the east industrializing are growing at about one third the rate of those in the industrializing world. As recently as 1960, East Asian economies contributed only a paltry 4 percent of world output. By the early 1990s, they had drawn even with the United States at 25 percent, and most experts believe that they will soon account for a third of total world output. By the year 2020, the World Bank predicts that nine of the world's top fifteen economies will be from what we patronizingly call today the "industrializing" world, including China, India and Indonesia.[3]

These phenomenal growth rates represent something of a two-edged sword for Western business. On the one hand, they clearly represent a threat to the West's historic economic hegemony and herald the emergence of a whole new set of formidable competitors from countries whose names Westerners can barely pronounce. Not only that, but new information and telecommunications technologies have leveled the international playing field to the point where ten-person software engineering firms in Bangalore, India can and do compete successfully with the best in Silicon Valley. Large law firms in London and New York not infrequently farm out such back-office functions as accounting and even typing to contractors in Taiwan or the Philippines. It has become much cheaper—and faster—than carrying it down the hall to your own colleagues.

On the other hand, the explosive growth rates of the industrializing economies have also created unprecedented opportunities for Western companies. For one thing, these countries have an insatiable appetite for infrastructure to support their growth. Roads, bridges, airports, power dams, telecommunications networks, sewage treatment systems and even entire new cities must all be financed, built and operated. The price tag for this will run well into the *trillions* of dollars over the next decade and represents not only an extraordinarily lucrative target for Western companies, but an increasingly indispensable one, given the stagnation in their own domestic markets.

Globalization has thus revolutionized the world of business. It has simultaneously created the imperative for companies to internationalize their competitive strategies and the means to do so. Companies can and do now shop in a single global supermarket for capital, employees, customers, suppliers, raw materials and strategic alliance partners. We now have 24-hour global financial markets and the ability to shift billions of dollars halfway round the world with a few computer strokes. New manufacturing and information technologies allow transnational companies to locate different parts of their "value chains" wherever it makes the most economic and political sense to do so, at any given time.

Of all of the potential beneficiaries of globalization, none face more exciting and unprecedented opportunities than small and medium-sized enterprises (SMES). Historically, SMES have lacked the opportunity, the necessity and especially the wherewithal to attack international markets. Today, technology and liberalized trade rules have changed all that. In this new global free-for-all, small boutiques of knowledge rich specialists can leverage powerful databases instantaneously, and go head to head in niche markets with huge multinational competitors, eight time zones away. Not only that, but many of the same information and communications technologies are also enabling ten-person outfits to station senior people in six different countries and still stay in daily contact.

This is not to imply that all will be sweetness and light in the new corporate global village. Global snake pit might be more like it. Markets are infinitely more complex, turbulent and far-flung and competitors can come at you from anywhere and at any time. The term "politial risk" takes on new meaning: If McDonalds can have a major real estate lease canceled overnight in Beijing, what hope can there be for lesser mortals like you and me? Managing global companies across borders, time zones and cultures calls for a level of talent and subtlety light years beyond what was necessary only a decade ago. Strategy, marketing, logistics, recruitment and training must all be rethought if not reinvented altogether to cope with the new challenges.

This will be a particularly difficult task for North American executives, who tend to lack the necessary linguistic, cultural and attitudinal skills for this job. They certainly lack the formal educational background; until embarrassingly recently, even the most prestigious business schools in North America nearly ignored the international dimension of corporate strategy. Even today, only a handful of schools offer a special concentration in international business at the same status as the traditional fare of marketing, finance or manufacturing.

International business is not for the faint of heart, but it never has been. The only difference is that as the 21st century approaches, companies now have no choice. Let's make the heroic assumption that you've finally screwed your courage to the sticking point and are now prepared to give serious thought to how you might actually begin to internationalize your company. Here is a short list of tips:

- **Develop and promote a psychology of internationalism.** This one's a toughie, but it's a fundamental precursor to all the others: you have to create a gut realization that international success is no longer the icing on the cake to your traditional domestic markets, it's rapidly becoming the cake itself. Until and unless this ethos permeates most of the key players in your firm, your globalization efforts are unlikely to amount to much more than very expensive dabbling.

- **Get good partners.** Even domestic markets have become so complex and demanding that strategic alliances with outsiders are often needed to assemble the full range of competencies required. The need for strategic alliances to attack international opportunities is that much more powerful. If gigantic multinationals like Asea Brown Boveri, Mitsubishi and Royal Dutch/Shell have the organizational humility to take on outside partners for new international projects, it's highly unlikely that you and I can successfully avoid it. There is simply no substitute for first-rate local knowledge about market opportunities, competitors, talent and emerging government policy.

- **Take the long view.** Rome wasn't built in a day and the Romans were using local talent. If you stop and think how long it took to establish and stabilize your company in your home market, you'll realize it's patently absurd to expect earth-shattering results and profits from your new venture in Malaysia within the first three years. You might achieve them, but don't count on it.

  You're going to need staying power, both financial and psychological. Don't let minor annoyances like a 50 percent drop in the value of the Mexican peso dampen your ardor for your Mexican initiative, provided the strategic reasons for going there in the first place were valid and still are.

- **Become an international learning machine.** In an international company, the challenges may become more daunting, but the learning opportunities also become infinitely richer. The companies that will really dominate the 21st century will be those that figure out how to disseminate and leverage knowledge *throughout* a global company. International job rotations are one proven method of disseminating two-way learning throughout the company. Frequent international meetings and workshops are another, only don't restrict them to senior executives: Send the people who actually do the work and have the knowledge. The development and use of on-line, company-wide "lessons learned" databases is another leading-edge tool to minimize the necessity for reinventing the same wheel in ten different countries. Recruitment, training, evaluation and compensation policies should also be structured to create and enhance an international workforce oriented to continuous learning. None of this is easy and none of it will happen on its own. It takes serious work and commitment, but the rewards can be prodigious.

- **Strengthen your corporate culture.** Global organizations are more vulnerable to the centrifugal forces that may tear them apart than are purely domestic ones; the challenges of coordination and integration are disproportionally great. The most effective—indeed, perhaps the only—"glue" available for counteracting those tendencies and holding far-flung global organizations together is a strong corporate culture. Even military "command and control" type organizations have extreme difficulty trying to stretch chains of command halfway round the world; your firm is unlikely to do much better. Your best bet is to commit the time and resources necessary to ensure that your corporate culture is strong and coherent enough to help guide the myriad decisions that must, both by preference and by necessity, be made quickly and on the spot by local managers.

- **Flexibility is key.** One of the commonest mistakes made by newly internationalizing companies is to over-react to the global coordination challenge by superimposing a corporate straitjacket of one-size-fits-all procedures on the entire company. A strong, coherent corporate culture is one thing, but trying to treat business in Bangkok as if it were Omaha is a certain recipe for disaster. You've got to be flexible. Flexibility starts with tailoring product and service offerings to unique local requirements. This may sound self-evident and trite, but it's not that long ago that American automakers were trying to sell American-style cars in Japan, where both consumer tastes and driving conditions are radically different. (Then they had the gall to blame their poor results on Japanese protectionism.) Global flexibility must go well beyond tailoring goods and services to local markets; it must also embrace every aspect of your business, including organizational structures and human resource policies and practices. This is often a difficult pill for us ethnocentric North Americans to swallow.

- **Just remember: All "solutions" are temporary.** There's nothing CEOs normally like better than announcing grand, sweeping organizational solutions to the challenges and complexity of global management. One year, it's centralization, the next year it's decentralization. One year, the company is organized by product line, the next year by geography. Or maybe, just for fun, the CEO will try out that newfangled "matrix management" approach he or she heard about at an executive seminar, which attempts to combine both functional and geographic reporting responsibilities.

The point is not that any of these solutions is intrinsically good, bad or indifferent. I am simply saying that none of them should be regarded as anything more than a temporarily adequate response to constantly changing circumstances. Employees understandably develop "reorganization fatigue" and skepticism after three different organizational "solutions" are unveiled in five years, each one touted as definitive. It would be more honest and far more effective if everyone accepted that the world is now changing too fast and too unexpectedly for any solution—organizational or otherwise—to endure. The best that anyone has a right to expect is a constant cycle of self-examination, learning, adjustment and improvement.

Let's take a look at seven companies that have done outstanding jobs of building *global* strategic architecture with which to attack their 21st century competition.

## *Rupert Murdoch: Australia's Sun King of Media Technology*

In projecting his business acumen around the world, Rupert Murdoch has few if any peers. Not since Queen Victoria has one person presided over such a vast global empire. Through a series of bold and debt-defying acquisitions, Murdoch succeeded in positioning himself as *the* global communications czar for the 21st century. This Aussie is literally all over the map and his $11 billion empire is showing no signs of slowing down. In Queen Victoria's time, they said the British Empire was so vast, the sun never set on it—it was always shining somewhere on British-controlled soil. So it is with Rupert Murdoch, the world's first truly global media tycoon.

First there was his print empire. Through his Sydney-based parent company News Corp. Ltd., Murdoch owns newspapers on four continents: Australia, Great Britain (including the prestigious *Times* of London), Hong Kong and the Pacific Basin and the United States, where his holdings include *The New York Post*. He owns magazines in Australia and the U.S.; among them *TV Guide*, with a weekly circulation of over 14 million. In the late 1980s, Murdoch added book publishing to his portfolio when he acquired Harper & Row and later William Collins, which were subsequently merged to become HarperCollins. That company now has offices in Australia, the

U.S. and England. For some people, this might have been enough. Murdoch was just warming up. The next frontier to conquer was the world of entertainment media.

In the U.S., Murdoch bought Fox Broadcasting Co., Twentieth Century Fox Movie Studios, a host of independent television stations, FX (cable) and SF Broadcasting. In Great Britain, he acquired British Sky Broadcasting; in Australia, Seven Network; in East Asia, Star Television; and in India, Zee TV. Although he was uncharacteristically late getting into the feeding frenzy over American cable rights, Murdoch has made up for lost time by prying channels away from American distributors by trading them for some channels he controls in Britain or Asia. His is a classic illustration of the power, synergy and leverage that can be generated from a global competitive platform.

Murdoch's Asian holdings have a potential client base of two billion people. He is poised to tackle this market with much the same strategy as he used in the U.S. and Britain: Namely, give the people the music, the sports and the entertainment they like. This formula worked well for bringing BSkyB into the black when it negotiated the rights to broadcast Premier League soccer to a soccer crazy British populace. Following similar logic in North America, Fox Television bought the broadcast rights to four years of NFL football for $1.6 billion. Star Television will concentrate on cricket in India and soccer and gymnastics in China.

Murdoch invests in undeveloped and potentially risky media properties in Asia, and the numbers alone would seem to justify his gamble. Look at India. It has a population with over half a billion people living in squalor and poverty, but it also has a population equal to that of the entire United States living in middle class or better conditions, learning English as a second language—and many of them just dying to watch Fox TV's Bart Simpson. The title of a recent *Forbes* article about Murdoch says it all: "There are more Patels out there than Smiths."[4] In China, the number of households receiving Star TV jumped from almost five million to almost thirty-one million— more than the entire population of Canada—in a mere twelve months during 1993. Lots of Western entrepreneurs have recognized the extraordinary potential of the bourgeoning consumer markets in Southeast Asia, but few have positioned themselves as successfully as Murdoch to exploit it.

As communications and computing technologies continue to converge with dizzying speed, it is clear from Murdoch's most recent acquisitions that he is also determined to play a dominant role in the information technology revolution. On a world scale, of course. His digital publishing holdings already include News Electronic Data and Delphi Internet Services. The plan is to leverage every aspect of Murdoch's global empire, using every medium it controls, which is pretty much all of them. This new technology-driven competitive platform which Murdoch is currently assembling is almost frightening to contemplate. Chris Holden, one of Murdoch's vice presidents at HarperCollins, says: "We now have to think of polymedia deals. When we sit down to strike a deal, we'll talk movie, on-line, CD-ROM. At the end of the day, we'll derive as much revenue from on-line media as from current traditional media."[5] Books, magazines and newspapers can leverage new value by going on-line. Television programs and movies can be reformulated and reissued as interactive software. Educational materials will continue to merge with entertainment into a new gestalt dubbed "edutainment."

Murdoch understood and exploited the meeting of two unprecedented and compelling megatrends: The emergence of the first truly global markets for popular entertainment (viz. "The Simpsons Go to Bombay") and the convergence and convertibility of the new media technologies. And so Rupert Murdoch stands, like a 21st century colossus astride five continents, owning and leveraging almost every kind of modern information technology to distribute news, entertainment and education to a potential audience of 2.5 billion people.

## Ikea: Sweden's Global Invasion Force

Today, Ikea's distinctive blue and yellow logo is widely recognized far beyond its native Sweden, whose flag provides the store's basic color scheme. Last year alone, founder Ingvar Kamprad's stores were visited by 116 million people, or roughly 2 percent of the Earth's entire population. Given Ikea's humble beginnings as a grocery and general store in the tiny village of Smaland in southern Sweden, these staggering numbers are an eloquent testimonial to a globalization strategy with few equals in the business world.

The original store developed into a mail-order firm, which expanded again in the early 1950s when Kamprad took over an abandoned workshop and opened the doors of his first furniture showroom. From the start, Kamprad published a product catalogue and delivered orders by the village dairy milk truck, until a routing change left him stranded without a distribution system. This turned out to be a blessing in disguise; he promptly asked his customers to come and collect their own furniture from his showroom. This innovation was followed in 1956 by Kamprad beginning to sell his furniture in self-assembly flat packs, which saved space and were easy to transport. These seemingly simple innovations turned out to be big hits and continue to define Ikea's distinctive business concept to this day. From that first store in southern Sweden, Ikea has since expanded to 108 stores in eighteen countries, earning revenues of $4.5 billion in 1994.

Ikea sells simple but high-quality Scandinavian designs, sources its components globally and sells furniture in kits that customers transport and assemble at home. The company passes on a portion of what it saves on low-cost components, efficient warehousing and customer self-service to customers in the form of lower prices, anywhere from 25 percent to 50 percent below those of competitors. An Ikea store, with its free baby-sitting and Scandinavian café is designed to be a "complete shopping destination" for value-conscious, car-borne consumers.[6]

The foundation for Ikea's global success is the way it cleverly reinvented the furniture retailing business. Traditionally, the furniture industry was highly fragmented, divided among department stores and small, family-owned shops. All sold expensive products for delivery up to two months after a customer's order. Ikea, by contrast, displays its enormous range of more than ten thousand products in huge stores built in less expensive, out-of-town locations with plenty of parking and amenities. (Ikea basically invented the superstore, some twenty years ago.) The firm reaps huge economies of scale from the size of each store and the big production runs made possible by selling the same furniture all around the world. This in turn allows the firm to match rivals on quality, while undercutting them on price.

Ikea also redefined value and the roles of the key players in the value chain. With Ikea, customers also become suppliers (of time, labor, information and transportation) and suppliers become customers (of Ikea's business and technical services). The result is an integrated, reinvented business system that creates value by matching the various capabilities of participants more efficiently and effectively than was ever the case in the past.

The company's vast size and international supply network have made global logistics management another key ingredient of its continued success. Ikea now counts some 2,300 suppliers in sixty-seven countries in its fold and was one of the first companies to expand production into Eastern Europe, where it now has some 500 suppliers. Suppliers receive long-term contracts, technical advice and leased equipment. Ikea designers work closely with suppliers to build savings into products from the outset. In return, Ikea demands an exclusive contract and low prices.

The supply network uses fourteen warehouses, the largest located in Almhult, Sweden, which holds enough items at any given time to furnish thirty-thousand three-bedroom apartments. Most ordering is done electronically. Cash registers at Ikea stores around the world relay sales information to the nearest warehouse, as well as to operational headquarters in Sweden, where information systems oversee and analyze sales and shipping patterns worldwide. The efficiency of Ikea's global logistics system ensures that when the back and seat of a chair are made in Poland, the legs in France and the screws in Spain, the chair will actually hold together. The company orders parts in high volumes, allowing it to insist on low costs from suppliers.

But such a diverse global company needs much more than fancy, computerized logistics to hold itself together. Ikea's distinctive corporate culture is also a major contributor to its success and has been effectively transplanted around the world. Strong beliefs rooted in Swedish egalitarian traditions encouraged Ingvar Kamprad to create a company with few management layers, only four levels currently separate new chief executive Anders Moberg from his checkout and warehouse workers. Senior managers share secretaries and fly economy class. Employees dress as they feel most comfortable, no titles are used and all employees eat in the staff canteens—there are no directors' dining rooms. It is also very important for Kamprad that managers not lose touch with the actual substance of their business. Accordingly, there is a roster for all managers right up to the top executives to spend a week each year working as ordinary warehouse attendants and sales people. Kamprad often drops in on his stores to check on things personally.

Ikea has cheerfully and successfully broken two of the iron rules of international retailing: Never enter a market without conducting exhaustive studies first; and gain local expertise through acquisition, joint ventures or franchising. Ikea typically does neither of these things. According to Moberg: "We don't spend much money or time on studies. We use our eyes and go out and look and say it will probably do quite well here. Then we adapt, but quite often we stick to our opinions."

Ikea uses a specialized, headquarters "SWAT" team to investigate and develop new store locations. The team picks the sites, plans the buildings, supervises their construction and launches the stores. The team also operates them for the first year and then hands over management to a permanent, fully trained local team. The SWAT group then moves on to its next store-opening project. This approach allows the central team to specialize in store development and management, consolidate the lessons learned all over the world and then share this knowledge with local managers in the first year.

Tackling the North American market wasn't easy, despite Ikea's outstanding success all over continental Europe. Potential customers, complaining of long lines and frequent stock-outs, were leaving American Ikea stores empty-handed. Imitators cashed in on Ikea's marketing effort to introduce Americans to Scandinavian furniture design. Worse, it became increasingly difficult to offer low-cost furniture made in Europe when the value of the

U.S. dollar dropped some 30 percent relative to the Swedish krona between 1985 and 1991. Moberg went to the U.S. to see what was going wrong. "We were behaving like exporters, which meant we were not really in the country," he explained. "It took us time to learn this." While many other retailers might have been tempted to retrench and refocus on their successful European operations, Ikea persevered. "If you're going to be the world's best furnishing company, you have to show you can succeed in America, because there's so much to learn here," explains Göan Carstedt, who took over North American operations in 1990.

Moberg found that North Americans' tastes and even their physiques represented major barriers to purchase. Swedish beds are narrow and measured in centimeters. Ikea did not sell the matching bedroom suites that North Americans liked. Its kitchen cupboards were too narrow for the large dinner plates needed for pizza. Its glasses were too small for a nation that fills them with ice (Carstedt noticed that North Americans were buying the firm's flower vases to use as glasses). Customers stored sweaters in chests of drawers, and Ikea's drawers were too narrow. To their credit, Ikea's executives decided to adapt. The firm now sells king and queen-sized beds, in inches, as part of complete suites. After deepening drawers by a couple of inches, sales of these chests rose 30–40 percent. In all, Ikea has redesigned about a fifth of its product line specifically for the North American market. The company also began doing more local sourcing as the exchange rate moved in favor of American manufacturers. Today, 45 percent of the furniture in the American stores is produced locally, up from 15 percent only four years ago. This helped the firm cut prices in its American stores for three years running.

Ikea learned three vital lessons from its North American experience. The first was the importance of flexibility and adaptability. The second involved giving more autonomy to Carstedt than his European counterparts typically enjoy. "You can't steer America from Europe," he says. The third resulted in a typically unconventional move: In 1992, Ikea abolished internal budgets. "We realized that our business planning system was getting too heavy; now we can use the time saved for doing other things better," Carstedt continues. Today, each region must merely keep within a fixed ratio of costs to turnover. The American operation is finally booming; sales have tripled since 1990 to $480 million in 1994, and the company has begun turning profits.

What's next for Ikea? In November 1994, the company announced plans to move into China, where it will open up to ten stores in the "foreseeable future." The firm is sticking to its tradition of jumping into big new markets feet first. Ikea's managers stress that its North American experience demonstrates it is easier to make changes to the product range once critical volume has been achieved. But the company is also applying other lessons learned in North America to China. It has already set up the bones of a supply network within the country itself, and is leaning towards a more decentralized system of management. In the U.S., Ikea's Swedish identity is evolving into a "new alloy," according to Carstedt. "It's still blue and yellow, but with the stars and stripes mixed in." In the People's Republic of China, the alloy should soon gain an even redder hue.

## Bombardier: Poised for Global Take-Off

When Canadian Joseph Armand Bombardier designed the world's first snowmobile, he couldn't possibly have created a more apt symbol of his country's image as a parochial, isolated, snow-covered, frozen wilderness. It is therefore ironic that, thirty years after Bombardier's death, his family has built his company into an enterprise that is a veritable metaphor for the 21st century globalization imperative.

In the early 1970s, when the snowmobile industry took a dramatic nose dive due to the energy crisis, Bombardier Inc. was faced with two alternatives: diversify quickly or cease to exist. Thus began a business odyssey that would see Bombardier products literally traversing the cities and countrysides, waterways and skies of countries all around the world. The company began by manufacturing subway cars that were sold in Canada, the U.S. and Mexico. Diversifying further into the mass transit industry, Bombardier produced double-decker Superliner train coaches for Amtrak in the United States, cars for Disney World's monorail, light-rail mass transit systems in Malaysia and Turkey and shuttle-train cars for the Chunnel linking Britain and Europe. In one of its most recent coups, Bombardier won the right to comanage China's largest passenger rail factory in late 1994, thereby acquiring a strategic toe-hold in south Asia, potentially the largest market in the world for mass-transit equipment.

But Bombardier has not forgotten its humble beginnings in motorized consumer products. It continued producing Ski-Doo snowmobiles and built on this core competency to develop the highly successful Sea-Doo personal watercraft.

Then Bombardier really took off. In 1985, the Canadian government put the publicly owned aircraft manufacturer Canadair on the block. Canadair was hemorrhaging money even though it produced the respected Challenger business jet. With no experience in the aerospace industry whatsoever, Bombardier jumped at the chance to add airplanes to its line of transportation equipment. A rapid initiation into the tumultuous world of civil aviation convinced Bombardier CEO Laurent Beaudoin (son-in-law of the late Joseph-Armand Bombardier) that the future of his company lay in the production of small personal and public aircraft, i.e., business jets and small commuter passenger jets. In quick succession, he bought up three more ailing companies: de Havilland, maker of the Dash 8 commuter jet; Learjet of Kansas, maker of excellent short-range corporate jets; and Short Brothers PLC (Shorts) of Belfast, Ireland, which gave Bombardier an entree into the burgeoning European market. In 1994, Bombardier Inc. posted earnings of US$4.3 billion, over half from its aerospace division. Since 1989, Bombardier's sales more than tripled, with 1994 profits up over 150 percent from the previous year. Fiscal 1995 promises to be even better. Almost all of Bombardier's remarkable success is due to globalizing its strategy and operations.

In just twenty years, Bombardier has gone from a small purveyor of Ski-Doo snowmobiles in a single market to an aggressive, diversified international company employing 36,500 people, with plants in Canada, the U.S., the U.K., Mexico, Austria, France and Belgium. International markets now account for fully 90 percent of Bombardier's revenues.

Bombardier's products are themselves metaphors for the globalization phenomenon. Barriers to trade and business are crumbling, borders are disappearing and continents are figuratively moving closer together. Bombardier not only recognizes and responds to this fact, the company has actually accelerated it through its choice of product lines and industries.

Consider its participation in the massive Chunnel project. For the first time since the Ice Age, people can now travel from England to continental Europe without leaving the ground. Step into a Bombardier shuttle coach and overcome the splendid isolation that defeated the Spanish Armada, Napoleon and Hitler.

A second example of surmounting the legal, psychological and time barriers among trading nations is Bombardier's development of one of the world's first ultra-long-range personal jets. Bombardier believes that as the Asian market, with its three billion consumers, continues to open up, business executives will want to be able to fly to these markets faster. Bombardier is developing an ambitious project to build a corporate jet capable of flying from New York to Tokyo in thirteen hours without refueling. It has assembled a global team of talent and money from Canadair, de Havilland, Learjet, Shorts, BMW Rolls-Royce, Mitsubishi, Honeywell, Dowty Aerospace and Sextant Avionique to accomplish the task. The jet will be called the Global Express, and will carry a price tag of about US$30 million.

By building a plane to meet the needs of a geographically expanding business world, Bombardier reveals a company that not only understands the globalization process, but actually accelerates it a little bit by itself.

## Daewoo: The Korean Colossus

Kim Woo Choong will go whereever he must to make money, and since he himself has said: "I can smell money everywhere,"[7] that is pretty much where he has gone. It would be difficult to find a country where his gargantuan company Daewoo has not made its presence felt. A partial list of its global activities would include making textiles in Burma, videocassette recorders in Northern Ireland, computer chips in Silicon Valley, trucks in Vietnam and, to top it off, Chairman Kim is currently promoting a $70 billion natural gas pipeline from Siberia to Korea. At the moment, Daewoo is South Korea's fourth largest industrial group or *chaebol*, and first place is by no means out of reach.

Less than thirty years ago, Mr. Kim started Daewoo trading in textiles out of South Korea. He must have had global ambitions even then: Daewoo translates as "great universe"—a reasonably cheeky name for a five-person start-up. The company has grown considerably since then, adding another 79,995 employees worldwide. Kim's competitive advantage initially lay in the potent combination of South Korea's cheap labor market and a devalued *won*, the South Korean currency. Fed up with depending on Japanese trading firms to sell his textiles overseas, Kim opened his own sales offices abroad and Daewoo began marketing its own products. Thus started the globalization of Daewoo. Like Toshiba, which originally entered the American television market through Sears, Daewoo initially sold its ready-made garments in North America through Sears Roebuck & Co.

These early successes only served to whet Kim's appetite for diversification and international expansion. Kim followed a deliberate strategy of diversifying into businesses that had the least competition in South Korea, such as financial institutions. It is interesting how often successful entrepreneurs credit fate for a defining moment in their business's history. (Laurent Beaudoin of Bombardier Inc. has said that his company was not particularly looking to get into the aerospace industry, but took the opportunity simply because the federal government decided to privatize Canadair at a time when Bombardier was looking for diversification projects.) Daewoo took a similar path when the South Korean government decided to privatize a hopelessly inefficient machinery plant and offered it to Kim. By the time he had the business back on its feet, Daewoo was firmly established as a machine parts supplier for companies around the world. This expertise then led to further diversification into the automobile industry, which in turn led to collaborations with, over the years, GM, Honda and Suzuki, among others.

In 1995, the list of businesses, joint ventures and products under Kim Woo Choong's control and/or direction is mind boggling. In addition to textiles, garments, auto parts and automobiles, Daewoo now makes electronics equipment and aerospace products and builds ships, pipelines, plants, hotels and roads. Daewoo also invests in banks and insurance companies and even operates its own oil refinery. As befits a global conglomerate, Kim is ever alert to opportunities to create synergies between different parts of his far-flung empire. In one recent—and fairly typical—transaction, Daewoo constructed schools, roads and a medical college in Libya. Daewoo accepted payment (up front, of course) in crude oil, which Kim immediately transferred to his recently acquired refinery in Antwerp, Belgium for upgrading and distribution.

Kim, the youngest of the current crop of Korean *chaebol* chiefs, has constructed a complex global-value chain, with a growing number of opportunities to add value at different geographic stops. Luckily for him, there is no international equivalent of American anticombines legislation, though the South Korean government has in recent years expressed concern about the intense concentration of wealth in the hands of a few individuals.

Daewoo's basic approach to globalization has been to make haste, slowly. In the company's early days, when Kim opened sales offices overseas to market his textiles, he learned the value of examining a market carefully from the inside before investing in new ventures. This became Daewoo's modus operandi. Before the company commits to expansion in a region, it first opens a sales office for its existing products and then studies the internal system for potential areas of growth. This methodical approach has contributed to successful ventures in Ireland, the U.S., Europe, Asia, Russia, China and Africa. It also provides a sobering lesson in globalization for international wannabes: If a global titan like Daewoo invariably walks before it runs into new global markets, then maybe it's not a bad strategy for the rest of us mere mortals as well.

In the 1990s, however, the *won* began to recover against the American dollar and South Korean labor costs started to rise along with it. Although Kim didn't need much encouragement to expand the global reach of Daewoo in the first place, these developments put even more pressure on the company to transfer manufacturing to other Asian, Middle Eastern and African countries and the republics of the former Soviet Union, where lower labor costs and higher government subsidies could help maintain Daewoo's competitve advantage. Daewoo has subsequently expanded into Uzbekistan, Tatarstan, the Philippines, Burma, Libya, Vietnam, Thailand, Pakistan and North Korea.

There appears to be nowhere Kim won't take his company. As he says: "To survive in competitive times, you have to find places that people have never been to and do things that people haven't done yet."[8]

## Methanex: Building A Global Value Pipeline

In the late 1980s, a diversified Canadian company called Ocelot Industries was bleeding cash at the rate of about a million dollars a week. It looked ready to go down for the count. By the mid-90s, a slimmed down, ruthlessly focused survivor company, Methanex Corporation, had risen phoenix-like from the ashes to become a dominant competitor in the growing international market for methanol. Methanex's story provides a textbook illustration of a successful globalization strategy.

The principal architect of that strategy was Brooke Wade, who began as a young controller with Ocelot in the early 1980s. In 1987, at the ripe old age of thirty-three, Wade drew the short straw and was put in charge of the faltering company. Few people envied him the opportunity.

By 1991, Wade had largely stanched the financial bleeding and had not only reinvented the company, but also renamed it Methanex. He reduced Ocelot's grab bag of loosely related interests to a single product—methanol—and determined he would build a world-class, world-scale, focused company. Methanol is an industrial chemical derived primarily from natural gas and has applications in the housing and construction, textiles and plastics industries. It is also used as an ingredient in the clean-fuel additive methyl tertiary butyl ether (MTBE), for which the environmental concerns of the Eco-Industrial Revolution are creating a brisk and growing international demand. As environmental legislation such as America's tough Clean Air Act continues to bite, the demand for MTBE (and therefore methanol) is certain to increase. This trend is well advanced in many OECD countries, notably Germany, Finland, Sweden and the United Kingdom. It is also becoming evident in several of the more progressive, newly industrializing countries, including Mexico, South Korea and Thailand.

By the mid-90s, Methanex's strategy of aggressive global acquisitions and logistics leverage had completely transformed the company. From a single-plant, largely domestic operation four years earlier, it has grown to the point where Methanex now does business in thirty countries and twenty-five languages and has production facilities in Canada, the United States, New Zealand and Chile. Along the way, it increased its production capacity by a factor of ten and its market capitalization ballooned from $100 million to $2 billion. Today, Methanex produces over 20 percent of the total world supply of methanol and markets over 35 percent.

The key to all this was the creation and leverage, on a global scale, of what Methanex executives like to call "strategic flexibility." They assiduously constructed a unique, integrated, worldwide infrastructure of production, marketing and logistics that gives the company an unsurpassed ability to adapt quickly to changing customer requirements. They refer to their international network of plants, terminals, ships, rail cars, vehicles and marketing and logistics professionals as the company's "global pipeline." Depending on local market conditions, this global pipeline can switch production from Chile to New Zealand or Louisiana in a matter of hours. It can also shift readily from one grade of methanol to another. At its New Zealand plant, Methanex can even switch to a different product altogether: synthetic gasoline. This "swing capacity" is a major competitive advantage for Methanex, and a direct result of the company's globalization strategy. Swing capacity is also the source of Methanex's ability to guarantee customers a steady and secure supply. Security of supply is *the* single most important issue for methanol customers and, for several of Methanex's competitors, it is not always something that can be taken for granted.

Having painstakingly constructed this global strategic architecture, Wade and his colleagues then set about leveraging as much value out of it as humanly possible. One of the company's most important elements is its international human resource infrastructure. Methanex consciously uses both international job rotations and multicountry "SWAT teams" as instruments for diffusing knowledge and learning throughout the company. The design and construction of Methanex's Louisiana plant, for example, profited from the experience and contributions of staff from Canada, New Zealand and Chile, as well as from the U.S.

In 1994, Methanex entered a new phase in its corporate growth cycle. Brooke Wade, the aggressive dealmaker who had created Methanex's global architecture in an incredibly short space of time, left to try to repeat his success formula with another natural gas derivative: acetic acid. Pierre Choquette, Methanex's new CEO, is a veteran of the international natural gas marketing wars and recognizes that a different role is now required. The company's competitive infrastructure has now essentially been put in place; what's now required is a concerted effort to consolidate and leverage it. For Choquette, that means only one thing: An all-out crusade to energize and focus Methanex's increasingly diverse human resource base, to wring full value out of it.

Accordingly, in 1994, Choquette introduced a new, worldwide performance management system, to ensure his rapidly growing international workforce of nine hundred could maintain a coherent framework of values, learning opportunities and performance measurement. "Business as usual" simply wouldn't cut it anymore. As part of the new system, each employee was asked to develop a statement of personal career objectives, as well as an explicit strategy for integrating them with Methanex's overall corporate agenda. This was no empty exercise. More than one employee was stunned—and flattered—to have his or her paper returned with detailed, handwritten comments and suggestions from the CEO himself.

As this suggests, Choquette takes his job as chief coach and mentor very seriously. At least once a quarter, he has two- or three-hour, uninterrupted "fireside chats" with each of his ten direct reports—and he strongly encourages them to do the same with their own teams. He sees this interaction as the only way to infuse his rapidly-growing company with the necessary coherence, urgency and collective vision. For the same reason, Choquette added another key element to his global learning infrastructure later in 1994, with the creation of the President's Council. The council is really the centerpiece of Choquette's campaign to strengthen and leverage the company's global knowledge-building capabilities. Comprising a dozen of the company's most senior executives from all over the world, the President's Council meets in person at least bi-monthly to figure out new ways to generate additional value from Methanex's growing international experience and knowledge base.

There can be no single, standardized formula for successful globalization strategies. But based on Methanex's meteoric growth rate and the commanding competitive position it currently enjoys internationally, this much seems safe to say: You can't go too far wrong emphasizing focus, flexibility and company-wide organizational learning.

## Compagnie Lyonnaise Des Eaux-Dumez

When asked to name a French water company, most people immediately think of such classy names as Perrier or Evian. But with revenues in the range of $17 billion, Lyonnaise des Eaux dwarfs these mineral water companies by dealing with a decidedly more prosaic commodity: tap and waste water. Lyonnaise des Eaux and its 140,000 employees currently supply water to 22 percent of the French population. But France represents only one-third of Lyonnaise's customers. The company also supplies tap water and treats waste water for some thirty-six million people in thirteen other countries around the world, including Spain, Argentina, the U.K., Italy, Australia, the U.S. and Canada. Although it remains firmly rooted in France, global expansion is the cornerstone of Lyonnaise's corporate strategy.

Much of Lyonnaise's current prosperity can be traced back to 19th centu-

ry France. In most Western countries, the public sector is primarily responsible for infrastructure. Local public works departments prepare
specifications and tenders, issue bonds to pay for new facilities and then
maintain them. However, France has operated a much different system for
over a century. Its 36,000 municipal *communes* select private companies to
act as long-term *concessionaires*, designing projects and specifications, raising
capital, building infrastructure, managing assets, bearing risks and pocketing
profits. The government delegates nearly all its public service duties to a private company, retaining only an overall political responsibility for the quality of the end product. The system has allowed France to develop its water
infrastructure without using public money. And competition among the private companies for concessions has helped keep costs down.

Lyonnaise des Eaux, with other French concessionaires, benefitted enormously from this system, gaining the financial, political, social, legal, managerial and technical engineering skills to ensure the smooth operation of
public-service infrastructures. Today, local governments from London to
Bangkok are rushing to privatize the construction and management of much
of their infrastructure. With decades of experience already under its belt,
Lyonnaise is extraordinarily well positioned to capture a disproportionate
share of this exploding international market. Not only that, but the years of
fierce competition have obliged the company to stay on the cutting edge of
research. Lyonnaise currently spends about $100 million each year on R&D.

To accelerate and reinforce its globalization strategy, Lyonnaise has also
taken pains to acquire and develop a broader, more integrated package of
skills. In buying Dumez, the second largest construction company in France,
in 1990, the company increased its debt load heavily, but it was for the first
time able to offer clients a fully integrated package of construction and environmental services. It can now build a facility with its construction arm,
then run it using its utility arm. The "bundled" packages Lyonnaise can now
put together for clients are hard to beat for competitors with only one side
of the business. Lyonnaise has also developed a substantial capability in the
energy field, which nicely dovetails with the company's traditional strengths
in waste management. In Paris, for example, 10 percent of the homes are currently heated with the energy Lyonnaise generates from its waste-to-energy
garbage incinerator.

One other key to Lyonnaise's globalization strategy is the fact that it is resolutely committed to taking a long view of international market penetration.
Lyonnaise sends representatives to countries such as Vietnam as much as ten
years in advance of any real profit expectations. During those early years, the
representative builds up a network of contacts and gains knowledge of the
local market. In this task, he or she is usually assisted by the extremely help-

ful French embassy down the road. When the developing country finally decides to put projects out to tender, it is very difficult to compete with the entrenched Lyonnaise des Eaux.

To improve the odds even more, Lyonnaise routinely buys stakes in foreign companies that act as footholds into markets in which it has a long-term interest. It also puts together consortia with local firms to bid on Build-Operate-Transfer projects, and it has signed more of these agreements than anyone else in the world. In 1992, a consortium led by Lyonnaise des Eaux won a thirty-year concession to produce and distribute water, and treat waste waters for Buenos Aires, the largest such contract ever signed. Again, its local subsidiary had been on the ground a few years earlier working on an Argentine dam project and making contacts. Lyonnaise also has won other concessions in Malaysia, Australia, Mexico and Macao.

Organizational learning is another key part of Lyonnaise's globalization strategy. To ensure the entire organization learns from its international successes (and the occasional failures), Lyonnaise rotates its managers and scientists internationally and across subsidiary boundaries. The result is a global network of mutually supportive companies and individuals.

Lyonnaise des Eaux made its American debut in 1982 by taking over General Waterworks, a Delaware-based company serving one million people in fourteen states. In early 1994, the company merged General Waterworks with Harrington Park, adding the latter's million customers in New Jersey to its American holdings. Although these moves represent a useful toehold in the American market, they remain a drop in the proverbial bucket of the total American market, which could reach $54 billion.[9] Why? Because municipal governments still own and operate 86 percent of the drinking water systems and nearly all waste water. But with federal water standards becoming ever tighter and municipalities' budgets shrinking, the market for private water companies in the U.S. is expected to represent a growing portion of Lyonnaise des Eaux's international revenues.

The company's skill in dealing with the American political system is also improving, which should boost sales even further. It is now adapting its European experience to the stateside political context, and is actively courting American politicians: forming consortia with local firms, agreeing to hire laid-off workers and investing some of its profits in local communities.

Lyonnaise's coziness with government occasionally lands the company in hot water. One of the company's subsidiaries was accused of paying kickbacks to secure a water contract with the French city of Grenoble. The scandal forced Grenoble's mayor (and France's communication minister) Alain Carignon to resign. He is alleged to have received political contributions from a Lyonnaise subsidiary in return for public works contracts in Grenoble. Lyonnaise des Eaux vigorously denied any wrongdoing, but it decided to halt contributions to political campaigns nonetheless.

Despite such occasional setbacks, however, the company has little cause for alarm. Lyonnaise des Eaux is predicting profits of over $200 million for 1994, an increase of some 25–30 percent from the previous year. And with the integrated competitive platform it has carefully constructed, Lyonnaise is well positioned to capitalize on the interplay among three of the most powerful trends of the late 20th century: privatization, environmentalism and, of course, globalization.

## *Nokia: Finland's Cellular Flash*

When most people think of Finland, they usually think about Santa Claus, reindeer and snow, though not necessarily in that order. But these days a few might also think of an upstart company called Nokia, which though once specializing in toilet paper and rubber boots, has more recently become the second largest producer of cellular phones in the world (after Motorola), and the twelfth largest telecommunications manufacturer. Nokia has succeeded by moving quickly in an exploding digital electronics market, proving that even small, agile players can develop and execute aggressive global strategies. "They set out to build a new industry for themselves and that's what they've done," says Herschel Shosteck, a cellular industry analyst in Silver Springs, Maryland. "These guys are tough, entrepreneurial street fighters."[10]

Nokia has sold over five million cellular phones worldwide and currently has an impressive 20 percent share of the world market. With estimated 1994 revenues in the order of $6 billion, up 50 percent over 1993, Nokia is now one of the largest employers in the Nordic countries. It earned 1994 profits in the range of $400 million and accounts for more than 25 percent of the value of the Helsinki Stock Exchange.

From its inception in 1865 as a small pulp mill in the village of Nokia, north of Helsinki, Finland, the company gradually expanded beyond paper into rubber, chemicals, floorings, ventilation systems and power cables, mostly serving the five million-strong domestic market. In the early 1960s, the company entered the telephone business, manufacturing paging equipment and radio-telephones for both military and civilian use.

By the mid-1980s, however, slumping sales led chief executive Kari Kairamo to go on an acquisition binge, buying up four European color television manufacturers and a large Swedish computer company. These additions made Nokia a big European player, but the company was still too small to compete in markets that were increasingly global and profits began to nose dive. In 1988, Kairamo committed suicide and a management committee took over, selling off most businesses not related to the company's new priorities: telecommunications, mobile telephones and consumer electronics.

Jorma Ollila, then forty-four, took over Nokia in 1992 and immediately began cleaning house. He dramatically changed Nokia's strategy and culture, pouring both money and people into the mobile phone and telecommunications businesses. "There was a turnaround in the summer of 1992," says Nokia's chief financial officer, Olla-Pekka Kallasvuo. "Our new management decided to take a clear and committed approach to becoming a telecoms company."[11] The new Nokia that emerged from the complete restructuring within had hammered was much leaner, more tightly focused and more entrepreneurial. It was also determined to become a truly global player.

Ollila was also at pains to change Nokia's stodgy, centralized management style. He worked hard to promote the entrepreneurial, high-tech culture that had always been alive in scattered pockets of Nokia and to extend it to the company as a whole. He hired dozens of young new managers, many of whom had studied outside Finland and brought a decidedly international flavor to the company. All employees and managers were encouraged to get on a first-name basis. The average age in the mobile phones division plunged to thirty-four.

Ollila next turned his attention to Nokia's crown jewel: cellular phones. There were a number of reasons for this division's remarkable success, including a quirk of history. When the Finns plotted to revolt against the heavy-handed rule of the Russian Tsar Nicholas II in the late 1800s, they used an obscure technology the rulers in St. Petersburg had ignored: the telephone. Finland developed a network of makeshift telephone lines and has kept to locally run networks ever since, boasting fifty autonomous, local phone companies. The number of companies and resulting price pressure forced Nokia to hustle for business in its home market, unlike the cosy situation its major competitors enjoyed with their state-owned telecom monopolies.

Nokia was also helped in the late 1970s when the telecommunications authorities of Sweden, Denmark, Norway and Finland decided to build the world's first international cellular system. When this system was switched on in 1981, Nokia was there with both equipment and phones. But the small size of the Nordic market meant it also had to look for international opportunities in order to grow. This forced the company to become familiar with a variety of different technical standards, which would prove to be of great value later on.

Finland's sparsely populated and inhospitably cold temperatures have encouraged the growth of cellular technology, as it would have been too costly to lay wire throughout the country. The cold weather also meant many people wanted to have cellular phones in their cars in case of mechanical trouble.

Ollila's strategy revolved around the global leverage of Nokia's core competence in cellular phones. The company's hot (digital) products, low-cost manufacturing and "we try harder" attitude helped it gain market share quickly. For example, when British personal communication network operator Orange PCS asked bidders to design novel features for its new $75 million network, such as a mobile handset with two phone numbers and two different ring tones, most failed to deliver. "Nokia was the only manufacturer that listened to us and didn't tell us what to do," says Paul Craig, general manager at Orange.[12]

The company also worked hard to trim manufacturing costs. To minimize the factory changeover downtimes needed to produce phones for differing Japanese, American and European technical standards, Nokia began redesigning its phones to be as similar as possible. Nokia is focused like a laser on user friendliness, using icons and scrolling to help the user tap popular features like speed dialing, call forwarding, call screening and voice mail—unlike many of its competitors, who focus simply on reduced phone size. The company hopes these efforts will boost its market share beyond its current 20 percent of the twenty-five million mobile phones sold worldwide in 1994, up from fourteen million in 1993. These 50 percent growth rates are expected to continue for at least another couple of years as new markets in Asia, Latin America and Eastern Europe come on stream.

With a cellular phone penetration rate of only 7 percent (compared with 9–12 percent in the Nordic countries), the United States remains a major source of untapped growth potential. Although Nokia entered the North American market in 1983, it was initially hampered by its lack of brand recognition outside of Scandinavia. Nokia's solution was to team up with Tandy Corp, and Nokia got its phones into over six thousand Radio Shack stores under the Tandy brand. Together, the companies built factories in Korea and Texas in the mid-1980s. Tandy's obsession with costs also forced Nokia to cut manufacturing costs to the bone. Ollila also increased Nokia's American advertising and promotion budget. More than half that money will go into joint promotions with big customers like the Bell companies, emphasizing the Nokia name, whose Japanese-like sound makes for a confusing image. Results have been impressive. In the exploding American market for cellular phones, Nokia's market share quickly jumped from 10 percent to its current 20 percent. According to Ollila, Nokia's goal is to boost market share in the United States even further, although just hanging on to its existing share will mean growth rates of about 50 percent per year.

Even first-rate cellular technology will only buy you an admission ticket into the hypercompetitive markets that lie beyond the year 2000. By then, Ollila reckons mobile phones will have become simply low-cost commodity items—remember your 1986 pocket calculator? For Nokia, therefore, the future is in technology convergence. By the year 2000, mobile phone makers will likely be producing hardware that works on both cellular and satellite networks and experts predict that by 2010, mobile phones will also be jam packed with video and computing power. Executives might tune into CNN on their video mobile phone en route to catching a plane, holding a video conference, tapping into the Internet, or dictating a message that appears as a fax seconds later halfway around the world. The Multimedia Age is almost here, and Nokia intends to be smack in the middle of it.

Nokia continues to take a long view of further international market expansion. Despite the near disappearance of the former Soviet market for Finnish products, Ollila is laying the groundwork for future development. "We have to build new trading relations for the future," he says, "and maintain contacts with those who will be the decision makers."[13] Nokia is setting up joint ventures and trying to arrange different forms of payment to overcome the acute shortage of foreign exchange in the former U.S.S.R.

By any measure, Nokia has traveled an enormous competitive distance incredibly quickly. From a small base in a tiny Scandinavian market, it has not only become a global corporate superpower, but it has done so in an industry squarely situated in the middle of the emerging global information superhighway.

## CONCLUSION

Even successful and sophisticated executives often have only the most rudimentary grasp of political, economic and market dynamics outside the rather cloistered—and economically stagnant—confines of their own regions or, at best, the G7 countries. But competitive circumstances are changing rapidly and both the target markets and the relentless struggle to dominate them have become decidedly global. To be competitive in those markets, companies must develop an unprecedented level of global capability themselves. It is worth recalling that the G7 countries represent no more than 12 percent of the world's population and a shrinking proportion of its consumers.

Corporate globalization is no small task, and it has so far attracted far more rhetoric than concrete initiatives and results. The experience of the seven companies profiled in this chapter provides some important lessons about how to translate that rhetoric into reality:

- **Successful globalization requires heroic measures.** Many executives seem to think that a globalized version of their company would look pretty much like the current one, only with bigger long-distance phone bills. Wrong. As companies like Methanex demonstrate, extracting full value and learning potential from a globalized operation takes both conscious effort and fundamental changes. New organizational mechanisms and different recruitment, training and evaluation programs and criteria must all be developed and implemented. Perhaps even more important, a genuine global worldview and *culture* must be developed, and that never happens spontaneously or overnight.

- **Coherence comes from vision, not operating manuals.** Arguably the single greatest challenge for far-flung global companies is creating sufficient cohesion, coherence and focus amidst geographic, linguistic and cultural diversity. Companies such as Sweden's Ikea have demonstrated convincingly that the most effective source of coherence and "glue" in a global company is a common and compelling corporate vision and value set. As dysfunctional as hierarchical, "command-and-control" approaches have become in purely domestic companies, they are even less effective in global ones. Standardized operating procedures and manuals can only take you so far.

- **There is strength in diversity.** This is the flip side of the same coin as corporate coherence. While a certain degree of commonality of vision is indispensable to offset the centrifugal tendencies of a global company, it must be balanced by a healthy respect for decentralization and diversity. In practice, this means the devolution of a tremendous amount of decision-making power to the local level and a high tolerance for different approaches and solutions in different parts of the empire. Invariably, huge international companies like Lyonnaise des Eaux run into trouble when they try to superimpose standardized, one-size-fits-all approaches into geographic and cultural contexts where they simply don't and can't work.

Make no mistake: Globalization will require the reinvention of a good chunk of your company's innovation infrastructure and intellectual capital base, from corporate culture to strategic alliance strategies to human resource development. But the effort will prove well worth it. At a minimum, strengthening the company's global infrastructure will at least allow the firm to stay in the next round of global hypercompetition. And if it can be done superbly, it can itself become a major source of actual competitive advantage. And here's the best part: You don't have to be big to play the globalization game effectively; technology has seen to that. So what's holding *you* back?

### CHAPTER TEN

# THE ECO-INDUSTRIAL REVOLUTION

## ENVIRONMENT AS A COMPETITIVE WEAPON

*"The environment will provide one of the largest opportunities for technological and managerial innovation—and profitable enterprise—that the industrial world has ever seen."*

PERCY BARNEVIK CEO/ ASEA BROWN BOVERI

In a single day, June 13, 1994, the share price of Exxon fell by fully 5 percent ($2.88), with news of the company's exposure to additional legal damages for the *Exxon Valdez* disaster. Despite what should have been a dramatic wake-up call, Wall Street analysts, investors and CEOs continue for the most part to conduct business as usual, unpersuaded that environmental considerations are anything more than a superficial and temporary blip on their Quotron screens. Well, they're dead wrong. What they're currently sleeping through is nothing less than the beginnings of a profound, global industrial restructuring.

From Zurich to Singapore to San Francisco, ever-tightening environmental regulations, multimillion dollar cleanup costs, exploding lender liability and even executive jail sentences have begun to impact on corporate bottom lines with unprecedented speed and ferocity. In future, managing environmental risk and investment opportunities effectively will make the difference between outperforming your competitors and lagging behind—or worse. Access to capital, customers, suppliers and committed employees will become more and more dependent on companies' environmental performance and efficiency. Taken together, these changes amount to what some senior Asian industrialists have recently termed an "Eco-Industrial Revolution." It is a revolution that will reshape the global business environment in ways that are, to most senior executives, as mysterious as they are unprecedented.

In this unsettled new world of environmental considerations, the competitive ante will be jacked up even higher than it already is. Not only individual companies, but entire industrial sectors will become obsolete and disappear. Conversely, those who can adapt and innovate will enjoy rich opportunities in supplying and improving new products, processes, technologies and services to an international market projected to exceed $600 billion per year by the end of this decade, in the OECD countries alone. It is growing even faster in the newly industrializing countries.

Given that existing corporate strategies were all generated in the "dark ages" before the Eco-Industrial Revolution, most will need to be completely reinvented. What is now urgently required are corporate strategies that take as their premise the need to derive a substantial portion of the firm's competitive advantage from superior environmental performance. *Everything* needs to change: new strategic directions and alliance partners for companies, new roles for CEOs and directors, new products and services, markets and customers, manufacturing processes, hiring and evaluation criteria, technology and R&D strategies and, most far-reaching of all, new corporate cultures.

Recent surveys by McKinsey and Arthur D. Little give rise to both optimism and concern about the ability of international business to come to terms with the Eco-Industrial Revolution. The good news is that environmental awareness among CEOs has increased dramatically over the past five years. The bad news is that this awareness is generally not accompanied by any clear sense of what the CEOs can actually *do* about it.

This can scarcely be considered surprising. Almost nothing in either their formal educations or their previous business careers could possibly have prepared contemporary executives for dealing with the implications and effects of the Eco-Industrial Revolution. Even today, it is the exceptional business school or management writer who takes the environmental problematic on board in a serious way. Contemporary executive programs and MBA courses at even the top business schools in the world are only now beginning to address the question of how corporate strategy and profitability might best be integrated with environmental imperatives. "Leading" business and management journals are similarly mute on the subject.

These days, when I discuss the Eco-Industrial Revolution with groups of (usually skeptical) international CEOs, one of the most important points I try to make to them is this: Environmental issues have acquired not only operational but strategic significance. In bygone days, it may have been sufficient either to ignore environmental questions altogether or to marginalize them in the organizational gulag of the "health, safety and environment" department. But those days are over for most companies.

Environmental questions must now be brought from the periphery to the strategic center of a company, and must command the serious attention of both board members and CEOs. There are at least nine reasons why:

- *Long-term corporate survival.* Nonsustainable harvesting practices undermine the very resource base on which the futures of many companies and even entire industries depend. The forestry, energy, agriculture and tourism sectors are particularly at risk. Others, such as the chemicals industry, have already started their painful journey up the environmental learning curve, but still remain vulnerable.

- *Market opportunity.* The sheer size of the environmental market is now simply too large to ignore. Banque Paribas has estimated the market for environmental goods and services at more than $600 billion per year, in the OECD countries alone. And the fastest growing environmental markets are not even included in this figure: countries such as Taiwan, South Korea, Indonesia, Thailand, Malaysia, Singapore and China.

- *Competitiveness.* Harvard Business School professor and competitiveness guru Michael Porter has argued persuasively that tough domestic standards produce companies that are superior performers in world markets.[1] His thesis would appear to be amply borne out in the environmental sector by the example of Germany, whose companies have already parlayed that country's notoriously demanding environmental regulations into a 20 percent share of the growing world market for "green" technologies.

- *Short-term operating ability.* Particularly in the OECD countries, increasingly rigorous environmental standards are leaving few industries unaffected. The chemicals, forestry, energy and automobile industries are merely the most obvious ones. Compliance with environmental standards has become an important factor for companies simply to retain their "social license" to do business.

- *Finance.* Because of new regulations and an aggressive litigation climate, a clean environmental bill of health is becoming increasingly vital to securing investment and project financing. From Wall Street, where environmental due diligence is delaying and even killing mergers and acquisitions financing, to parts of the former East Germany, where it has ground the government's privatization program to a near standstill, environmental considerations are starting to move into the financial mainstream.

- *Legal and criminal liability.* Astronomical environmental cleanup, compliance or litigation costs (not to mention the increasing incidence of jailed executives) are causing badly squeezed profits, huge contingent liabilities and even bankruptcies. In the U.S. alone, the Environmental Protection Agency has estimated that its environmental regulations will have cost American industry some $2 trillion by the end of this decade.

- *Corporate reputation and image.* Companies are beginning to appreciate the increasingly direct link between environmental performance and corporate reputation. Union Carbide and Exxon are by no means the only examples of this, merely the most spectacular. In addition, companies are beginning to discover that they are no "greener" than their weakest link, which is frequently their outside suppliers. Major companies such as Boeing in the U.S. and Migros in Switzerland are giving their suppliers a stark choice: Clean up your act or we'll take hundreds of millions of dollars of business elsewhere.

- *Reinventing the company.* Above all, the environment is now a strategic, CEO-level issue because it requires reinventing most of the company's key strategic functions: board/CEO roles, stakeholder relations, corporate cultures, organizational structures, manufacturing/production processes, management-information systems, R&D and technology strategies, marketing, human resource management and development, finance and strategic alliances.

- *Strategic fitness barometer.* Environmental issues affect so many different dimensions of the company, and in such fundamental ways, that they provide an excellent barometer for a company's overall strategic fitness. In my experience, if you find a company that can manage *this* issue well, you'll find a well-managed company, period.

Even taken individually, these nine considerations qualify as strategic ones. Together, they constitute an unassailable case for bringing environmental questions closer to the strategic center of the company, where they can receive the sustained attention of the board and CEO.

But how, concretely, might this be done? Like most other strategic changes, the shift toward a fundamentally new paradigm must begin at the level of both corporate culture and individual mindset. Companies wishing to leverage the economic power of the Eco-Industrial Revolution must begin to:

- **Treat environmental efficiency as a *competitive* weapon.** In Japan, for example, superior environmental efficiency is estimated to give Japanese firms an immediate 5 percent cost advantage over their less "eco-efficient" international competitors.

- **Move beyond the essentially negative and constraining mentality of "environmental management" and instead seek *positive*, enabling** opportunities for new products, processes, services and technologies that combine profitability with environmental improvement. The international policy community refers to this new paradigm as "sustainable development," and it was the centrepiece of the historic Earth Summit in Rio de Janeiro in 1992. Leading companies such as Brazil's Aracruz Cellulose, the U.S.'s Southern California Edison and Canada's TransAlta have made this new approach a unifying principle driving much of their competitive strategy.

- **Move beyond static, remedial, "end-of-pipe" approaches to pollution control and focus instead on *preventive* measures well upstream in the corporate value chain.** In many instances, preventive measures can be literally hundreds of times more cost-effective than post-facto remedial ones.

- **Help mobilize and reorient the *international capital markets* to become major forces for environmental change.** In the OECD countries, this will mean adopting longer-term investment horizons and integrating environmental considerations more squarely into lending and investment decisions. In the developing world, priorities will also include aggressive debt reduction strategies such as "debt for environment" swaps and mobilizing the informal economy through such initiatives as "green microlending."

No one should be deceived about either the immensity or the difficulty of the changes that will be required. The Eco-Industrial Revolution will sweep away many of the comforting but obsolete notions about how companies ought to be managed, financed and led, and it will sweep away many companies too. And, as with any biological system, it will be those unable or unwilling to make the necessary adaptations that will disappear first.

Death, taxes and the Eco-Industrial Revolution. Each will inevitably affect us all; the only question is when. Depending on the alacrity of our response, the new eco-industrial paradigm will either make us better and more agile business people or it will bankrupt us. There isn't a lot of middle ground.

Let's look at some leading international companies that have not only got the environmental message, they have turned it into a competitive weapon.

## Northern Telecom: Environment as Competitive Weapon

Broadly speaking, there are three basic options for corporate strategists responding to environmental issues. The first and, until recently, the most popular response is to ignore them as much as possible, dismissing the environmental phenomenon as essentially a nonissue for business, or at worst a transitory one. The hallmarks of the Level 1 environmental strategist is the liberal use of lobbyists to water-down new legislation, and of lawyers to fight existing laws.

Higher up the evolutionary scale we have the Level 2 company, which tends to treat environmental considerations as a drain on profitability and an afterthought in the industrial production process. Their approach is an essentially defensive one, predicated on damage control and after-the-fact mitigation. The better practitioners of this second approach have installed elaborate systems to monitor potentially harmful emissions, to ensure corporate compliance with minimum legal standards and to alert the board and senior management to serious liabilities that may be looming.

Only a select few companies—by my extremely rough estimate, less than 1 percent worldwide—have taken environmental strategy to the highest Level 3: Embracing the "Eco-Industrial Revolution" as a new and central fact of business life, and as a potentially significant source of competitive advantage and new profitability. Northern Telecom is one of those rare companies.

Northern Telecom is one of the world's leading manufacturers of telecommunications equipment. Headquartered in Canada, Nortel has annual sales in the $10 billion range, roughly 57,000 employees worldwide, and over fifty manufacturing plants in North America, Europe and Asia. Like all major electronics equipment manufacturers, Nortel used the compound CFC-113 extensively as a cleaning solvent to remove flux residue from printed circuit boards, in order to achieve the extraordinarily high levels of cleanliness and reliability demanded in the industry. Until the late 1980s, CFC-113 was considered the safest and most effective cleanser available, and Nortel was using over two million pounds of the stuff each year. By 1987, however, new scientific evidence about the harmful effects of CFCs on the earth's ozone layer led to the signing of the Montreal Protocol. That document, subsequently amended and strengthened in 1990, committed its international signatories (over ninety countries) to eliminate CFCs altogether by the year 2000 within the OECD countries and ten years later in the developing world.

Like most of its competitors, Nortel initially took a somewhat jaundiced view of the Montreal Protocol, regarding it as the unwelcome and potentially expensive intrusion of remote, out-of-touch United Nations bureaucrats. Quite quickly, however, senior Nortel executives such as Margaret Kerr came to recognize the potential for both short-term cost savings and medium-term competitive advantage. Armed with this new realization, Nortel threw itself into an intensive corporate campaign to discover cost-effective substitutes for CFCs and, if possible, turn them to competitive advantage.

Within three years, Nortel had become the first major electronics company in the world to eliminate CFC-113 completely from its global operations, fully nine years ahead of the timetable set out in the Montreal Protocol. The financial payback was almost instantaneous: $4 million in immediate savings was realized from reduced inputs and waste-disposal costs. This level of savings was achieved through the investment of only $1 million, not an altogether bad return. What's more, by developing CFC alternatives, including an innovative "no-clean" system that bypassed the need for solvents altogether, Nortel figures to save an additional $50 million in purchasing costs by the year 2000. In recognition of its leadership role on the CFC issue, Nortel received two prestigious awards: the 1991 Stratospheric Ozone Protection Award from the U.S. Environmental Protection Agency and the 1992 UN Environmental Protection Award. But that was only the beginning. Having put its own house in order, Nortel then began to look around for opportunities to turn its improved environmental performance into a competitive weapon. It soon found that opportunity in Mexico.

The electronics industry is one of the fastest-growing sectors in the Mexican economy and it is also the largest single consumer of ozone-depleting solvents. The Secretaria de Desarrollo Urbano y Ecologia (SEDUE), the Mexican environmental agency, recognized that electronics companies would need assistance if the country was to achieve the targets set by the Montreal Protocol. Of even greater short-term strategic importance, Mexico was eager to make dramatic improvements in its environmental performance, in order to gain its much-sought-after acceptance into the North American Free Trade Agreement with Canada and the United States.

The whole industry required new technologies and techniques to reduce its dependence on ozone-depleting solvents. Nortel was approached to join SEDUE, the Mexican Association of Industries (CANACINTRA), the U.S. Environmental Protection Agency and others to attack the problem. Nortel agreed to provide technical assistance and cooperation for several reasons. The company was already selling products in the Mexican marketplace and was familiar with developments in the electronics industry. For another, sharing such expertise and technical information not only conformed with Nortel's commitment to environmental leadership, but could become an excellent market-penetration device as well. As senior environment VP Margaret Kerr told me: "The creation of a multistakeholder forum for transferring technology suited to the needs of Mexican businesses is an ideal extension of Nortel's activities in Mexico. Our involvement in this project simply made good business sense."

So Nortel took the lead in designing and conducting a series of hands-on demonstration projects and workshops with industrial companies throughout Mexico over the course of two years, absorbing all the costs itself. One result was a new-found understanding among Mexican industrialists of concrete ways in which improved environmental performance could be translated into better product quality, reduced costs and increased competitiveness. This in turn encouraged the Mexican government to become the first developing country in the world to commit to the more aggressive CFC phase-out schedule adopted by the industrialized countries.

For Nortel, the initiative's business benefits were substantial—and quick. The positive profile and new relationships with senior Mexican government officials and industrialists were instrumental in winning new telephone equipment supply and service contracts in Mexico worth over $60 million. It also brought Nortel widespread international recognition as an environmental leader and innovator, which should stand it in good stead elsewhere. Nortel already judges the experiment to be sufficiently successful that it is attempting to clone it in China and Thailand

Nortel's success in dealing quickly, effectively and profitably with the CFC issue created wider ripples throughout the company. It would be disingenuous to pretend that Nortel is now a seething mass of 57,000 committed environmentalists, but the CFC experience definitely opened eyes throughout the company to a set of wider possibilities. As Margaret Kerr observes:

> By taking a leading role in CFC solvent elimination, we demonstrated that the merging of environmental and business imperatives can result in direct cash savings. This has changed the attitudes of many of our senior executives and opened the door for other company environmental initiatives in areas such as energy conservation, design-for-environment and product life-cycle stewardship.[2]

Over the coming decade, superior environmental performance will become even more critical to Nortel's competitive success. In Europe, the most aggressive recycling legislation in the world will place a growing competitive premium on telecommunications products that minimize adverse environmental impact throughout their entire life cycle. This means Nortel and its competitors will be required to develop equipment that is environmentally efficient not only during its manufacture and use, but also in its ultimate disposal. Nortel's considerable front-end investment of time, effort and money in integrating environmental considerations throughout its design and manufacturing processes will place it at a distinct competitive advantage. Equally important, its environmental initiatives have triggered a much wider process of organizational learning throughout the company.

## Brazil's Aracruz Cellulose

Even today, the vast majority of corporate CFCs in the industrialized world remain extremely skeptical about incorporating environmental performance at the very core of a company's competitive strategy, and profiting from doing so.

Environmental awareness is even more limited among CEOs in the developing world. One Brazilian forestry company, however, has confounded the skeptics and taken a leadership role. Due to its long-term commitment to *sustainable* forestry development, Brazil's Aracruz Cellulose now finds itself extremely well positioned to compete internationally in the environmentally conscious 1990s.

The 1992 Earth Summit in Rio de Janeiro was a high-water mark for international recognition of the growing importance of environmental considerations in business. Aracruz was way ahead of the curve; it had already been practicing what the Earth Summit was advocating in Brazil for almost fifteen years. Under its visionary chairman Erling Lorentzen, Aracruz initiated its sustainable development strategy as far back as 1975, when it adopted the highest environmental standards in the world, drawing from Scandinavia and the United States. At that time, Brazil had next to no environmental regulations of its own, so Aracruz was forward-looking in the extreme. In stark contrast to the traditional "slash and burn" approaches dominating the forestry industry even today, Aracruz deliberately located its operations on land already badly degraded, with a view to reforesting and rehabilitating it.

Successive generations of farmers, loggers and livestock raisers had stripped and burned vast tracts of woodlands in the Espirito Santo region, leaving the area both financially and environmentally impoverished. Aracruz's first step was to create a company town, providing badly needed employment, schools, housing, health clinics and other social services for the local population. Next, the company invested heavily in research and genetic engineering to develop a species of eucalyptus tree that not only produces high-quality paper, but can be harvested every seven years, growing back from its stump three times before needing to be replaced. Thanks to the tree's remarkable growth rates, large areas that had been completely denuded experienced spectacular new growth. This work not only won the Aracruz team the coveted Marcus Wallenberg Foundation prize, but provided a sustainable source of new fiber for the company's pulp operation. To further reduce unsustainable logging of original forests for such basic needs as fuel and housing, Aracruz distributes nine million free eucalyptus seedlings to local farmers every year. The company also designed special tractors and wood-handling equipment to minimize soil erosion and other environmental damage from its harvesting operations.

Having created a stable, secure and environmentally sustainable supply of raw material, Aracruz then set about building a state-of-the-art pulp mill, one that still meets or exceeds the toughest environmental standards in

Europe, Scandinavia or North America. In addition to producing minimal pollution, the plant recycles most of its own waste heat and is 90 percent self-sufficient in energy. In an era when many of its competitors continue to fight environmental standards tooth and nail, Aracruz was one of the first forest products companies in the world to pioneer chlorine-free techniques for bleaching wood pulp. By taking dead aim on what is arguably their industry's greatest environmental problems, Aracruz is convinced they can parlay superior environmental performance into competitive advantage. And their financial results strongly suggest they're right.

Aracruz is not only one of the most innovative forestry companies in the world, but one of the most profitable. In 1994, it netted over $300 million in profits on sales of just under $1 billion. The company has also managed to become the cheapest cost pulp producer in the world, proving once and for all that high environmental standards and low costs are not mutually exclusive. The company's top environmental executive, Carlos de Oliveira Roxo, provided me with an eloquent summary of Aracruz's corporate philosophy:

> *It has been argued that one cannot serve both the needs of industry and of the environment. We believe that this is not an impossible task. Industry can no longer afford to ignore environmental needs. Business is the most forceful agent of change. As business leaders, we are responsible for change that is positive. We believe that a business cannot continue to exist without the trust and respect of society for its environmental performance.*[3]

Welcome to the Eco-Industrial Revolution. You *can* do well by doing good. Just ask any of Aracruz's seven thousand employees, 90 percent of whom come from the poorest areas of Brazil. Or ask one of the beneficiaries of the Brazilian Foundation for Sustainable Development, cofounded by Aracruz to propagate some of the lessons the company has learned about combining economics and environmentalism.

## Southern California Edison

Until very recently, the power utility sector was not the place to look for innovation of any kind, much less environmentally driven innovation. Utilities were a pretty sleepy—not to mention dirty—lot, operating what were essentially monopolies in stable, highly regulated markets. Incentives to compete, much less innovate, were few and far between. Well, hold onto your hat. California utilities are about to be caught in the withering crossfire of two apparently countervailing trends: financial deregulation alongside tighter environmental regulations. As of 1996, the utilities' major industrial customers will be free for the first time to buy power from any company of their choice, including out-of-state suppliers. With California power prices roughly 50 percent higher than the national average, the very notion of deregulated competition is enough to make utility CEOs—and shareholders—blanch. But that's not all. Environmental regulations have been tightened to the point that California air quality standards are now arguably the toughest in the world. For industry leaders like Southern California Edison, this juxtaposition of environmental reregulation and financial deregulation has moved the environment front and center in the company's strategic thinking.

For Southern California Edison, the economic benefits of environmental leadership are at least threefold. First, in a newly competitive, environmentally conscious marketplace like California, the perception of environmental excellence can be an important source of differentiation and advantage. Second, with an annual environmental expenditure tab of over $300 million, any improvement in SCE's "environmental efficiency" will drop rather decisively to the firm's bottom line. And third and most importantly, unlike 99 percent of industrial companies, SCE understands that environmental performance is far more than simply a question of defensive, damage mitigation. Approached creatively and opportunistically, in the words of chairman John Bryson: "Enhancing business oportunities and protecting the environment are not mutually exclusive, but mutually dependent goals . . ."[4] He also says: "There are great business opportunities in meeting environmental needs . . . an environmentally demanding future means bigger markets and better business."[5]

The importance—and novelty—of Bryson's mindset should not be underestimated. A disturbingly large percentage of corporate CEOs continue to regard the environment as a complete nonissue, or at most a fleeting, ephemeral one. Others see the environment as a disaster waiting to happen, viewing it entirely from the negative perspective of risk management. Such a purely defensive posture is almost intrinsically incapable of turning strategic environmental management into a true competitive weapon. By starting with the premise that environmental performance can and should be a source of both profitability and competitive advantage, Bryson and SCE are already way ahead of the game.

SCE's environmental strategy has three pillars: promoting energy efficiency and reduced power demand among its customers; ensuring the energy that *is* required is supplied in an environmentally superior way; and finding and exploiting new business opportunities driven by environmental considerations.

The first pillar is known in the utility business as demand-side management. It is based on what ought to be the incontrovertible principle that it costs far less to reduce energy consumption by a given amount than it does to create an equivalent amount of new generating capacity. Unfortunately, this insight took considerably longer to dawn on utility regulators, who continued to set rate structures that encouraged power companies to sell more, not less energy. SCE was a pioneer in helping convince regulators to radically overhaul that system and provide incentives to both the utilities and their customers for energy conservation. Under the new regime, SCE could finally begin to make better profits by saving energy than by producing it.

With a new regulatory framework in place, SCE developed a demand-side management program that has become a model for energy utilities all over the world. An important part of the program is the Customer Technology Application Center in Irwindale, California. The Center is a massive demon stration and education facility, showcasing state-of-the art energy efficiency technologies for residential, commercial and industrial users. Technologies such as thermal-energy storage systems, energy-efficient lighting and appli- ances and even alternative-fuel vehicles are demonstrated at the center. SCE's energy experts also make house-calls. They visit homes, businesses and facto- ries to discuss and develop customized solutions for saving energy. Some of those house calls can take them an awfully long way from Southern California. Through its participation in the "E-7," a group of some of the world's leading power companies, SCE provides advisory services to compa- nies and governments in the developing world. Closer to home, SCE teamed up with several major aerospace companies and the California Manufacturers Association to develop and transfer clean-air technologies to area businesses at no cost. All told, SCE spends over $100 million each year on energy-efficiency research and programs.

The second pillar of SCE's environmental strategy involves improving the company's own environmental efficiency and performance in producing power. In 1991, SCE chairman Bryson announced an ambitious new program to reduce the company's emissions of carbon dioxide by 20 percent by early in the next century. Since $CO^2$ is believed to be the greatest single contributor to global warming, reducing emissions has become a major priority with environ- mental regulators, policy makers and activists around the world. An important part of its efforts is SCE's emphasis on renewable energy sources, including solar, wind, geothermal and biomass-driven power. Typical of this thrust is SCE's Partnership with the Sun project, developing the most advanced solar-thermal generating plant in the world, a $48 million project in Barstow, California. By late 1994, SCE had already reduced its $CO^2$ output by 10 million tons. In one par- ticularly novel move, SCE engineered a 200-megawatt power swap with a utility in Oregon, thereby allowing SCE to reduce its own production during the smoggy summer season in Los Angeles.

Another innovation is SCE's pioneering work in helping establish a market for tradeable permits to emit air pollutants such as sulphur dioxide and nitrogen oxide. Under such a system, facility-specific emission limits are replaced by a collective, aggregate limit for a given region. Within that broader "bubble," individual companies are free to either make the necessary investments to reduce their own emissions, or alternatively, to purchase a "license" to release the surplus amount from another emitter that is under its limit. That way, the regional total of pollutants remains within acceptable limits and investment will gravitate toward the most cost effective solutions. If your neighbor is in a position to solve the problem more cheaply than you are, then economic rationality suggests that you should purchase some of his or her surplus entitlements. These types of market-driven win-win opportunities are very much on the cutting edge of current thinking.

The third and perhaps most exciting dimension of SCEs environmental strategy is the conscious pursuit of entirely new, environmentally based business opportunities. John Bryson is absolutely convinced that the early 21st century will belong to those who can understand and leverage the Eco-Industrial Revolution, and I fully agree with him. Bryson sees particularly attractive opportunity in electric vehicles (EVs), and SCE already has over fifty in service. In addition, the company is testing a prototype electric shuttle bus in the Long Beach area. So far, the new buses have achieved a 97 percent pollution reduction over conventionally powered vehicles. SCE is working with GM, Ford and Chrysler to develop electric vehicles suitable for large car fleets. The company is also developing and seeking to commercialize dozens of other, innovative environmental technologies, ranging from high-efficiency electric motors to high-tech electron beam guns for detoxifying contaminated soil. In one joint venture with Texas Instruments, SCE is working on photovoltaic technologies for use in inexpensive solar panels for residential rooftops.

Not all these initiatives will pan out. After all, most of them are breaking entirely new ground—or at least trying to clean it up. But merely by making such a concerted and imaginative effort, SCE demonstrates itself to be in the vanguard of the Eco-Industrial Revolution. Many of its contemporaries, by contrast, are still wasting huge amounts of energy trying to repeal the 21st century equivalent of the Law of Gravity.

## *TransAlta: Thinking Global, Acting Local*

You don't need to spend a whole lot of time with TransAlta CEO Ken McCready to realize that both the man and his company are something special. Ten years ago, TransAlta was an unremarkable, midsized electric utility with operations confined to its home province of Alberta, Canada. Today, while TranAlta remains relatively small (2,700 employees and annual revenues of just over one billion dollars), it is a recognized international innovator whose influence and business activities stretch from India to Argentina. Although McCready has been with the company for over thirty years, in person he exudes the energy, dynamism and eagerness to test the limits of a fresh recruit.

Four aspects of McCready's vision become apparent almost immediately. The first is the degree to which the ethos of sustainable development and environmental concern permeate nearly everything the company does. The second is the decidedly global nature of the company's outlook, both in terms of new business opportunities and its own sense of environmental responsibility. The third is TransAlta's exceptional openness to incorporating community and stakeholder input into its corporate strategy and decision making. And the fourth is the palpable sense of responsibility McCready and his people feel for helping change both public policy and corporate behavior well beyond their own direct sphere of operations. One or more of these attributes can be witnessed to varying degrees in any number of companies, but rarely does one see them integrated with such coherence in a single corporate culture.

It certainly wasn't always that way. One formative event in TransAlta's history occurred in the early 1970s, when local community opposition killed the company's attempt to build a coal-fired plant near Camrose, Alberta. TransAlta's failure to engage the community in early and meaningful consultations had cost them the project, but it was not a mistake they would repeat. Today, TransAlta's innovative community participation and outreach initiatives have achieved international recognition and are widely imitated.

TransAlta's other epiphany occurred in the mid-1980s, when the emergence of international concern over global warming shattered the company's insular worldview. This concern was reflected in national and international responses to the potentially harmful global environmental impacts of thermal power plants. Given that 90 percent of TransAlta's power was generated by these self-same thermal sources (coal), these findings had direct and sobering implications. Indeed, they triggered a profound reconceptualization of the entire company. TransAlta began to adopt a much more global conception of its sphere of responsibility and opportunity.

One of the many visible manifestations of TransAlta's new global consciousness was the company's active role on the Geneva-based Business Council for Sustainable Development, beginning in 1990. The BCSD included the heads of forty leading industrial corporations in the world, including

DuPont, Volkswagen, Royal Dutch/Shell, Mitsubishi and Asea Brown Boveri. It was created specifically to serve as the chief business and industry advisor to Maurice Strong, the secretary general of the historic 1992 UN Earth Summit in Rio de Janeiro. Over twenty different countries from all over the world were represented on the Council; the first chairman was a billionaire Swiss industrialist, the second a former prime minister of Thailand. McCready and TransAlta were invited to join this corporate pantheon, and he credits this involvement with dramatically accelerating and broadening his own global outlook. McCready's work with the BCSD is typical of TransAlta's two-pronged approach to environmental issues: In addition to a focus on its own performance, the company spends a good deal of time and energy trying to influence the evolution of global public policy. BCSD's 1992 book, *Changing Course*, has already had a major impact on both government policy makers and the international corporate leadership.

But McCready's international activities are not confined to stratospheric lobbying efforts at the BCSD. TransAlta is also putting at least some of its money where McCready's mouth is. The company is building a gas-fired cogeneration plant in New Zealand and in 1994 invested $100 million in a hydroelectric project in Argentina. In 1995, TransAlta also launched a series of initiatives in Canada and internationally to develop projects that would help offset emissions of greenhouse gases.

Closer to home, TransAlta is executing an aggressive array of programs to improve both its own eco-efficiency and that of its customers. McCready has publicly committed the company to stabilize its net emissions of greenhouse gasses—mainly $CO_2$—through a combination of internal and customer efficiencies, the increased use of renewable energy sources, and other domestic and international initiatives to counteract the deleterious impact of remaining emissions. There is a growing acceptance of the value of such "offset" programs: actions to neutralize the global impact of greenhouse gas emissions or to sequester additional $CO_2$ at other locations, nationally and internationally.

McCready is acutely aware that environmental education, like charity, must begin at home, and his efforts on the international stage are complemented by aggressive efforts within the company and the Alberta community. Within TransAlta, McCready has established the Environmental Citizenship Initiative, which elicits from all employees suggestions and actions to improve TransAlta's environmental performance. Outside the company, McCready served for several years as chair of the Alberta Round Table on Environment and Economy, a diverse group of business, government and community stakeholders working to set both public policy and corporate behavior on a more environmentally sustainable trajectory. Within the public school system, company initiatives include the Destination Conservation program, designed to create energy cost efficiencies and then recycle the savings back into new environmental education projects. The program is currently running in about 175 Alberta schools.

McCready and his team are clearly convinced that the Eco-Industrial Revolution is for real, that it isn't going away and that it is making environmental performance a key ingredient in corporate competitiveness. If they're right—and I firmly believe they are—they will have built a strategic architecture for their company that should carry it well into the 21st century.

## *Philip Environmental: Canada's Environmental Alchemists*

Few companies anywhere have leveraged the dynamics of the Eco-Industrial Revolution more aggressively or effectively than Canada's Philip Environmental. Five years ago, Philip was a simple, localized, unglamourous, family waste-hauling business in a working-class district in Canada's rust belt. Today, it is the fastest growing company in the country, with a diversified mix of services, growing international interests and a five-year revenue growth rate of a phenomenal 1300 percent. And the company is really only getting started.

Unlike many of their more established contemporaries in North America's waste-management sector, Allen and Philip Fracassi understood intuitively the long-term implications of the emerging new paradigm in their industry. Political, legislative and technological changes were all driving in the same direction, towards waste minimization and recycling. It was becoming both economically and environmentally preferable to prevent waste in the first place, than to spend time and money treating and hauling it away later. If factories and municipalities were aiming to create less waste, the traditional business of hauling, treating and managing it would seem to have extremely limited potential. A fairly obvious insight, perhaps, but subtle enough to have largely eluded several of the industry's dominant players, including Laidlaw and Browning-Ferris. They are now beginning to pay the price.

As for the Fracassis, they decided there was a much different and better business to be in: the business of providing comprehensive *solutions* to their clients' environmental problems. If the solution required redesigning the client's whole industrial process, then that's what they'd do. If the answer proved to be a combination of process redesign, recycling and landfilling what was left, then that's what they'd do. They'd be in the environmental *solutions* business.

The Fracassi brothers, products of working-class Hamilton, Ontario, saw two keys to their strategy for transcending the growing structural limitations of their industry: diversification and a dramatic intensification of the knowledge-value of their product and service offerings. Five years and over twenty acquisitions later, the brothers now preside over a growing, diversified and increasingly integrated empire that generated over half a billion dollars in revenue in 1994. The original core business of waste hauling and landfilling is now complemented with environmental testing laboratories, a chemical waste-management business, recycling and reprocessing plants for oil, metals and plastics and a full-blown environmental consulting business.

In 1994, the brothers really hit their stride. Their first move was to acquire a majority stake in a company with a committed management top-flight government laboratory specializing in waste-water treatment technologies. Next, the brothers combined their newly acquired technology base with their own impeccable track record as operators and promptly won long-term contracts to manage three municipal waste treatment plants. To top it all off, the Fracassi brothers teamed up with one of the country's most respected investment dealers and one of its largest pension funds to create a new venture capital company specializing in environmental R&D investments. In a single year, the size, value and potential of Philip's intellectual capital base increased by several orders of magnitude.

The conceptual thread holding the diverse pieces of the Fracassi empire together is this: Each business seeks in some way to harness and leverage new value from the Eco-Industrial Revolution. This common focus creates the potential for synergies and cross-selling opportunities among different companies within the group. The Fracassis place great emphasis on Philip's growing capability as a one-stop, full-service provider of environmental solutions. The company now has the capacity to go into a major industrial facility, conduct complete environmental audits and testing, recommend and implement new process efficiency solutions, profitably recycle some of the company's reduced waste stream and then dispose of what's left.

This is a far cry from the old-fashioned waste-hauling business and a good deal more knowledge intensive. Which is where the laboratories and technologies come in. The Fracassis see their recent acquisition of the private company managing the Canadian government's Wastewater Technology Centre (WTC) as particularly strategic; it gives them access to an ongoing source of new, value-adding technologies to embellish their other businesses and, for an added bonus, provides them with a toehold in international markets such as Mexico, where the WTC is establishing a presence.

However, it is one thing to identify potential synergies and quite another to actually deliver them. Any time a smallish company grows by over 1,300 percent through a largely acquisition-driven strategy, you're talking major integration and management challenges. Philip Environmental is clearly not exempt from this iron rule. Indeed, the challenges of integration and coherence are made even more difficult for Philip by the brothers' insistence on maximizing the entrepreneurial autonomy of their acquisitions. Most of them are companies much like Philip was itself five years ago: built, owned and operated by hardworking, independent-minded entrepreneurs. The Fracassis are understandably loath to tamper with the very entrepreneurial qualities which attracted them in the first place, so they tend to leave existing management in place and give them as much running room as possible. The downside, obviously, is that it makes coordination and synergy building among the group companies that much more difficult.

The Fracassis have developed at least two mechanisms to bring some level of organizational coherence out of the potential chaos. One is the inauguration of an integration committee, whose monthly meetings help plot group-wide strategies, identify joint opportunities and begin to develop the rudiments of a common corporate culture. The other is the judicious allocation of Philip treasury shares as partial payment for the acquisitions. This not only allows the entrepreneur to retain the motivation and incentive of an owner, but promotes a company-wide mindset by linking everyone's economic destinies.

Philip is still far from an industry behemoth. The industry's Big Three—wMx, Laidlaw and Browning-Ferris—are still much larger. Chemical Waste, wMx's specialized hazardous waste subsidiary, is three times Philip's size by itself. But none of Philip's competitors has built a similarly compelling strategic and competitive platform for the future. None is as broadly and synergistically diversified, knowledge rich, or more closely attuned to changing industry dynamics. Philip Environmental just may outdo the medieval alchemists by actually turning dross into gold.

## Wake-Up Call for the Money Men: American Captures the High Ground

If the world of commerce and industry in general has been slow to recognize both the dangers and the opportunities inherent in the Eco-Industrial Revolution, the *financial* sector in particular has been positively brain-dead.

One telling indication—but far from the only one—came in 1990, when Swiss billionaire industrialist Stephan Schmidheiny was assembling his high-powered Business Council for Sustainable Development. The BCSD was created specifically to provide a *business* perspective to Maurice Strong, the

Secretary General of the UN's historic Earth Summit in Rio de Janeiro, presumably to help counter-balance the other-worldly bafflegab which could reasonably be expected to emerge from the UN bureaucrats. At any rate, Schmidheiny had very little difficulty recruiting some of the leading industrialists on the planet, including the chairmen of companies such as Royal Dutch/Shell, Mitsubishi, Volkswagen, 3M, Chevron, Asea Brown Boveri, and DuPont. Despite all of this, however, he could not persuade a *single* senior banker or financial executive to join the group. Not that they were unsympathetic to his objectives, mind you; they simply couldn't see any direct connection between their lending and investment activities and environmental desecration. After all, *bankers* don't pollute; industrialists do. The titans of finance apparently didn't even see any *cosmetic* or PR benefit in joining Schmidheiny's group. So while their confreres in the manufacturing, chemicals, oil and gas, forest products, and myriad other industrial sectors were at least *trying* to come to grips with the Eco-Industrial Revolution, the bankers, investors, and insurers blithely continued their dogmatic slumber. With at least one conspicuous exception: American Re-Insurance Co.

At first glance, there is little about American Re's corporate profile to suggest any predisposition to storm the ramparts of financial orthodoxy and conservatism. After all, the company is a highly-respected, six billion dollar player in an industry not historically noted for wild excesses of lateral thinking or challenges to the corporate *status quo*. Nonetheless, at a time when most of its industry peers were either pooh-poohing the significance of environmental issues altogether or at best signing pious but somewhat empty declarations of concern[6], American Re decided to *act*.

The case, to Am-Re, was a simple and compelling one. As reinsurers, their whole corporate *raison d'etre* was risk: assessing it, pricing it, and helping clients manage it. *Environmentally*-driven risk was becoming an increasingly critical piece of the total corporate risk equation. In the words of then-U.S. Securities and Exchange Commission member Richard Roberts, "Environment costs have reached staggering proportions in recent years, and are one of the critical issues facing business today ... environmental liability, if it isn't already, will soon become a prominent concern for virtually all financial marketplace participants."[7] If American Re could understand that risk better than its competitors,—and better still—if could help their clients actually find *solutions*, then it stood to capture the strategic high ground in its industry *and*,—not incidentally,—make a lot of money in the bargain. So Am-Re plunged in.

In 1991, Am-Re's visionary CEO Paul Inderbitzin set up a special Technology Transfer Group within the company's consulting arm, Am-Re

Services. Headed by vice-president John Reynolds, the group now numbers eight professionals, and acts as a catalyst and *de facto* venture capital group within the Am-Re empire. Its focus is early-stage environmental technology companies—the cutting-edge innovators and solution providers which the group hopes will one day give their clients—and therefore Am-Re itself—a significant competitive advantage in tackling large-scale environmental problems. The intellectual and business challenges confronting Reynolds and his team are considerable: they must find and develop young companies capable of walking the extremely fine line which so often separates leading-edge technologies from compelling economics. And they must do it in a way which adds demonstrable value to inherently skeptical, corporate insurance clients. In pursing that daunting challenge, the group has two key assets: financial capital and intellectual capital, and it is quite prepared to invest both. Am Re recognizes the myriad barriers which so frequently prevent small, early-stage companies from reaching their technological—and financial—potential. Accordingly, Am-Re provides its investee companies with the sort of intellectual capital which is both rare and absolutely invaluable: credibility, high-level marketing contacts, and assistance in developing new partnerships and strategic alliances. Not only that, but unlike most garden-variety venture capitalists, Am-Re is back-stopped by six billion dollars, a gilt-edged reputation in the mainstream capital markets, and a global network of offices.

Am-Re typically invests this intellectual capital (think of it as the 21st century equivalent of "sweat equity") in return for stock warrants, which permit Am-Re to participate in its partners' ultimate commercial success. As the early-stage companies develop and achieve pre-set milestones, Am Re may inject financial capital as well. To date, the group's biggest commercial success story has been Molten Metal Technology (see the following section on "The Eco-Entrepreneurs"). Am-Re first became involved with MMT in 1991, when the latter had a grand total of three employees. After working with MMT for two years, Am-Re invested 5 million dollars in a private placement. Subsequently, MMT's share price has nearly tripled, and its total stock market capitalization is now closing in on a billion dollars. Today Am-Re's stake in the company is worth many, many times what it originally paid for it. Who said insurance companies made lousy investors?

But the benefits to Am-Re of its environmental technology initiative go well beyond short-term financial returns. Environmentally driven risk is rapidly emerging as *the* dominant issue for the insurance industry worldwide. (Global warming and climate change, for example, are now recognized as having literally catastrophic implications for insurers.) MMT is only one—albeit the most successful one so far—of the half-dozen technology investments which the technology group has made to date. Its other early-stage partners are developing leading-edge technologies for everything from air pollution control to the decontamination of toxic waste. The knowledge which Am-Re has gained about both the dynamics of environmental risk and, more importantly, about cutting-edge *solutions*, will position it as an industry leader for years to come. At six billion dollars, American Re may not be the biggest insurance company in the world; just the most strategically placed to exploit the emerging opportunities of the Eco-Industrial Revolution.

## The Eco-Entrepreneurs:
## *Molten Metal Technology and Catalytica*

The Eco-Industrial Revolution, like any major economic restructuring, is creating a host of exciting new opportunities for those with enough acumen to identify them and the guts to go after them. Almost by definition, out of any group of entrepreneurial wannabe's, there will be far more losers than winners. This is particularly true in the environmental sector, where capital markets remain skittish and skeptical, and regulatory regimes are constantly shifting. Two outstanding young companies who have defied those forbidding odds are New England's Molten Metal Technology and Silicon Valley's Catalytica.

The entrepreneurial genius behind Molten Metal Technology is the remarkable Bill Haney. By the ripe age of twenty-seven, he had already sold his first environmental company for $200 million and was wondering what to do for an encore. In walked Chris Nagel, a bright young MIT scientist who had patented an innovative new way to dispose of hazardous wastes by dissolving them in a super-hot molten metal bath. Not only did the technology have the potential to neutralize toxic waste (a multibillion dollar problem/opportunity in the U.S. alone), but it promised to produce valuable by-products such as industrial gases and metal alloys. The eco-entrepreneur and the scientist teamed up to commercialize the technology and they haven't looked back.

Molten Metal Technology's corporate strategy was conceived and executed in textbook fashion: Start with a compelling scientific concept well protected by an impenetrable wall of patents, recruit an all-star board of directors and sign up some of the country's most powerful and respected companies as customers and backers. Bingo. One of the driving forces on the board was Maurice Strong, the business visionary and environmentalist who served as the secretary general of the 1992 Earth Summit in Rio de Janeiro. Strong's global circle of colleagues and admirers runs from David Rockefeller to Mikhail Gorbachev to the Aga Khan and he proved a highly potent and credible salesman for MMT. Meanwhile, blue-chip corporate partners who signed up to fund parts of the commercialization process included DuPont, Fluor Daniel and American Re-Insurance, part of the heavy-hitting Kohlberg, Kravis and Roberts (KKR) financial empire.

Haney mixed this heady brew into a company that, in only its fifth year, has a market capitalization approaching one billion dollars. Not too bad, for a company with annual revenues of only $4.7 million which has yet to open its first commercial-scale facility. For much of Wall Street, MMT has become the flagship for the entire environmental industry. Should the company fail to deliver on its enormous early promise, it will cast a major pall over what could otherwise become a $40 billion industrial sector in the U.S. alone. Conversely, its continued success would make life an awful lot easier for other eco-entrepreneurs wishing to follow in its footsteps. My money's on Haney.

My other nominee for eco-entrepreneur of the year, or decade, is Catalytica's Ricardo Levy. A native of Ecuador, Levy was working on catalytic chemistry in an Exxon lab in New Jersey in the early 1980s. Wanting to make a distinctive contribution on his own, Levy left and founded Catalytica as a consulting company in 1984, along with fellow Exxoner James Cusimano and Stanford professor Michel Boudart. World headquarters was a cramped room in Levy's basement; paid-in capital was the princely sum of $30,000. Ah, the stuff of Silicon Valley legend.

Intellectually and strategically, Catalytica is definitely on the cutting edge of environmental management. Historically, environmental solutions were tacked on after the fact, as remedial, "end-of-pipe" measures. Two decades of painful experience later, it has become clear that moving the solution *upstream* in the industrial production chain is infinitely preferable, both economically and environmentally. It is usually several orders of magnitude cheaper to prevent the pollution from occurring in the first place, than trying to clean it up afterwards.

Which is precisely where Catalytica comes in. Its proprietary catalysts are designed to alter chemical reactions and thereby reengineer some key industrial and manufacturing processes to minimize their adverse environmental impact. Two examples: a new reformulation of high-octane, low-polluting gasoline and a new catalytic combustion system for gas turbines used to generate electricity. Both initiatives have the potential to produce enormous profits and substantial environmental benefits and they have attracted such heavyweight development partners as Conoco, Mitsubishi and Tokyo

Electric Power. Both products are expected to reach the market in 1996. Farther down the road lies some even more exciting potential: the elusive nonpolluting car engine, produced under a joint venture with a mystery automaker whose identity Levy won't reveal.

All of which is giving Catalytica's investors the fortitude to be patient as the company endures its inevitable early stage losses. (No one is anticipating seeing any profits for at least another year, despite annual revenues of over $10 million.) In private conversation, Levy likes to call Catalytica's negative cash flow "losses by design."[8] He has a point. His faith in the inevitability of Catalytica's success is both unshakeable and infectious, almost all the company's 120 employees are evangelists for the corporate cause. And that's no accident. Levy and Cusimano are deadly serious about changing the world, and they put prospective colleagues through some of the most exhaustive—and exhausting—preemployment testing in the business. If Catalytica doesn't succeed big time, it won't be for lack of brainpower, commitment, or a compelling and timely business concept.

The stakes for both Molten Metal and Catalytica are high indeed, transcending the particular fates of the two companies and their pioneering investors. In many respects, they are a combination of advance guard and metaphor for the entrepreneurial cutting edge of the Eco-Industrial Revolution. If they can't succeed in converting its power and dynamism into sustained profits, it is difficult to conceive of anyone who could. If they don't, it will be a long, long time before the lemmings of Wall Street summon the courage and vision to back anyone else. And that would be bad news indeed for the whole planet.

---

# CONCLUSION

---

The Eco-Industrial Revolution will require the reinvention of nearly all of a company's strategic architecture. For that reason, a company's environmental management capabilities provide a very useful proxy for its overall strategic fitness. Show me a company that manages this issue proactively and effectively, and I'll show you a well-managed company, period. These are the attributes to look for:

- A corporate attitude that views environmentalism positively, as a creative source of new efficiencies, products, services and technologies, rather than as an onerous burden.

- A corporate culture that embraces change rather than resisting it and learns from mistakes rather than punishing them.

- Entirely new conceptions of the role of the firm and its boundaries; central and earlier roles for suppliers, customers and strategic alliance partners in developing new, environmentally sound products and services.
- New internal organizational forms that promote rather than inhibit interdepartmental collaboration and learning.
- New manufacturing processes and technologies more directly predicated on environmental efficiency.
- New human-resource management approaches that sensitize staff to the environmental realities of the company's operations.
- More aggressive benchmarking of competitors' best practices in environmental performance.
- Radically improved environmental performance indicators and management information systems

None of this will be painless, but there are at least two consolations. First, these initiatives will pay dividends for the company's overall strategic fitness, adaptability and competitiveness well beyond the confines of the environmental portfolio. Second, on a more pragmatic level, such efforts will make it far more likely the company will actually survive into the 21st century and that its directors and senior executives will be able to lead from their offices rather than from their jail cells.

### CHAPTER ELEVEN

# ORGANIZATIONAL LEARNING
## THE NEXT CORPORATE JIHAD

*"The ability to learn faster than competitors may be the **only** sustainable competitive advantage."*

ARIE DE GEUS/ FORMER EXECUTIVE, ROYAL DUTCH/SHELL

O f all the 11 Commandments advocated in this book, none is of more fundamental importance than a thoroughgoing commitment to organizational learning. In a very real sense, it is a precondition to all the others.

One of the defining, driving forces of our time is the global mega-shift towards knowledge-value and away from the traditional, material sources of wealth creation. Conventional economic theory is now demonstrably bankrupt. The traditional building blocks of production—land, labor and finance capital—have been largely superseded by knowledge and information as the primary basis for generating wealth. MIT's celebrated, globe-trotting economist Lester Thurow makes the case succinctly: "Wealth is created by the capitalization of innovation."[1] Amen.

Indeed, there has been a complete role reversal. "Hard" tangible assets such as Dallas office towers used to be seen to have bankable value, while "soft" assets like Microsoft's programming talent were unquantifiable and therefore virtually impossible for financiers to evaluate. Well, which would *you* rather have invested in?

These are not new insights. Some of our more thoughtful social scientists have been talking and writing about them for years.[2] What *is* remarkable is how both theorists and practitioners of business have steadfastly ignored their compelling strategic and operational implications. This cannot last;

the forces of both history and competition are simply too strong to permit it for long.

In the 21st century, the case for the "learning organization," with knowledge creation as its primary strategic task, will be overwhelming. Propelled by the competitive imperatives of speed, global responsiveness and the need to innovate constantly or perish, learning will be the essential hedge against corporate extinction. Organizational learning will—or at least it should—replace control as the dominant responsibility and test of senior management and leadership. Despite the stakes, it is remarkable and depressing just how few companies and executives have really, at a visceral level, accepted the importance of organizational learning.

The intellectual assets of most companies are probably worth at least three or four times the company's tangible book value, yet no CEO I know could honestly claim to be actually utilizing more than 20 per cent of his or her firm's intellectual capital base. Can you imagine the fate of any CEO who could only manage a 20 percent utilization rate in his or her production capacity, inventory efficiency or any other traditional index of performance? It doesn't even bear thinking about. Yet in this, the most important wealth creating area of all, a 20 percent efficiency rate is considered normal, inevitable and acceptable. Well it isn't.

Organizational learning has always been important, but it is the geometric increase in the difficulty, complexity and speed of today's hypercompetitive environment that now makes it truly essential. One by one, most traditional pillars of competitive advantage, such as size, scale and even speed, have either come tumbling down or been turned into "commodities" that everybody must have, to get into the competitive game at all. And so we are left with organizational learning. Former Citibank CEO Walter Wriston puts the case bluntly: "The person who figures out how to harness the collective genius of the people in his or her organization is going to blow the competition away."[3]

Japanese management professor Ikujiro Nonara nicely summarizes the reasons why this is true: "In an economy where the only certainty is uncertainty, the one sure source of lasting competitive advantage is knowledge. When markets shift, technologies proliferate, competitors multiply and products become obsolete virtually overnight, successful companies are those that consistently create new knowledge, disseminate it widely throughout the organization and quickly embody it in new technologies and products."[4] In short, successful companies will be effective *learning organizations*.

Despite the ease with which the term learning organization trips off the tongue nowadays, actually building and maintaining one is a herculean and, by definition, an unending task. Let's start by defining it. Of the several dozen definitions I've seen, my favorite comes from Harvard's David Garvin: "A learning organization is an organization skilled at creating, acquiring and transferring knowledge and at modifying its behavior to reflect new knowledge and insights."[5] What I particularly like about Garvin's formulation is its recognition that, while acquiring knowledge and wisdom is all well and good, it needs to be disseminated and translated into action and changed behavior before it does anybody any good.

How do we actually build a learning organization? The companies profiled in this chapter have not only talked and written about organizational learning, they have used what they've learned to change their corporate behavior.

The place to start is by building an organizational culture that embraces change rather than fearing and seeking to minimize it—one that exalts continuous improvement and innovation above all else. However, while such a culture is a sine qua non for organizational learning, it is by no means sufficient by itself. Companies must also have the mind-set and organizational structures (or, sometimes, the lack thereof) to actively encourage interdisciplinary teamwork and collaboration.

Successful firms of the 21st century will also require superior infrastructure for knowledge building, gathering and dissemination. They will need to be capable of delivering strategically relevant information—i.e., qualitative and quantitative—to the right people and in real time. Professional service firms are a little further along the curve on this. Leading consulting companies such as McKinsey and Andersen Consulting have devoted much time, effort and money to figuring out how to extract, organize and disseminate even a fraction of the hard-won knowledge and experience residing in their far-flung intellectual empires. Other industries, where the knowledge content may be less obvious but no less important, will need to do likewise or face being trampled by competitors. I won't pretend this is easy. Most companies have reward structures that actually penalize people who take the time to think seriously about their last project and what lessons might be learned and shared. They're too busy hustling to find or do their next project, or to generate their next "billable hour," to do so. This has to change.

One important technique for maximizing organizational learning is benchmarking best practices—not just of direct competitors, but of absolutely anyone from whom something useful can be learned or adapted. One particularly inspired convert to the cause, having run out of things to benchmark, actually began benchmarking a competitor's approach to benchmarking! Not a bad idea, when you stop to think about it. Another useful but grossly underutilized instrument for gathering strategic intelligence is the training and deployment of the firm's front-line troops (delivery, sales, repair and secretarial staff, bank tellers and the like) as incredibly fertile sources of customer feedback and market information. A third technique is the strategic use of temporary personnel assignments and rotations not only between departments and geographic locations, but even with suppliers, customers and strategic alliance partners.

Organizational learning also has major implications for a company's training and evaluation programs. A company's attitude to training must change substantially to embrace lifelong learning for everyone and to stress group-learning experiences in addition to individual ones. The actual content of the training programs needs to change dramatically too, placing far greater emphasis on the "soft" process skills of managing change, innovation and learning, and less on "hard" factual knowledge, which has an increasingly short shelf life. People's success in strengthening both their own knowledge base and that of their colleagues needs to be factored more directly into promotion and compensation decisions.

---

# ORGANIZATIONAL FORGETTING

---

Perhaps most difficult of all, organizational learning also means surfacing and reexamining all those inarticulate assumptions about the firm and its business environment that, while rarely explicitly scrutinized or even acknowledged, drive much of what the firm actually does. These assumptions can cover everything from geopolitical analysis ("Mexico is far too politically and economically unstable to even contemplate doing business there") to consumer psychology ("Americans will never buy those funny little Japanese cars"). Thus, organizational learning is about more than simply acquiring *new* knowledge and insights; it is also crucial (and arguably more difficult) to unlearn the *old* ones when they have outlived their relevance. Thus, "organizational forgetting" is probably at least as important as organizational learning. Old cultural and psychological habits die extremely hard. Rigorously rooting out and challenging obsolete assumptions can expose critical discrepancies between external reality and the firm's internal mental models. It is these gaps that provide much of the creative tension and dynamic energy that drives organizational learning.

Today's competitive environment also creates qualitative changes in how organizational learning must be carried out. We have already seen that tomorrow's organization—learning or otherwise—will likely be a global one. This makes the task of organizational learning more difficult, but also creates a much wider and richer body of knowledge and experience to harvest. Frequent international meetings and rotations of staff (and not just executives) are an excellent way to begin and/or enrich the organizational learning process.

A second and more subtle shift in the quality of organizational learning is in the *source* of the knowledge. In the old days, companies tended to learn "from the outside in." While external sources of learning are still important, the balance is now shifting towards internally generated knowledge. Boundaries between companies and their competitive environments have become much more porous, and it has become increasingly difficult to tell what's outside and what's inside in the first place. Customers, suppliers and strategic alliance partners must become a much more critical part of the organizational learning equation and may be the most fertile sources of all. There has also been a huge increase in the democratization of information within a company. The old, top-down methods of analyzing, screening and disseminating knowledge have proven too slow and unworkable and are now largely unnecessary as vertical barriers are breached by technology. Horizontal barriers between disciplines, divisions and geographic locations are also eroding. The combined assault of empowerment, "delayering," cross-functional team, and the new information technologies has vastly increased both the variety and the availability of information within an organization.

Performance measurement is fundamental to organizational learning. If you have little or no idea how successful your last marketplace intervention was, and why, your prospects for learning very much of use for the next project are slim indeed. It is astonishing how often this seemingly obvious truism escapes otherwise capable senior executives.

Let's look at some different companies around the world that have made exceptional progress along the organizational learning curve. What they've already accomplished is impressive enough, but what's even more encouraging is their commitment to do even more in the future.

## *Motorola: The $17 Billion Learning Machine*

The alert reader will recall that a certain level of organizational humility is an absolute prerequisite for organizational learning. This being the case, Motorola must be a serious candidate for the Learning Organization of the Millennium Award. Why? Because most companies with 28 percent year-over-year sales increases, 77 percent profit increases and a Baldridge National Quality Award under its belt might assume that they don't have that much left to learn. But not Motorola. To quote Deborah King, Motorola's director of executive education: "As a company, we believe that to compete in a global marketplace, while technology is essential, it is not sufficient. People are what's going to make a difference. And people only contribute for as long as they continue to learn."[6]

Motorola has long had one of the finest reputations for quality of any American company. Unlike most of its competitors, however, Motorola understands that the dynamics of global hypercompetition are rapidly turning quality into a mere commodity. By the turn of the century, Motorola executives reckon their rivals will have caught up completely on quality, robbing it of its competitive power almost entirely. At that point, competitive advantage will shift to responsiveness, adaptability and creativity and organizational learning ability will become the greatest differentiator. Motorola fully intends to stay ahead of the pack. In the words of current CEO Gary Tooker: "If knowledge is becoming antiquated at a faster rate, we have no choice but to spend on education. How can that not be a competitive weapon?"[7]

Few companies anywhere approach organizational learning with greater fervor than Motorola. The company already spends nearly four times the American industrial average on training, and hopes to quadruple that figure by the turn of the century. If resource commitments count for anything, Motorola should have one of the best-trained workforces on earth. Then again, lots of companies are throwing tons of money at workforce training these days, without achieving Motorola's results. It's the strategic *quality* of a firm's investment in learning that counts, not the quantity.

Motorola's epiphany on organizational learning occurred in the mid-1980s. For several years, the company had been waging a corporate *jihad* on quality, an all-out war against manufacturing defects in pursuit of the elusive "six sigma" quality level.[8] On one level, they succeeded. In 1988, Motorola won the coveted Malcolm Baldridge Quality Award, the industrial equivalent of the Nobel Prize for physics. But they had unwittingly paid a heavy price for it. The company had become so obsessed with manufacturing quality and so internally focused, it had lost sight of the customer and his or her changing requirements. This misplaced focus was confirmed by the devastating results of an independent customer satisfaction survey. On a far more tangible level, it was further confirmed by a precipitous drop in profitability in the mid-80s. In a single year, earnings dropped from $350 million to $70 million. While there was some consolation in the fact that Motorola was the only major chipmaker to make any money at all that year, the reversal nonetheless served as a major wake-up call for the company.

Like any good learning organization, Motorola learned from its mistakes. Stung by the poor financial results and by the customer survey, the company set about reinventing itself, using its training infrastructure as the chief instrument. The most obvious and important requirement was to provide a stronger focus on the external competitive environment. A new customized, sixteen-hour training module on "competitive awareness" was developed and given to over 2,500 Motorola managers. The new module is almost entirely focused on the external competitive environment and benchmarks some "best in the world" practices of other companies, including some in ostensibly unrelated industries.

Aside from the sheer magnitude of the resources it dedicates to training, Motorola's approach is impressive in two other respects. The first is the unusually tight links it has forged between the content and style of its training programs and the company's real-world business strategies. Typically, Motorola executives will articulate a new strategic objective—reduced cycle times, improved teamwork or stronger customer linkages—and then develop customized training packages to support the strategic initiatives directly. In the words of an admiring outsider, retired AT&T training chief Donald Conover: "The intimacy between education and business strategy is tighter at Motorola than anyplace I know." [9]

The second hallmark of organizational learning at Motorola is the way it extends throughout the company's entire value chain. I have argued strongly that the time has come to break corporate barriers of all kinds, whether they exist between departments, or between companies and their customers and suppliers. Motorola has certainly practiced what I preach: It runs special courses for its customers and suppliers and even for its future employees. Understandably concerned about the quality of its future workforce, Motorola is actively working in the public schools in states such as Illinois, Massachusetts and Florida, home to many Motorola workers. Through special pilot projects and curriculum development work with local school boards, Motorola tries to inculcate such neglected skills and values as teamwork, problem solving, communication and interdisciplinary learning, which it considers critical success factors for the workforce of the future. Motorola is actively involved with over one hundred public school districts throughout the U.S.

The backbone for the company's organizational learning infrastructure is its famous Motorola University. With fourteen "campuses" from Tokyo to Schaumberg, Illinois to central China and an annual budget of $120 million, Motorola U. is clearly a good deal more than a token nod in the direction of training and education. And Motorola U. teaches much more than the nuts and bolts of the business. It is also an important source of the corporate cultural "glue" so necessary in binding such a diverse and far-flung company together. But Motorola U. should not be regarded as merely a tool for spreading American "we know best" business techniques and ideas around the world. New training programs are just as likely to be developed in Singapore and exported to America. The importance Motorola attaches to learning is further reinforced by day-long teaching stints by senior executives like CEO Tooker or COO William Weisz. Workers are sometimes startled to receive a personal visit or phone call from Tooker or Weisz to follow up on a training program and make sure it fit the bill. The message is unmistakable: "At Motorola we place a tremendous priority on learning and development; we consider it worthy not only of our money but our own time."

As important as Motorola U. is, learning at Motorola is by no means confined to the classroom. The company is very bullish on learning by doing, or what it calls "embedded learning." Sometimes that takes the form of Motorola's "away teams." corporate SWAT teams that fan out around the world to acquire state-of-the-art knowledge and techniques, and then bring them back to build, say, a new world-class chip plant in Texas. Or sometimes it takes the form of a modified apprenticeship program, where new recruits earn regular wages while learning under the tutelage of a more experienced worker. A similar emphasis on "action-learning" pervades the executive suite. In the early 1990s, Motorola revamped all its executive learning programs, making real-world business problems the fodder for team-learning exercises and building in new feedback mechanisms to ensure that executives were doing "double-loop learning"—learning about what and how they'd actually learned so they could do it even better the next time.

Motorola is not without its faults and Achilles heels. Perhaps the most worrisome of them is the fact that, as with any company, its strong corporate culture could become a two-edged sword. On the one hand, its culture is a competitive imperative, providing indispensable coherence to an incredibly diverse and scattered workforce. At the same time, however, the Motorola culture may ultimately prove to be so strong, rigid and regimented that it strangles the very creativity and innovation its executives have rightly identified as the key success factors of the early 21st century. Only time will tell, but Motorola's track record of organizational learning provides considerable grounds for optimism.

## *Samsung: Global Learning in Action*

South Korea's Samsung Group has always believed in knowledge as the primary basis for long-term business success. Chairman Lee Kun-Hee's clearly stated objective is to turn Samsung into one of the top ten "technology powerhouses" in the world. And he's not off to a bad start: Samsung has already become the top producer of semiconductors in the world. In the field of genetic engineering, Samsung pioneered the breakthrough development of interferon and it also developed the first industrial robots used in the precision machine industry. The company has now become a major player in chemicals, electronics, heavy machinery and even financial services. As if that weren't enough, Samsung is actively looking to expand into automobiles, aerospace and entertainment, negotiating deals with the likes of Nissan, Boeing and Walt Disney Co. And Lee Kun-Hee is firmly convinced that the basis for success is a company-wide commitment to global learning and continuous improvement.

For Samsung, global competitiveness involves a relentless pursuit of knowledge about foreign markets, customs and competitors. Accordingly, his staff are routinely sent to study and immerse themselves in foreign countries targeted by Samsung for expansion. These employees are expected to learn the language of their host country, note trends, identify opportunities and, effectively, stop thinking like a Korean and start thinking like a native consumer. The expectation is that this knowledge and acculturization will then be shared with fellow employees in South Korea to maximize knowledge and the return on investment in training and development. The commitment to overseas postings and foreign-language training has yielded the further dividend of making Samsung the consistent number-one choice as a future employer among South Korean university students. Samsung can therefore choose from the cream of graduates.

Learning in the Samsung corporate family is a two-way street, and South Koreans are not the only ones to benefit from overseas training. Samsung hires employees in countries around the world and brings them to South Korea to train in the Samsung corporate philosophy. International procurement offices operate in countries around the world to ensure that local needs are matched with accurate information about Samsung technologies.

In 1990, Samsung established an Advanced Technology Training Institute to pursue R&D and train employees in leading-edge technologies. Over 1,500 Samsung employees train there every year. In addition, most of the Samsung Group's individual companies have in-house "technical universities" that focus on advancing and disseminating the development of their particular technologies. There is also a twelve-month program to train specialists in the politics and competitive environments of target regions around the world. Perhaps best of all, Samsung employees do not learn and work in isolation. There is a strong bias toward interdisciplinary product-development teams, where engineers, marketers and financial people work side by side on projects. Both the final product and the team members benefit from the exposure to the variety of disciplinary perspectives. Occasionally, as in the case of Samsung's magneto-optical disk, the development team actually evolves into a full-fledged independent business unit, taking over the entire responsibility for producing, marketing and distributing the product. Samsung has also invested heavily in joint-venture businesses in the former Soviet Union and developing Asian countries, transferring its technical knowledge to them and providing training opportunities to these start-up ventures. The company believes that this strengthening of its partners' ability to produce high-quality goods and manage themselves well is, in the long run, a wise use of resources.

The real hallmark of a learning organization, however, is its ability to adjust to changed competitive circumstances. In recent years, Samsung has begun to suffer from the same problems besetting other giant South Korean *chaebols* such as Daewoo. Their competitive advantage is being steadily eroded by a strengthening local currency and by increases in South Korean labor costs. In Samsung's case, an additional problem is its traditional reliance on downstream companies to sell its products. With the exception of semiconductors, less than two-thirds of Samsung's products are actually sold under its own name. Fully half of Samsung's electronics are sold on an original equipment manufacturer basis. Although this practice conserved resources for Samsung's in-house technology development, it has also been responsible for relatively low returns on sales. Too much of the final product's value is captured by the downstream partner, not Samsung. As a result, earnings in 1993 were only a modest $600 million on $54 billion in sales.

Lee decreed that a company-wide shake-up was needed. The management system his father, company founder Lee Byung-Chull, had put in place had worked extremely well in its day, but new competitive realities demanded radically different approaches. To remain successful and to move into the top rank of truly world-class companies, Samsung needed to become more nimble, innovative and externally focused. It needed new investment priorities, tighter product development focus, and better quality and marketing. Most challenging of all, it also needed to become less hierarchical and its managers more independent minded and entrepreneurial. In short, Lee is proposing to reinvent the entire company. This, in an organization that has already enjoyed a considerable measure of success and in the teeth of a conservative and tradition-bound Korean business culture. But Lee has never been accused of complacency—or timidity.

The success of the shake-up will inevitably depend on how well and how quickly Samsung employees can adapt themselves to the demands of the new corporate culture. Lee deliberately made himself unavailable to his employees to encourage them to make more decisions, become bolder in their operations and display more individuality. And, in a symbolic gesture meant to underline the completeness of the break from the old ways, Lee switched Samsung's office hours to 7 A.M. to 4 P.M., instead of the traditional South Korean work day of 9 A.M. to 8 P.M. Newly freed-up evening hours are for self-improvement courses. In a country where old habits die particularly hard, this is pretty radical stuff.

Another important part of Lee's new learning infrastructure is Samsung's own School, established in 1993. The school provides mandatory six month "reeducation" courses to Samsung's 850 senior executives. Three months of the courses take place overseas, where the executives learn about non-Korean cultures by living with local families. (Lee has also forbidden his executives to travel by air in these countries, figuring that buses, trains and cars will give them much better learning opportunities.) Lee also runs his own private, informal CEO school, which is more like a high-level corporate boot camp. Lee drags his senior executives along on a breakneck round of meetings, sometimes around the clock and all over the world, so they can see and experience first hand the shortcomings that the perfectionist Lee can invariably identify in Samsung's products or marketing strategies. These "private tutorials" with the chairman tend to leave an indelible impression on Lee's executives.

In another of Lee's global-learning initiatives, four hundred managers each year are given cash and the freedom to go wherever they want for twelve months, to learn a language and a different culture. When they return, they are expected to become specialists in selling Samsung products in that country and to share their new knowledge with their colleagues through reports, workshops and daily interaction. This new five-year program will train two thousand such specialists and cost $100 million.

For some at Samsung, change will not come easily. Decentralized decision making and empowerment are almost entirely foreign to the traditional Korean business culture. Lee himself says candidly: "About 5 percent of them can't change at all, so I'll fire them. Another 25 percent to 30 percent may find change difficult, so we'll give them less responsibility."[10] In other words, in this particular learning organization, you'd better learn.

It may be of some metaphorical significance that one of Chairman Lee's favorite "relaxations" is driving one of his customized Porsches at 200 miles per hour, either on Germany's Autobahn or on private racetracks. While he will find it more difficult to put the new Samsung through its paces quite as quickly, it won't be for lack of trying. Or for lack of faith in both the power of organizational learning and its growing importance in global competition.

Samsung's top human-resource executive, Jong Toe Kang, sums up Samsung's view: "The new global business situation requires excellent global managers who have international perspectives and flexibility. Training and cultivating outstanding global managers will be one of the most important tasks for our company."[11]

## Singapore Airlines: Learning's Air Force

We've all seen it, on billboards, in magazines and in newspapers. The beautiful, smiling face of the Singapore Airlines girl, dressed in the traditional female costume of Singapore. She has come to represent the best in airline service around the world, offering "in-flight service even other airlines talk about." It all seems so natural, so effortless. Well, don't believe it. Behind that beguiling smile is one of the most thorough and intensive training programs in aviation history.

When Singapore Airlines (SIA) separated from Malaysia Airlines almost twenty-five years ago, it established a corporate strategy that recognized the airline business for what it is: a service industry. After all, the industry's basic "product"—an airline seat—is a pretty standard commodity; when you've seen one, you've seen 'em all. But, the way SIA treated its customers would be the defining factor that differentiated it from its competitors. The *service* package was the key: ticketing, baggage handling, check-in, reservations and, of course, in-flight service. SIA never had a monopoly on this realization, it simply put it into action better and more thoroughly than anyone else. While its competitors were focusing on such tactical issues as schedules and fares, SIA pioneered a strategic emphasis on service innovation. The quality of SIA's service was solely dependent on the training and knowledge of its personnel—all of them, from ground crew to management, flight crew to technicians. The infrastructure that SIA built over the years to support and sustain its commitment to organizational learning is the real source of its differentiation and competitive advantage.

SIA's strategy is a reflection of the thoroughgoing commitment to excellence and competitiveness that pervades the entire island city-state. Former Prime Minister Lee Kuan Yew, still a towering figure in Singapore, is blunt about what's at stake: "Maintaining high standards is not a favor SIA workers are doing for management or the government. It is what you have to do to keep jobs in a very competitive industry. In the airline business, to stay still is to stagnate, and to stagnate is to be overtaken."[12]

The competitive imperatives facing SIA have become even more acute recently, with the advent of a major assault on the burgeoning Asian air travel market by such fearsome Western competitors as British Airways, Delta and

United. To make matters worse, SIA is also facing renewed competition from rivals within its own region, such as Hong Kong's Cathay Pacific, Malaysia Airlines and Thai Airways.

The key, in SIA's view, is an uncompromising commitment to training and learning throughout the organization. SIA Chairman J. Y. Pillay, one of Singapore's most influential businessmen, summarizes his company's commitment this way: "We do not treat our employees as mere economic digits. Our objective is to enable each of them to develop through training and career development his or her full potential. So we train and retrain our employees."[13]

A perfect example is the outstanding in-cabin service for which Singapore Airlines is justifiably famous. Its best-in-the-world quality is assured by the thorough training flight attendants receive before they even see their first customer. In mock aircraft cabins in SIA's $2 million training center, they study and practice all aspects of in-flight service, including repeated drills in safety procedures. Flight crews train in their own center using computerized flight simulators specific to the aircraft operated by SIA. There is also a commercial training center, an engineering center and a computer training center. In fact, each of the major divisions within the airline has its own training department that handles job-specific instruction. Staff training and development routinely consume more than $100 million from SIA's annual operating budget and each department must commit to a process of ongoing learning. This process is further facilitated by a system of regular staff communiqués that keep employees informed of SIA's activities at the corporate level.

In 1987, Singapore Airlines established a management development center to coordinate organization-wide learning for its senior staff. This center employs faculty and executives from top universities and corporations in Asia, Europe, North America and Australia. The curriculum includes courses on management and personal development. The sessions are organized across disciplines to achieve the maximum cross-fertilization of ideas among staff, which in turn accelerates organizational learning.

In effect, Singapore Airlines is operating its own minibusiness school through the center, but it's not restricted to SIA personnel. Programs are open to management staff from other businesses in the region. This unorthodox sharing of expertise and facilities serves several agendas. First, it improves the long-term prospects of Southeast Asia's overall corporate competitiveness, on the theory that a rising tide of learning and competence in the region will raise all corporate boats. The stronger and more competitive the other industrial and service companies in Southeast Asia become, the more they will need to use airlines—preferably SIA. Second, the inclusion of executives from outside the airline industry introduces SIA employees to an additional source of cross-fertilization for experience, knowledge and ideas.

Is all this commitment to organizational learning worthwhile? Let's put it this way: despite an increasingly competitive industry environment, Singapore Airlines is still the most profitable airline in Asia and continues to receive the highest customer satisfaction ratings in the world. It must be doing something right. By 2010, airline industry experts expect that nearly two-thirds of all international passengers will be flying to cities in the Asia Pacific region. My own bet is that a healthy percentage of their backsides will be nestled comfortably in Singapore Airlines seats.

## Andersen Consulting: Just-In-Time Knowledge Transfer

Andersen Consulting, the management and information technology consulting arm of international accounting giant Arthur Andersen, is about as pure an example of a knowledge-driven company as you're likely to see. Information and knowledge are its stock in trade, and its effectiveness in expanding and leveraging them will totally determine its commercial destiny. Lots of other consulting firms proudly proclaim themselves to be "in the knowledge business," but few have grasped the full impact of what that means as well as $3.3 billion Andersen Consulting. Companies like Andersen are the archetype for the knowledge-driven business of the future. How Anderson goes about acquiring, disseminating, applying, leveraging and learning about knowledge will have much to teach us about how to survive and thrive amidst 21st century global competition.

Andersen's information technology (IT) and systems-integration practice is the intellectual and financial cornerstone of the company. It churns out over $2 billion in fee revenue every year and employs over fourteen-thousand professional staff. But Andersen is more than simply a one-trick information technology pony. It also has a growing presence in strategy consulting, corporate change management and business-process reengineering services. Together, these new practice areas already represent nearly $500 million in annual revenues and 2,500 professional staff. They also represent the wave of the future. The market for traditional IT consulting services is leveling off and becoming even more viciously competitive. And, of course, potential synergies among Andersen's various practice areas abound; newly reengineered businesses generally need new IT software, hardware and systems as well. Other firms such as EDS and France's CAP Gemini Sogeti are attempting similar "migration" strategies from their roots in IT, but none has moved as far or as fast as Andersen. Geographically, though its world headquarters remain in Chicago, Andersen is now active in over fifty different countries worldwide, and generates 54 percent of its global revenues outside the United States. Indeed, the Asia Pacific practice is currently the fastest growing, with annual growth rates currently exceeding 25 percent.

Capturing, disseminating and leveraging the knowledge and experience of 27,000 employees in over fifty different countries is a prodigious challenge, but it is one to which Andersen has devoted itself with uncommon zeal and ingenuity. Andersen's size, complexity and explosive growth rates have far eclipsed the ability of individual partners to tap their own networks for information— including information about who would have the necessary information. Conscious mechanisms had to be developed to provide *systematic* knowledge capture and dissemination capability throughout a company. The ultimate objective is what Andersen's managing director Robert Elmore calls "just-in-time knowledge information transfer."[14]

At the center of Andersen's knowledge infrastructure sits the Knowledge Exchange, a series of infrastructure databases wired together with Lotus Notes software. The Knowledge Exchange is an ambitious effort to leverage Andersen's global intellectual capital base, and to transfer the just-in-time knowledge to its consultants. The Knowledge Exchange tracks and codifies client engagements, lessons learned and particularly innovative approaches, and is organized around Andersen's major industry and practice areas. There is also an electronic bulletin board, Group Talk, which allows consultants to raise business problems with their colleagues around the world and get real-time answers. Elmore reckons that at least one thousand Andersenites use Group Talk at least once a week, and that each shares what they learn with another five to ten colleagues, thereby further amplifying the impact of the system. There are also CD-ROM systems that allow peripatetic Andersen consultants to carry the equivalent of the firm's entire central library into their clients' offices, anywhere in the world.

Andersen's enthusiasm for high-tech knowledge transfer has done nothing to reduce its appetite for the old-fashioned, face-to-face kind. The company currently spends an astounding $200 million each year on training, roughly 6 percent of its total revenues. The average Andersen employee spends 135 hours each year in formal classroom training. The mecca for structured learning at Andersen is the Center for Professional Education and Development in St. Charles, Illinois, an hour's drive from Chicago. A typical week at the center would have one thousand Andersen employees from forty countries in residence. Smaller learning centers exist in Eindhoven, the Netherlands, and in Asia.

The "hardware" side of Andersen's organizational learning machinery is impressive enough on its own, including the Knowledge Exchange, Group Talk, the CD-ROMs and its aggressive—and expensive—commitment to more structured learning. But it is their "software" that really sets Andersen apart. As any decent IT consultant can tell you, even the jazziest information technology in the world is of no use whatsoever unless people have both the skills and the inclination to use it. In Andersen's case, building the tangible elements of its global knowledge infrastructure was the relatively easy part; the tricky bit was creating the climate of collaboration necessary to unleash its real potential.

As a former senior partner of one of Andersen's competitors, I can testify that the single most difficult challenge confronting global, knowledge based organizations is developing mechanisms that actually promote, rather than retard, international teamwork and information sharing. Most do a wretched job. Andersen doesn't. It starts, quite rightly, with its compensation and reward systems. Whereas most consulting firms are broken into a series of discrete profit centers (read "introverted fiefdoms"), Andersen organizes itself so that partners share in the total, company-wide profits. As a result, when a partner in Chicago receives an urgent call for help from a confrère in Singapore, there are no company-inspired barriers preventing him or her from giving enthusiastic assistance. Unlike other firms, he or she will not need to justify the "waste" of potentially billable hours on some frivolous activity outside of the local profit center. At Andersen, when Singapore succeeds, so do Chicago, San Francisco and Frankfurt.

This apparently simple device of pooling compensation is probably the single most powerful instrument for promoting cross-boundary and cross-border collaboration—and learning. A close second would be the evaluation criteria the firm uses for promotion to the coveted rank of partner. It is well known throughout Andersen that an individual's willingness and ability to share his or her knowledge is one of the paramount criteria for promotion. The number of case solutions contributed to the Knowledge Exchange, and the general reputation of being a team player, are major factors in the Andersen evaluation process. The entire corporate culture is consciously and carefully managed to promote information sharing and, as we have seen, it is underpinned by hardware and software tools that support and amplify that goal.

Another part of Andersen's organizational learning strategy is its recent emphasis on recruiting talented outsiders. Historically, the company preferred to "grow its own," recruiting recent graduates with a first degree and then educating (indoctrinating?) them in the Andersen system. As the competitive environment grew more extreme, however, and as Andersen began to branch out beyond IT, a new approach was needed. Andersen is reaching out aggressively, recruiting top talent from McKinsey, Boston Consulting Group and other top-strategy consulting houses. Andersen quite rightly reckons that recruiting experienced outsiders adds a perspective and a richness to its knowledge base that insiders could simply never match. A straightforward insight, perhaps, but one that seems to have escaped some of Andersen's leading competitors, who doggedly refuse to bring in top-level outsiders, apparently for fear of contaminating the purity of their corporate "gene pool." In the 21st century knowledge economy, such approaches will breed only intellectual incest and commercial disaster.

Just how effective is Andersen's approach to building the infrastructure of a learning organization? In 1989, Andersen Consulting officially separated from its accountancy sibling, citing irreconcilable differences of corporate culture. Since then, Andersen Consulting's revenues have more than tripled. After spending some time lecturing at their Eindhoven training facility in Europe, I can't help but feel that the Andersen learning machine is just getting cranked up. Take a corporate culture built around organizational learning and knowledge transfer, add a world-class IT capability and infrastructure and throw in a heavy dollop of organizational humility and what do you get? Big, big trouble for Andersen's competitors.

## *Learning the South American Way*

If a company is consistently successful, it is safe to say that it must be, at least to some extent, consciously or otherwise, a learning organization. Learning from mistakes and moving on; soliciting and acting on feedback from all levels of staff; listening to customers and incorporating their needs into both R&D and operations; encouraging open discussion and collaboration among all employees; providing all levels of staff with opportunities for personal and professional development. These are the hallmarks of a learning organization.

But when a company *consciously* creates institutional structures for learning, that's when things get really interesting. We saw one example of this when Singapore Airlines opened its management school to employees of other companies so that the entire regional economy can become more competitive. When a company does this amidst political and economic turbulence, and in a traditional culture of political and managerial autocracy, it becomes truly remarkable. South America has already demonstrated its capacity for organizational innovation through such examples as Semco's empowerment strategies and the Caja Social's leverage of hidden value potential among the urban poor. Now we return to South America for a couple of textbook illustrations of organizational learning.

Amil Assistencia is a Brazilian health insurance company that has constantly registered growth rates of 40 percent a year. At the center of its business strategy is the continuous improvement of its employees through learning. For example, the company established its own MBA program, which is also open to non-Amil employees. Amil's MBA program offers sixteen courses and attracts over 150 internal applicants each year for the sixty available spaces. One entire working day per week is devoted to classroom learning. Directors of the company personally teach as many as one hundred hours a year. The president of the company, Edson de Godoy Bueno, devotes as much as 90 percent of his time to teaching, on the unassailable logic that no executive function could possibly be more important to his company's future. As Bueno says, "The best way to learn is to teach." Much of the learning is one on one. Employees formulate and discuss five to ten year personal career plans with de Godoy Bueno, including specific action plans for reaching their goals. In groups, Amil employees study and discuss leading-edge management theories, and attempt to identify potential applications for Amil Assistencia. Practical business problems are the subject of periodic Sunday morning study and discussion groups. Employees are even sent into the community to encourage Brazilians to pursue further education.

Incentives for participation in skills development and cross-training programs include large cash bonuses of up to 40 percent of workers' base salaries. As is usually the case, however, the most effective reinforcement is often nonfinancial. You can't beat peer recognition and Amil provides plenty at raucous company celebrations of both personal and team achievements. At the end of the day, though, it's all about one thing: personal and organizational learning. As de Godoy Bueno says: "There is only one way to increase the wealth of a nation, and that is to train and develop people all the time." At Amil it's hard for an outsider to tell whether he's stumbled across an insurance company or a teaching institution. Let's hope it stays that way.

Cali, Colombia has acquired most of its international reputation for being the Avis of the international cocaine smuggling business: Number two, but trying harder. But there is a lot more to Cali than unsavory characters in sunglasses, flashy chest jewelry and Mercedes. The Colombian city is also home to Latin America's largest transnational manufacturing concern, Carvajal Inversiones. And Carvajal is second to none in the business of organizational learning.

Carvajal Inversiones is a family-owned printing and publishing business started by Manuel Carvajal Valencia and his two sons over ninety years ago, using a hand-operated printing press. Today the company employs over thirteen thousand people, uses state-of-the-art technology, some of it self-developed, and is active throughout South America, with a growing presence in both North America and Europe.

Long before the term "mission statement" had been invented in trendy North American business schools, Carvajal drafted a document called General Principles of Our Organization, which still guides the company over twenty-five years later. The Principles are replete with such phrases as "respect for human dignity," "self fulfillment of each human being," and, perhaps most importantly, "self-criticism capacity." In short, the key constituents of the learning organization. At Carvajal, the high-minded rhetoric is backed up with concrete action. The company established Carvajal College as a center for the education and training of its employees, on the theory that the more self-actualized people are both personally and professionally, the more willing and able they will be to contribute to the success of their employer.

In order to operationalize the company's concept of human-resource development as a humanistic quest for self-improvement, Carvajal also created the Institute for Human Development in 1992. Programs at the Institute are strategically focused on both "soft" skills such as leadership training and self-actualization, and "hard" skills like marketing and second-language skills, particularly English. Given Colombia's socioeconomic circumstances, basic skills in reading, writing and mathematics are also emphasized. Unlike most garden-variety worker training programs, Carvajal teaches employees to think for themselves and to ask tough questions. The goal of these courses, aside from raising the basic managerial and technological knowledge level of the company, is to create leaders with the appropriate skills to expand the company into new markets and in new directions. For every five employees, Carvajal Inversiones believes it can produce at least one leader—and four good team players.

Carvajal's commitment to organizational learning and empowerment is now extending even further, to the next generation of workers. Seeking to positively influence educational standards from a very early age, the company created its own kindergarten for the children of employees. The company expects that many of these children will follow their parents into the business and they want the ethos of learning to start on day one. This commitment is all the more remarkable given Carvajal's base in Latin America, a region where authoritarian, hierarchical management approaches have long dominated. North American and European companies often evince the impression that if they didn't actually invent organizational learning, they have certainly elevated its practice to the highest levels in the world. Far from it. Like all management innovation, organizational learning knows no geographic boundaries and some of the most compelling examples can be found far beyond the cloistered boardrooms and business schools of the OECD countries.

---

# CONCLUSION

---

These days, every company worth its salt purports to be a learning organization, but precious few actually deserve the label. How can you tell the real thing? The companies I presented in this chapter come in a wide variety of shapes, sizes, industries and nationalities, but they all share a number of key attributes. Those attributes are both the hallmarks and the preconditions of organizational learning:

- **Intellectual curiosity:** A passion to understand the changing forces swirling around their organizations, an eagerness to learn to master them, and a recognition that the quest for mastery is an unending one.

- **Organizational humility:** A pervasive acknowledgment, starting with the CEO, that neither he nor she nor the whole organization can ever have all the answers; that customers, suppliers, partners and even competitors have much to teach; and that the learning process never ends. In short, a willingness, preferably an eagerness, to learn from others.

- **Vigilant self-criticism:** A logical extension of organizational humility. A constant questioning of conventional company wisdom, and a keen awareness that complacency about today's success will invariably sow the seeds of tomorrow's failure.

- **A capacity to imagine alternative futures:** Notwithstanding lip service to the contrary, most companies have real difficulty accepting, at a visceral level, that the future could be anything much more than a straight line extrapolation of the past. Learning organizations can and do.

- **A high tolerance for ambiguity, complexity and change:** Organizational learning is intrinsically iterative, experimental and often nonlinear. Learning organizations are not only not threatened by change; they actually thrive on it and look for ways to turn it into competitive advantage. Complexity and ambiguity are simply part of the corporate existential condition.

- **An embrace of constructive contention:** Conventional wisdom and "group-think" are mortal enemies of both organizational learning and innovation. To avoid them, constructive contention and well-reasoned dissent must not only be tolerated, they must be encouraged and celebrated.

- **A proclivity for experimentation:** This is part and parcel of organizational learning. It is only by experimenting with new approaches, monitoring the results and incorporating the feedback into new initiatives that organizations can possibly learn and grow.

- **An appetite for feedback:** Another corollary of organizational humility. A genuine eagerness to reach out and get performance feedback from a variety of sources, and a willingness to actually listen to it and make changes. Lessons learned from past projects can become a rich source of knowledge and insight, if one is genuinely ready to listen to the feedback.

- **A preference for learning by doing:** This is a corollary of having a bias for experimentation. The extensive use of pilot and demonstration projects and real-world market tests is a much more fertile source of organizational learning than abstract speculation, market studies and team retreats, as useful as all of those can be.

- **A high pain threshold for "constructive failures":** Most CEOs would probably concede that they've learned more from their corporate mistakes than their successes. Sadly, they tend to have a much higher tolerance level for their own mistakes than for those of subordinates. Learning organizations and their leaders view experiments as desirable, mistakes as inevitable and failures as the raw feedstock for the learning process.

- **Conscious mechanisms for creating, collecting and disseminating knowledge:** Learning organizations recognize that knowledge-value is very rarely created and shared by accident. Conscious mechanisms must be put in place to acquire it, and considerable energy expended to disseminate and leverage it.

- **A taste for creative destruction and self-obsolescence:** Good companies understand intuitively that no competitive advantage can last forever. The best companies take this insight one step further. They try to ensure that they are the ones to render their best products or services obsolete. Sometimes this means "attacking" their own successful products with a new version before the original ones run out of useful economic life. It's the price world-class innovators gladly pay for staying ahead of the pack. Myopic competitors find that, in trying to milk the last ounce of profit from an existing offering, they've surrendered the future to more innovative and courageous rivals.

This list is an ambitious one. Ideally, it is not even a fully attainable one. For the true learning organization, the journey is never completed; there will always be room for further learning and improvement. But the conscious and consistent pursuit of the ideal of organizational learning is what really counts. Not only is the learning odyssey extremely beneficial in its own right, but it is rapidly becoming a competitive imperative as we move more fully into the Age of Knowledge-Value. Organizational learning must become much more than glib rhetoric; it must become an abiding corporate jihad. There could be no more strategically compelling task to which 21st century companies should dedicate themselves.

### CHAPTER TWELVE

# WAKE-UP CALL FOR WALL STREET
## STRATEGIC PERFORMANCE MEASUREMENTS

*"The accounting system doesn't capture anything, really."*
JUDY LEWENT/ CHIEF FINANCIAL OFFICER, MERCK

Throughout this book I've suggested—even demanded—measures designed to create a whole new strategic architecture for innovative and dynamic, 21st century companies. There's just one problem: How will we be able to tell if we're actually making any progress? While we've been busy flattening hierarchies, building innovative, multifunctional teams and strategically repositioning the company, chances are we're still using essentially the same old, tired performance metrics that Henry Ford used to monitor the progress of *his* company back in the 1920s. It is highly questionable whether those unidimensional, finance-driven performance indicators were good enough even then; they certainly aren't today.

The new reality is that most companies' most valuable assets are intangibles, such as organizational learning ability, technological know-how, proprietary databases and software, market knowledge, communications networks, distribution channels, customer loyalty, staff morale, strategic alliance partners and corporate culture. Yet none of these assets is ever seen within a country mile of the corporate balance sheet or profit and loss statement. What's really happening is that we've gotten more and more precise and sophisticated at measuring less and less of the true value of the company. In the words of Merck's highly respected chief financial officer Judy Lewent: "The accounting system doesn't capture anything, really."[1]

Innovative, 21st century companies will need performance metrics as dynamic and forward-looking as they are themselves. That will mean discovering, capturing and reinforcing the key strategic and competitive drivers of the *future* performance of their businesses, *not* looking into the rearview mirror with six-decimal-place accuracy. At present, the entire focus of financial analysts and investors is on "the numbers," despite mounting evidence that they're the wrong numbers.

In the 21st century, business leaders will need to place much less emphasis on measuring such static symptoms of performance as the last quarter's financial results. Instead, ways can and must be found to capture the more forward-looking, strategic drivers *behind* the numbers: innovation rates, the growth of the company's intellectual capital base, customer-satisfaction levels, employee motivation, corporate environmental performance and so on.

Unfortunately, the road to 21st century, strategic performance metrics is squarely blocked by a snarling, six-headed dog called Wall Street (or, depending on your country of origin, Bay Street, the City of London or the Nikkei). It is difficult to conceive of the scale of seismic shock required to produce a true wake-up call for Wall Street. So far, neither the global mega-shift to knowledge-based wealth creation nor the Eco-Industrial Revolution has made so much as a dent in Wall Street's impervious modus operandi for evaluating corporate performance and worth. There is, however, some good news. While making the first few converts to the cause of strategic performance metrics will be unspeakably difficult, the next three thousand or so should be easy. After all, nobody ever went broke underestimating the lemming factor on Wall Street.

Broadly speaking, conventional approaches to corporate performance measurement have at least three cardinal deficiencies. First, they tend to provide at best only a retrospective snapshot of a business reality that existed at a particular, bygone moment. This is like looking through a powerful telescope at a distant galaxy that actually ceased to exist 200 million years ago but whose light is only now reaching Planet Earth. Interesting, but not all that useful.

Second, not only is the analysis inevitably static and out of date, it is also grossly incomplete. Even if you're a financial genius like Michael Milken, studying "the numbers" yields few if any clues to the real dynamics and changing profitability drivers of a given business. Traditional financial indictators tell us absolutely nothing about *why* the overall results are the way they are, or about *which* underlying organizational capabilities need improving to meet the company's bottom-line objectives. To take but one common example, slashing the company's R&D budget will probably improve short-term profits and shareholder value (read share price). What the numbers won't tell you is how badly the company has mortgaged its future and allowed competitors to gain advantage in the crucial new technologies or competencies that will translate into market leadership five years down the road. Nor will the numbers tell you much about the company's environmental performance or liabilities, even though in some cases they could literally bankrupt the firm. Ditto for the growth of the company's intellectual capital base. From a strategic perspective, the list of what traditional financial metrics don't tell you is much longer than the list of what they do.

Third, conventional indices tend to simply reflect and perpetuate the same functional divisions and isolation that landed many declining businesses into dire trouble in the first place. The marketing department tracks market share, finance measures cost and return on investment, production follows inventory levels, and so on. The problem is that *customers* never experience the companies that sell them goods or services as a collection of discrete, functional fiefdoms. All they see and experience is the gestalt of the total service or product package itself—good, bad or indifferent. Fragmented, functionally-driven performance metrics obscure that fact, and make it inordinately difficult for companies to monitor the net impact of various departmental efforts. The only cross-functional measures are the purely financial ones that got us into this mess: gross margins, earnings per share and so on. Nobody gets the whole picture. Does the whole exceed the sum of the parts or not?

A partial list of the strategic, leading performance indicators that conventional accounting metrics tell us little or nothing about include:

- Organizational learning capacity and potential.
- Innovation rates for new products and services.
- Rate of growth and development of core competencies and intellectual capital.
- Customer satisfaction.
- Customer retention rates.
- Employee morale and turnover.
- Capacity for teambuilding and interdisciplinary collaboration.
- Value of strategic alliances and outside distribution channels.
- Speed: time to market for new products.
- Environmental performance and liabilities.

I would argue that any two of these indicators would provide more useful insights about the future competitive strength and performance of the company than the past five years' financial statements put together. For example, the percentage of company sales derived from products or services introduced during the past three years provides a crude but highly useful proxy for a company's capacity to innovate, as 3M and others have convincingly demonstrated.

Let's be clear. I am not advocating that traditional financial performance measures be simply thrown overboard; sooner or later, such exotica as organizational learning and strategic-partnering ability do need to get translated into such old-fashioned financial incarnations as cash flow and profit. All I ask is that the traditional financial metrics be supplemented, both within the company and by external analysts, with a series of more dynamic, forward-looking indices tailored to a company's individual competitive circumstances.

Nor am I recommending developing a whole phalanx of clever new performance metrics. Like all good ideas, strategic performance measurement can be overdone. Provided that the measures selected are truly strategic and that they go to the heart of the company's competitive capability, eight to ten key indicators would probably be more than sufficient.

As well, I have four important caveats. First, the whole notion of strategic performance measurement makes one critical and heroic assumption: That managers and executives can actually develop an accurate understanding of the value drivers and critical success factors of their business in the first place. This is no straightforward or easy task; indeed, it lies at the very heart of innovation and strategy. But if it is not done, all performance measurement bets must perforce be off.

The second caveat is to remember that performance is intrinsically relative, and the most important benchmarks probably lie outside your organization, not within it. What's really important is how you stack up against the competition, not your own historical performance. Accordingly, you should attempt whenever possible to integrate three variables: the metric itself, your own performance, and that of the best in the world. Sooner or later, that's who you'll have to outperform.

The third caveat can't be taken for granted either. Let's suppose that, after the expenditure of considerable brainpower, your company has produced a spiffy new set of unspeakably brilliant and strategic performance metrics. That's great; you've just entered the corporate pantheon reserved for the top .01 percent of innovative companies. There's just one more thing: Don't forget to link your new metrics directly to your compensation and incentive schemes. For example, it's all well and good to decide that the critical success factor in your business is service quality, as measured by customer satisfaction levels. But you'd better be sure that you're not still rewarding your frontline people on some other basis, like the gross number of service calls they make each week. In short, make sure your performance metrics are *directly* wired back into the compensation and power structures of your company.

The final caveat is the one that reverberates throughout this book: Nothing lasts forever, and that goes double for performance metrics. It is crucial to monitor the continuing relevance of your company's performance indicators on an ongoing basis. As your corporate priorities and competitive circumstances evolve, so should your indicators. So don't be afraid to reexamine and reinvent them on a regular basis.

In the pages that follow, we look at four exceptional companies that are pioneering the development and use of 21st century performance metrics. It is my fervent hope that, in five years, they will have lot more company.

## *Starting the Journey: Chicago's FMC*

The odyssey from conventional financial metrics to indicators that are dynamic, strategic and forward-looking is a long and tortuous one, but it has to start somewhere. Chicago's FMC Corporation has clearly begun its journey.

FMC is an ideal, if challenging candidate to launch some sort of comprehensive effort to get a more strategic handle on its operations. It is one of the most diversified companies in the United States, with over twenty divisions, three hundred different product lines and interests in everything from industrial chemicals to military defense systems. Like many diversified conglomerates, FMC's senior executives traditionally viewed their primary role as one of redeploying assets from divisions that were mature cash generators to parts of the business seen as having both immediate growth potential and cash requirements. FMC historically placed enormous emphasis on such conventional financial metrics as return-on-capital-employed (ROCE). Like most companies, FMC's management attention—and compensation schemes— were focused almost entirely on short-term financial performance. They were also directed almost entirely inward, within the company itself. Performance benchmarks overwhelmingly tended to compare the performance of one part of the company against another part, rather than against outside competitors and changing market conditions.

In the early 1990s, there was an important sea change in strategic thinking at FMC. Senior management began to reconceptualize its own role substantially, placing new emphasis on both external market dynamics and on identifying and leveraging synergies among the different business groups. It was quickly realized that this new strategic approach would also require a fundamentally different approach to performance measurement. In FMC's case, that approach turned out to be the "balanced scorecard."[2]

As the name implies, the balanced scorecard approach attempts to supplement and counterbalance traditional financial indicators with new performance metrics that are more comprehensive and robust. FMC's approach provided an entirely new perspective, which forced operating managers to think far more strategically about their business. For many of them, it was the first time they had systematically considered fundamental questions about their comparative advantages (or lack thereof) and competitive vulnerabilities.

With a company as diversified as FMC, there could be no question of developing a single, one-size-fits-all set of performance metrics, no matter how ingenious they might be. Cycle-time improvement, for example, might produce breakthrough gains in FMC's agricultural machinery business, but would have very little impact on its defense business. So each division was charged with creating strategic indicators customized to the unique circumstances and competitive requirements of its particular industry.

There were, however, some important commonalities across all the new indicators. First, there was a distinct and unprecedented orientation towards external, not internal, targets. Measures of customer satisfaction and service, for instance, proved far more indicative of FMC's ability to create real value and long-term competitiveness in the marketplace than the largely internal metrics they replaced. So did benchmarking the performance of the best in the world, wherever they might be found. Second, FMC's new indicators were more strategic and attempted to uncover the company's true competitive advantages and vulnerabilities, not merely their superficial symptoms. Third, unlike traditional benchmarking, which tends to measure process, FMC's indicators were explicitly focused on outputs and *results*. This forced the company's managers to assess their performance in the broader context of the external competitive environment. And finally, having specified the desired outcomes, FMC's senior management deliberately refrained from prescribing how those results were to be achieved. This was a deliberate attempt to foster greater creativity and lateral thinking among the operating staff. To quote executive VP Larry Brady: "We have been deliberately vague on specifying how the target is to be accomplished. We want to stimulate a thought process about how to do things differently rather than how to do existing things better. We want to identify the opportunities for breakthrough performance."[3]

Like many executives, Brady and his colleagues were seeking a conceptual bridge between the short-term, control-oriented function of FMC's one-year budgets and the more strategic vision and time frame of its five-year plan. Historically, the two documents had existed in splendid isolation from one another, each prepared by different teams, serving sharply different functions and fundamentally unconnected. FMC's balanced scorecard went a long way towards building a bridge between the two.

Most divisions decided to focus on no more than ten indicators, aware that attempting to use many more would defeat the whole point of the exercise. (After all, 650 variables can't all be "strategic.") Significantly, more than half the performance indicators were entirely new to FMC: metrics such as relative market position, penetration rates for new markets, innovation and new product development rates and customer-satisfaction levels. The new performance indicators provided FMC with a far more dynamic strategic and forward-looking picture of its competitive fitness and much more guidance about how to actually improve performance.

## MEASURING, MANAGING AND LEVERAGING INTELLECTUAL CAPITAL

I would suggest that the last real intellectual advance in financial analysis probably occurred in 1494, with the introduction of double-entry book-keeping by the Venetian monk Luca Pacioli. Since then, accounting and financial analysis have been pretty much on cruise control. To be fair, things actually didn't work out too badly for the next four and a half centuries or so. But as the global mega-shift towards knowledge-based wealth continues apace, traditional balance sheets will continue to reflect less and less of a company's true value and competitive strength.

Of all the strategic performance indicators neglected by conventional Wall Street analysis, none is more critical than the state of a company's intellectual capital base. By now, even the most retrograde CEO would have to confess to at least a vague suspicion that knowledge-value and intellectual capital are becoming increasingly important to his or her company's competitive strength. Unfortunately, this dawning realization rarely triggers much more than some platitudinous declaration in the annual report, along the lines of "Our People Are Our Greatest Asset." Wonderful. But now what?

### Breaking New Ground: Sweden's Skandia AFS

Very few companies have moved far enough beyond platitudes to seriously manage and develop their intellectual capital bases, systematically and strategically. Of that elite number, fewer still have had the gumption to try to measure their performance in doing so, much less publish the results. The task's sheer complexity, ambiguity and intellectual effort have intimidated all but a handful of leading-edge companies. Sweden's Skandia AFS is one of those rare exceptions, and its effort is breaking new ground internationally.

The Skandia Group is the largest financial services company in Scandanavia. Its Assurance and Financial Services subsidiary, AFS, sells life insurance, annuities and other savings and insurance products from offices in ten countries, including the United States. AT&T revenues of $2.2 billion account for nearly 40 percent of the group total.

Innovation at Skandia seems to be a way of life and the tone gets set at the top. Executive Vice President Jan Carendi means it when he says: "Skandia's greatest asset is innovation and pioneering ideas . . . good leaders reward those who dare to stick their chins out."[4] Given the stress placed on innovation at Skandia, it is scarcely surprising that the company's intellectual capital is a top priority. As CEO Björn Wolrath puts it: "Auditors, analysts and accounting people have long lacked instruments and generally accepted norms for accurately evaluating service companies and their intellectual capital. At Skandia, we have always maintained that our intellectual capital is at least as important as our financial capital in providing truly sustainable earnings."[5] In 1991, Skandia gave concrete expression to those sentiments by hiring Leif Edvinsson as the corporate world's first Director of Intellectual Capital. Later, the company added Tove Husell as Intellectual Capital Controller, and now has a full-blown team dedicated solely to the growth and development of Skandia's intellectual capital base.

It is crucial to an understanding of Skandia's approach to recognize that this new title is not simply an updated, '90s equivalent of "human resource manager." Edvinsson has far more corporate clout than that; he is one of the highest ranking executives in the entire company. Equally important is his mandate, which both embraces and goes far beyond the usual human resources functions and challenges. His team's mission is nothing less than to capture and leverage as much of the company's intangible value potential as possible.

The skills, knowledge and talents of Skandia's workforce are an obvious element in that equation, but Edvinsson is looking for more—much more. He is particularly interested in what he calls "structural intellectual capital"—the pathways and infrastructure through which individual knowledge can be leveraged, disseminated and turned into real value. Structural intellectual capital includes things like:

- Customer and supplier networks.
- Databases.
- Distribution and marketing channels.
- Management information systems.

- Team-building capabilities.
- Strategic alliance networks.
- The organizational structure itself.

In short, structural intellectual capital includes any asset that allows the company to propagate and *generalize* knowledge-value throughout the organization.

Let's take a hypothetical example. You've just set up a ten-person strategy consultancy. Unlike most consulting outfits of this size, your board of directors includes a former finance minister from a G7 country, the former executive chairman of one of the largest, most respected and most profitable banks in the world and a former senior director of the World Bank. Now, what would you say are the most valuable assets and comparative advantages of your new company? Your opening financial balance sheet? Not likely. Seems pretty obvious, doesn't it? Apparently not to most bankers, though. Because none of the company's most potent weapons for wealth creation show up anywhere on its balance sheet, even the venture capitalists will probably shun your company like a leper. Just try raising money from conventional financiers on the strength of your "structural intellectual capital"!

Intellectual capital—structural or otherwise—is an extraordinarily amorphous and difficult asset to even define, much less to measure. At Skandia, Edvinsson starts with three basic assumptions. First, the value of a company's intellectual assets normally exceeds by many times the value of the assets reflected on its balance sheet. Second, intellectual capital is really the raw material from which financial results must then be manufactured. And finally, it is important to distinguish between two kinds of intellectual capital: human and structural. Human intellectual capital in individuals is clearly the starting point; it is the original source of innovation, knowledge and insight. Structural capital is the means by which the value of human capital can be leveraged and amplified many times over. Both types need to be measured and developed.

Human capital can and should be upgraded continuously by aggressive investment in training, but it cannot be leveraged into real value for the company without structural capital. Sadly, the converse is also true; just as structural capital can amplify the value of individual talent and knowledge, it can also diminish it. Anyone who has witnessed the corrosive effects of excessive corporate bureaucracy on talent and initiative can vouch for that.

Most companies, even relatively enlightened ones, focus the vast majority of their energies on their human intellectual capital, but the real leverage (and value for the company as a whole) exists with structural capital. In

Skandia's view, and mine, that's where the real focus of effort and attention belongs in the 1990s and beyond.

The first publicly available fruits of Edvinsson's labors was a ten-page document published in 1993: *Skandia* AFS: *Balanced Annual Report on Intellectual Capital.* The most interesting (and sensible) thing about the document is its avowed purpose: To serve as a tool to help the company manage its intellectual assets more strategically and effectively. For that purpose, it was judged unnecessary to engage in the futile exercise of trying to quantify the intrinsically unquantifiable with great precision. For purposes of managing and building value for the company, it is much less critical to quantify precisely the intellectual assets than to know what and where they are, and to then make sure value is added to them and not subtracted. To quote the report: "Direction is more important to follow than precision in the reporting."[6]

The report itself is both brief and basic, as befits a self-described "project in process." As the company's first report of its kind (and, to my knowledge, the first of its kind anywhere in the world), the document is understandably light on historical, comparative data. It's therefore not possible to attempt any time-sequenced correlations between the growth of the company's intellectual capital base and its financial performance. Edvinsson promises these, along with additional indicators, in future iterations. What the report does accomplish, however, is the creation of a solid baseline for assessing future progress on such key value indicators as innovation rates, the intensity of the company's use of information technology, its per capita investment in training, customer retention rates and so on.

The report's other major achievement has been to focus the company's attention on its real business: "Transforming human capital into structural capital . . . gaining productivity growth by systematically linking human capital with various dimensions of structural capital. This then becomes a continuous process of knowledge-creation and competence development for global competitiveness."[7]

The true test of the report's ultimate value, then, must be the extent to which it helps reorient Skandia's thinking, attention and *behavior*, refocusing them on the areas with the greatest potential leverage for value creation. Early indications suggest that it is already having an impact. Skandia has already been able to codify, clone and transfer its procedures for setting up new international offices (more structural capital), halving both the time and expense involved. Even more encouraging, Skandia has begun using similar knowledge-transfer techniques to amplify cross-border synergies and sales opportunities from products developed in other countries.

Skandia issued its second major report in 1995, *Visualizing Intellectual Capital in Skandia.*[8] Distributed as a supplement to the company's 1994 annual report, the newer document is lengthier, more detailed and extends the analysis to a wider cross-section of Skandia subsidiaries. A few new wrinkles are added, including corporate computer literacy rates and an intriguing Empowerment Index, but the basic thrust remains the same: to provide management tools to identify and amplify the single most crucial source of Skandia's future value—its intellectual capital base.

In nuclear physics, the Heisenberg Uncertainty Principle teaches us, among other things, that the mere act of attempting to observe and measure subatomic particles with powerful microscopes changes their energy levels and therefore their positions. Measurement itself actually changes behavior. So it is with intellectual capital. The mere act of trying to measure it creates change—most of it positive—and moves the object of study to new and higher energy levels. Given the extraordinary importance of intellectual capital to 21st century competitiveness, the art of capturing, measuring and leveraging it can only assume greater importance.

## CIBC: Leveraging the Knowledge-Value Revolution

Brace yourself. My recent international meanderings have yielded a genuine anthropological curiosity: a thoughtful, imaginative, farsighted group of *bankers*! Honest! In my previous experience, commercial bankers as a genus only rarely exhibited flashes of transcendental insight, innovation or leading-edge thinking. As one senior North American banker recently confided: "We don't like innovation around here; there's no money in it. We make most of our money on the trailing edge." Rarely have I heard a more candid—or accurate—self-assessment. Bankers certainly can be enormously creative, at the margin. They are capable of spinning out an endless stream of new financial products demonstrating great wizardry and imagination. But none of them is likely to call into question any of their industry's long-standing, time-tested assumptions.

Arguably their most fundamental assumption of all concerns what constitutes real, "bankable" value. For centuries, the only assets with meaningful value for bankers were the tangible ones: office towers, industrial machinery, oil in the ground and so on. Today, leading-edge bankers recognize that a global mega-shift is underway, and that it favors knowledge-value at the expense of more traditional sources of wealth. The big question is what to do with that realization.

Those few bankers who deign to acknowledge the existence of the knowledge-value revolution generally content themselves with proclaiming their new-found dedication to the cause in annual reports and media interviews. A few have gone so far as to set up special "Knowledge-Based Lending" units. But few banks anywhere in the world have gone as far as the Canadian Imperial Bank of Commerce in attempting to systematically measure, manage and leverage its own intellectual capital base.

The point man for CIBC's intellectual capital initiative is Hubert Saint-Onge, a bright, intense young man whose business card captures his distinctly 21st century approach. It proclaims him to be "Vice President, Learning Organization and Leadership Development." Saint-Onge's herculean challenge is to translate the rhetoric and conceptual underpinnings of the learning organization into terms and actions that are meaningful and credible to the hardnosed bankers with whom he works. He practices this modern alchemy from his command bunker in the bank's special new learning center in an idyllic, ranch-like setting north of Toronto, with frequent sorties to the bank's head office downtown.

The somewhat woolly intangibles that are Saint-Onge's stock-in-trade have traditionally been referred to as "goodwill" by analysts attempting to evaluate corporate assets during a purchase transaction. The crucial distinction is this: CIBC doesn't want to get a better handle on its intangible assets in order to sell them; it wants to be able to manage them better and grow them.

CIBC's wake-up call came in 1989, with the precipitous plunge in real estate values throughout North America. If formerly rock-solid assets could lose up to 50 percent of their value only in six months, what was value, anyhow? Maybe tangibles weren't so tangible after all and, conversely, perhaps intangibles had greater and more durable value than was previously thought. CIBC wasn't the first or only North American bank to be shaken by the collapse of real estate values. But it was one of the very few to assess the damage within the broader context of the knowledge-value revolution.

Saint-Onge's starting point is exactly where it ought to be: Acknowledging that the knowledge-value revolution has changed virtually everything about how the bank, and its customers, create, measure and amplify value. He firmly believes that conventional corporate lending has long since become yesterday's business and that banks need to find innovative ways to create value or else go out of business. He begins with three basic propositions.

First, the advent of the knowledge era has radically changed our understanding of what creates value in organizations. Second, the long-term prosperity of organizations depends to an increasing extent on management's ability to leverage *hidden* value, which can now be made more explicit by measuring the dynamics of intellectual capital. Third, valuing and measuring intellectual capital will promote strategic organizational learning and the generation of the organizational capabilities required to meet customer expectations on an ongoing basis.[9]

Saint-Onge uses a particularly clever metaphor to get his point across, something he calls "the iceberg balance sheet." He literally diagrams a pyramid of value, only about 10 percent of which appears above the water line. That 10 percent represents the bank's financial capital, as captured and reported through conventional accounting metrics. That, in Saint-Onge's view, is just the tip of CIBC's value iceberg. The bulk of it, 90 percent or so, is made up of the bank's intellectual capital base, largely unrecognized, unmeasured and certainly undermanaged. As Saint-Onge puts it: "Intellectual capital has remained invisible, not only to managers but also to market analysts and competitors, because they do not take into account the submerged part of the iceberg balance sheet."[10]

CIBC divides intellectual capital into three distinct varieties: individual staff skills and attributes (human capital); organizational capabilities, including corporate culture, which add value to customers (what Skandia calls "structural capital"); and the strength of its customer franchise, which CIBC calls "customer capital." Each type of intellectual capital requires a different management and investment strategy. Similarly, just as no single financial indicator can fully capture the complexity of a company's financial situation and performance, there can be no one-size-fits-all metric for measuring intellectual capital.

On the human capital side, CIBC has developed what it calls competency models for various positions, detailing several dozen skills required to give first-class service to customers. Such skill inventories are not particularly unusual in and of themselves, though CIBC is innovative in its explicit recognition that employee attitudes and mind-sets are a major resource—or liability. Intangibles such as capacity for teamwork and for generating and executing new ideas are an important part of CIBC's metric for human capital. But what's even more interesting is what CIBC does with the profiles. The bank has essentially used them to turn its entire set of training programs upside down. (The word "training" is something of an anachronism at CIBC; Saint-Onge and his colleagues are attempting to expunge it from the corporate vocabulary, regarding it as excessively paternalistic and unidirectional. They much prefer the word "learning.") Rather than force-feed standardized or even somewhat customized programs down the throats of their employees, CIBC has completely reversed the onus. The bank now arms its employees with profiles of both what's required and where they are now, and then turns them loose to create their own learning menus from CIBC's large smorgasbord of training resources. The employee thus assumes principal responsibility for upgrading his or her own portfolio of competencies. Saint-Onge told me he considers this an important part of his broader campaign to inculcate "a culture of personal responsibility and ownership"[11] within the bank and contrasts it with the previous culture of dependency and paternalism. Any way you slice it, the whole process provides a far more useful and dynamic measure of the state of the company's intellectual capital base than such limp, traditional indices as hours of training per employee per year.

Structural capital also requires its own metrics. Like Skandia, CIBC views structural capital as both the process and the result of transforming individual knowledge and competencies into a *collective* intelligence and capability that actually becomes imbedded in the organization. In order for this to happen, Saint-Onge reckons at least three things are required: a common purpose or vision; a common "nervous system" to wire the organization together; and a common "memory" to capture, codify and leverage the individual experiences into an effective corporate knowledge base. Saint-Onge identifies what he considers the five key building blocks of structural capital: strategy, structure, systems, culture and individual leadership (not leadership from the rarefied heights of the executive suite, but individual leadership and a willingness to accept personal responsibility). Needless to say, these qualities are extraordinarily elusive and difficult to define, much less to measure. For the moment, Saint-Onge and his colleagues must content themselves with such relatively crude proxies for the bank's structural capabilities as the rate of new product introduction, transaction processing times and cost and complaint resolution times.

Customer capital is somewhat easier, though still challenging, to capture and measure. Saint-Onge is acutely interested in the dynamics of the bank's interaction with its customers. How early has it been able to participate in the customer's business decision cycle? Is the span of contact between the two organizations broad or narrow? How much congruency can be developed between the two corporate value systems? It's subtle stuff. For now, CIBC uses such performance indicators as customer satisfaction and retention rates, levels of profitability by customer and also the bank's ability to grow single-purpose customer relationships into deeper, longer, more multifaceted ones.

Perhaps the most powerful ingredient of CIBC's model of intellectual capital is its explicit recognition and emphasis of two key insights:

- **Each component of the intellectual value system is connected to all the others.** Thus, there is a constant interplay between and among the three sources of intellectual capital: human, structural and customer. Each is capable of adding value to and converting itself into the others and all of them should ultimately be converted into financial capital that even an accountant could measure.

- **Value transfers can be either positive or negative.** This is probably the most compelling—and frightening—part of the entire analytical model. It explicitly acknowledges that there is absolutely nothing that guarantees the interactions will generate positive value. Without conscious and careful attention, it is entirely possible the bank's structural characteristics will actually rob value potential from its human capital base, its customer capital or both.

There's one more thing: The value of the bank's intellectual asset base is both relative and dynamic, not absolute or static. The real test of its value is its strength over time relative to outside market expectations. It's not enough even to make sure that the intellectual capital base is growing in absolute terms; "if customer expectations grow at a faster pace than the sum of human and structural capital, then the total capital value will decline exponentially."[12]

This is pretty heady stuff, especially for bankers. But Saint-Onge and his merry band at CIBC are clever about their intellectual marketing strategy. They have adopted guerrilla tactics to spread their revolutionary gospel about intellectual capital. Recognizing that a frontal assault on the bastions of corporate orthodoxy would be futile and even counterproductive, Saint-Onge chooses to integrate its key precepts in bite-sized doses, spread in nontoxic concentrations throughout a variety of CIBC's different learning programs. Acutely aware of both the futility and the dangers of overt preaching, Saint-Onge relies instead on what he calls "third party endorsements" to spread the message. Key clients of the bank and other influential outsiders who have bought into the group's leading-edge approach to leveraging intellectual capital have proven to be forceful and highly credible salesmen with other CIBC executives.

Perhaps the most powerful weapon in Saint-Onge's arsenal is his clarity of purpose. For him, measuring intellectual capital is, pure and simple, a tool for identifying, managing and leveraging the bank's assets. It is a way—about the best I've seen so far—to focus everybody's attention on at least two things. First, the supreme importance of intellectual capital to the bank's future financial health; and second, what's required to maintain and upgrade those assets. To find such an approach within the bosom of the very industry that has traditionally demonstrated an almost visceral aversion to real innovation is both surprising and enormously encouraging.

## MEASURING ENVIRONMENTAL PERFORMANCE

### *E. B. Eddy: In Search of Sustainability*

We have seen how the Eco-Industrial Revolution is rapidly adding another whole dimension to the competitiveness equation: environmental performance and efficiency. We also saw that only a few, leading-edge companies have come anywhere close to making this new industrial paradigm a central feature of their competitive strategy. Of that short list, fewer still have made meaningful efforts to actually measure their progress. And of that elite group, virtually none has taken that aspect of strategic performance measurement all the way to its logical conclusion: measuring the company's progress not only towards environmental efficiency, but towards "sustainable development." E. B. Eddy, a midsized ($530 million) Canadian forest products company, is one of only a handful of companies in the world to have attempted it.

To the environmental cognoscenti, sustainable development is an advanced step on the evolutionary ladder of consciousness, where mere environmental protection is viewed as a distinctly lower life form. Environmental protection harkens back to the bygone dark ages of unproductive, zero-sum confrontations between environmentalists (the Forces of Good) and the rapacious forces of capitalism and development (the Forces of Evil).

The doctrine of sustainable development[13] offers a way out of this impasse, and holds at least the potential of reconciling economic and environmental considerations. Environmental protection has always been an essentially negative concept of damage avoidance and control; sustainable development is more positive, enabling and facilitative. It is also a good deal more ethereal, elusive and slippery. To attempt a brief definition of what is a very subtle and complex concept, sustainable development is economic development that does not undermine the environmental or social basis of future growth and development. To quote the United Nations Commission that first popularized the term: "Sustainable Development is development that meets the needs of the present without compromising the ability of future generations to meet their own needs."[14]

As a forest products company making pulp, paper and lumber, E. B. Eddy is up to its neck in environmental issues from the get-go, so it comes by its interest in sustainable development quite honestly. The company depends on the environment directly for its raw material, and its environmental performance is increasingly fundamental to retaining its "social license" to stay in business. E. B. Eddy has developed its own definition of sustainable development, and it's a good one: "Sustainable development becomes a reality when social and environmental factors are integrated with economic needs to produce growth that is responsible."[15]

It would be an understatement to observe that any attempt to measure progress towards sustainable development requires the use of data and indicators that are rarely, if ever, used even internally, never mind publicly reported to outside stakeholders.

E. B. Eddy's public reporting on its odyssey towards the Holy Grail of sustainable development began with the publication of its 1993 landmark report, *A Question of Balance: Status Report on Sustainable Development*. Perhaps the most impressive aspect of the report is the ethos of humility and organizational learning that pervades it: "*A Question of Balance* is not intended to be the final word on sustainable development, but more an opening gesture. We welcome constructive comments and criticisms of this report and will endeavor to incorporate suggestions for improvement . . . although a relatively simplistic input-output model, it will provide a baseline of information with which to assess progress."[16] The 1994 report a year later exhibits a similarly refreshing openness to being challenged and, more importantly, to challenging itself: "By creating dialogue, we are providing stimulus to challenge our current thinking on all aspects of our operations . . . Only through the measurement of our actions can we show proof and only through the sharing of that measurement will we be trusted."[17]

It must be stressed that the E. B. Eddy sustainable development reports are far from soft-headed, dewy-eyed paeans to unfettered environmentalism. CEO Ted Boswell, a burly, no-nonsense, straight-talking industry veteran, wouldn't sit still for woolly-minded, tree-hugging environmental naiveté for one second. These are business documents, all right: "sustainable development will require financial profit . . . sustainability, of community and company, is clearly linked to competitiveness."[18] But they're business documents like none you've ever seen before. The boys at Price Waterhouse and Peat Marwick must still be scratching their heads over them.

The inaugural report in 1993 breaks the company's activities into four major impact areas:

- Socioeconomic impacts. This includes the company's impact on the resource communities where its operations are located. The report acknowledges E. B. Eddy's special responsibilities in this regard; in many cases, the company is the major source of employment for an entire community. The socioeconomic impact section also addresses the changing demographics, skill levels and training needs of its employee base—the company's sustainability from a human-resource perspective.

- Resource use and efficiency. The report examines the long-term sustainability of the company's wood-harvesting and reforestation practices; its ability to minimize waste in converting the forest resource into final products; its efficiency in using key inputs such as energy and water; and its ability to improve its recycling performance.
- Environmental impacts. This includes air and water emissions, and the volume of solid waste the company produces that require landfill.
- R&D. The document reports on E. B. Eddy's research initiatives in such areas as developing chlorine-free pulping processes and new approaches to treating toxic waste.

The report's detail and sophistication are truly impressive, forming a comprehensive baseline for monitoring further progress. It certainly holds the company's own feet to the fire, which is clearly its overriding purpose. As an example of strategic performance measurement in the emerging and elusive new area of sustainable development, the E. B. Eddy report sets a new world standard.

## CONCLUSION

One of the very few management maxims that *has* stood the test of time is this: You *do* get what you measure. This being the case, it would seem the height of naiveté to expect 21st century strategic performance out of companies still stuck in the time warp of 19th century measurement systems. It is of critical importance that companies constructing the new innovation infrastructure recommended in this book also devote considerable energy to devising metrics that not only capture the new performance, but actually *promote* it.

A few words of caution to temper any new-found lust for strategic performance metrics. There is always a danger that the measurement exercise will turn into an intellectual Frankenstein and become an end in itself. It is all too easy for executives to get so caught up in their new measurement toy that they lose track of why they built it in the first place. Performance measurement, whether strategic or otherwise, has little if any value in and of itself. It exists—or should exist—for one reason only: To enhance performance. No matter how elegant a set of strategic performance metrics may be, they will be totally useless if they fail to meet four key tests:

- They must help executives and staff identify priorities they should pursue to maximize the company's value-added potential. They must be truly aligned with the strategic drivers of the company's future success.
- They must help focus attention on those priorities once they have been identified.
- They must help assess the company's progress in pursuing them.
- They must lead to an observable difference in the company's actual behavior and performance. This means that they must be consciously reinforced in practice, with both monetary and intangible rewards and compensation.

Without these four conditions, strategic performance measurement can become a sterile, wasteful and even a counterproductive exercise. But if these conditions are met, forward-looking performance metrics can become an indispensable part of the strategic arsenal of the 21st century company.

# CONCLUSION
## BUILDING AN INNOVATION
## INFRASTRUCTURE FOR 21ST CENTURY
## COMPANIES

*"To stay still is to stagnate, and to stagnate is to be overtaken. We must press forward to ever-higher performance."*
LEE KUAN YEW/ FORMER PRIME MINISTER OF SINGAPORE

Throughout the industrialized world, we are fast approaching both the intellectual and the financial limits of "slash and burn" cost containment and sterile corporate reengineering. These approaches have been driven almost entirely by cost-control imperatives, and very little by strategic efforts to generate new and enduring sources of innovation, value and profits. It is now time to move beyond retrenchment.

The CEO's traditional preoccupations—managing the share price, tarting up the profit-and-loss statements and even today's trendy reengineering efforts—have become yesterday's game. Tomorrow's—and, increasingly, today's—critical focus is identifying, managing, and leveraging the company's *intellectual* capital base. That is how 21st century CEOs will add real value to their companies.

But it won't be easy; under today's conditions of chronic volatility and tectonic change, there can be no hope of achieving "sustainable competitive advantage," or of finding "the definitive solution." All "solutions" and competitive advantages should be regarded as temporary at best; *the only thing which should be regarded as permanent is the quest for the next advantage.*

In tomorrow's hypercompetitive business environment, doing one or two things well or even superbly won't be enough. Companies will need to develop the ability to fight strategic battles on multiple fronts simultaneously, and to excel at all of them. Observing one or two of the 11 Commandments, while difficult enough by itself, is unlikely to be enough; three or four will be a bare minimum. Those who can't or won't achieve that level of mastery are unlikely to be overly troubled by the turbulent competitive environment of the 21st century; it is highly improbable that they'll even be *around.*

In writing this book, I have been forcibly struck by the fact that the exceptional companies discussed here are almost always exceptional *across several dimensions simultaneously.* Few have been corporate one-trick ponies; companies which have been profiled for their ability to use speed as a competitive weapon might just as easily have been chosen for their capacity to leverage hidden value potential, build strategic alliances, or act entrepreneurially. But despite this, remarkably, none of the companies seems willing to stand pat with its current competitive weaponry; each is in constant search of the next source of value or advantage. It is this cultivation of a climate of relentless but constructive dissatisfaction and impatience that really sets them apart.

## THE "GALES OF CREATIVE DESTRUCTION"

A half-century ago, Austrian economist Joseph Schumpeter coined the memorable expression "gales of creative destruction" to describe the essence of the capitalist dynamic—the unending process of creation, obsolescence, destruction and rebirth through which new and better products, services and technologies emerge and then are themselves superseded. By the late-1980s, Schumpeter's "gales of creative destruction" had turned into a full-blown, unrelenting, force-10 hurricane, as the decimated ranks of the Fortune 500 can attest. Today, both the velocity *and* the unpredictability of those competitive gales have increased to the point where there seems to be an awful lot more corporate destruction than creation.

What makes the companies in this book and others like them exceptional is their ability to harness those forces of creative destruction and turn them into new sources of urgency, value and competitive advantage. Unlike their competitors, they take it as a given that even their best products, services, and technologies are destined to be superseded. Even more important, they are implacably determined that, since somebody is bound to render their offerings obsolete anyway, they might as well do it themselves! And out of the ashes of the obsolete product rises a new and improved one—even if the old one still appeared to have lots of commercial life left in it. Such is the price of getting, and staying, on the leading edge. Hypercompetitive times call for hypercompetitive firms! And hypercompetitive firms need superior innovation infrastructure. That infrastructure needs to be capable of not only withstanding the gales of creative destruction; but also of actually *creating* a few constructive gales of its own.

## The Iceberg Balance Sheet

The starting point for building this kind of 21st century innovation infrastructure, it seems to me, is with a fundamental reconceptualization of where the real value in a company actually resides. In the Industrial Age, a company's primary value lay in the tangible productive assets it controlled: natural resources, physical plant, machinery, finance capital and of course, the work force—and the more of all of them, the better. Today, in the era of knowledge capital and innovation driven value creation, traditional balance sheets and profit-and-loss statements can capture only a tiny and declining fraction of a company's true value. This entire book has been about how to recognize, manage and leverage the other 90 percent.

A central contention of this book is that this largely invisible part of the "iceberg balance sheet" must preoccupy the leaders of tomorrow's companies, not the 10 percent which currently consumes 90 percent of their attention and energy. But first, it must be made far more visible and explicit.

The key components of this submerged iceberg of corporate value are the three principal elements of the company's intellectual capital base and innovation infrastructure:

- Human capital
- Stakeholder capital
- Structural capital

Human capital—the skills, knowledge, and value of individual employees —is already receiving an enormous amount of attention from executives, human-resource specialists and academics alike. What has historically received far less attention, however, is the firm's *stakeholder* and *structural* capital. "Stakeholder capital" is our term for the wealth-creation potential inherent in the company's network of strategic alliance partners, customers, suppliers and distributors. "Structural capital" refers to the constellation of intangible attributes and channels through which individual human capital can be knitted together into an *organizational* capability. Structural capital includes such elusive assets as organizational learning and innovation ability, strategic vision and culture, team-building capability, management information systems and, in short, the rest of the 11 Commandments put forward in this book.

Together, stakeholder and structural capital comprise the principal strategic architecture, or innovation infrastructure, of the firm. Without that infrastructure, there can be no opportunity to "wire together" the individual competencies of the firm's human capital base into a corporate whole which can become greater than the sum of its parts. A company's innovation infrastructure provides the means to convert human capital into collective, *organizational* capability and intellectual capital, and ultimately into greater competitiveness and profitability.

We have seen that the relationship among these key variables looks something like this:

### *Intellectual Capital = Human + Stakeholder Capital ± Structural Capital*

It is important to recognize, however, that a company's innovation infrastructure can be a decidedly two-edged sword and is very rarely a neutral instrument. Designed well, it can create and leverage enormous new value; designed or executed badly, it can actually rob the organization of strength and vitality, and can easily make two and two add up to three—or even less. Just ask the dispirited, underutilized employees at a badly led, visionless company.

In my ceaseless quest to assist current and future executives to confront this frightening existential void, I have attempted to sketch the outline of the sort of innovation infrastructure which tomorrow's companies will need to remain competitive. The key building blocks of that 21st century infrastructure are the 11 Commandments. Armed with them, you too can build and run a $10 billion company with only a little practice, and all in the privacy of your own home. Or, if you'd prefer, *don't* build a $10 billion behemoth; build a nimble ten-person, virtual organization instead. And that's the best part. If this book has demonstrated anything, it's that you don't need to be big—or small—to be innovative. Leading-edge innovators can be found in huge conglomerates or small start-ups, and in Silicon Valley or Communist enclaves like Ho Chi Minh City. Size and geography have very little to do with it. What *really* makes the difference is the fit between a company's innovation infrastructure and the onerous requirements of 21st century, global hypercompetition. That, and the passion and commitment with which you pursue innovation. Just remember: Get Innovative or Get Dead!

Oh, and one last thing: there's also a kind of Twelfth Commandment, which may well be the most crucial of all: **Regularly, at least once a week, revisit the other 11 Commandments to make sure that they're still relevant and helpful in your own particular corporate circumstances.** In the vortex of 21st century global business competition, nothing lasts forever, not even the 11 Commandments.

# END NOTES

### Preface

1. This compelling term was, as far as I know, coined by business writer Richard D'Aveni. See *Hypercompetition,* New York, The Free Press, 1994

### Chapter 1

1. George Gilder, "The Network as Computer." Essay reprinted in *Northern Telecom 1994 Annual Report,* 1995, pp. 15–17.
2. James Brian Quinn, *Intelligent Enterprise,* New York: The Free Press, 1992, p. 243.
3. Kenichi Ohmae has provided particularly compelling commentaries on this phenomenon. His most recent is *The End of the Nation State,* New York: The Free Press, 1995.
4. I am indebted to my colleague Hubert Saint-Onge at the Canadian Imperial Bank of Commerce for first drawing my attention to this striking metaphor.

### Chapter 2

1. See, for example, *Business Week*'s 1996 cover story "The Fall of an American Icon," February 5, 1996.
2. *Ibid,* p. 37.
3. Quoted in Robert Cringley, *Accidental Empires,* New York: Harper Business, 1992, p. 53.
4. From General Magic's initial public offering prospectus.
5. *Business Week/Enterprise,* 1993.

6. George Gilder, "Telecosm: The Coming Software Shift," *Forbes ASAP*, August 28, 1995, pp. 156, 162.
7. See Gary Hamel and C.K. Prahalad, *Competing for the Future,* Cambridge: Harvard University Press, 1995.

### Chapter 3

1. Gary Hamel and C.K. Prahalad, "Strategic Intent," *Harvard Business Review,* May–June, 1989, p. 69.
2. I am indebted to Tom Peters for this memorable aphorism. See T. Peters, "Get Innovative or Get Dead." *California Management Review,* Fall 1990 and Winter 1991.
3. Quoted in Steven Prokesch, "Managing Chaos at the High-Tech Frontier," *Harvard Business Review,* November–December 1993, p. 136, emphasis added.
4. *Ibid.*, p. 138.
5. *The Globe and Mail,* Wednesday, February 8, 1995, p. B4.
6. Quoted in Gale Eisenstadt, "Crazy is Praise for US," *Forbes,* November 7, 1994, p. 176.
7. Quoted in William Taylor, "The Business of Innovation," *Harvard Business Review,* March–April 1990, p. 98. Emphasis added.
8. *Ibid.*
9. Richard Pascale, *Managing on the Edge,* London: Viking, 1990, p. 256.
10. *Ibid.*
11. *Automotive News,* January 31, 1995.
12. Quoted in Alan Deutschman, "How H-P Continues to Grow and Grow," *Fortune,* May 2, 1994, p. 90.
13. *Ibid.*

### Chapter 4

1. Robert Cassidy, "Corporation of the Year: A Perpetual Idea Machine," *Research and Development,* November 1989, p. 55.
2. Based on Financial Times/Price Waterhouse peer-group survey of top executives, June 1994. The executives were asked to name rival companies they admired.
3. Alison Smith, "Survey of UK Consumer Credit and Asset Finance (8): Range of Participants Widens," *Financial Times,* November 3, 1994.
4. Neil Buckley, "Europe's Most Respected Companies: Three-P Principles Pull M&S Through," *Financial Times,* June 27, 1994, p. 8.
5. Quoted in "A New Spirit of Partnership," *Canadian Business Review,* Summer 1994, p. 10.
6. Quoted in *Forbes,* August 29, 1994, p. 58.

### Chapter 5

1. See Joseph Bower and Clayton Christensen, "Disruptive Technologies: Catching the Wave," *Harvard Business Review,* January–February, 1995, p. 45.
2. *The Economist,* March 4, 1995, p. 64.
3. *Automotive News,* December 5, 1994.
4. Quoted in Tom Peters, *Liberation Management,* New York: Alfred A. Knopf, 1992, p. 34.

5. *Business Week*, January 22, 1996, p. 73.

6. See, for example, Sun Microsystems, *Annual Report,* 1994.

7. Quoted in *Fortune,* August 17, 1987, p. 89.

8. Quoted in Stalk and Hout, *Competing Against Time,* p. 142.

9. *Business Week*, January 22, 1996, p. 66. Another indication of McNealy's inveterate iconoclasm was his choice of the name for his new son: Maverick.

10. Quoted by Larry Farrell, in *Searching for the Spirit of Enterprise,* New York: Penguin, 1993, p. 133.

11. See Joseph Cosco, "Black and Deckering Black and Decker," *Journal of Business Science,* January 1994, p. 60.

12. Donald Reinertson, *Developing Products in Half the Time,* New York: Van Nostrand and McKinsey and Co., 1991.

### Chapter 6

1. Kevin Kelly, "Out of Control: the Rise of Neo Biological Civilization," *Whole Earth Review,* Spring, 1994, p. 94.

2. Quoted in William Burger, "Up, Up and Away: Peter Pan's Empire," *Newsweek,* June 13, 1994, p. 31.

3. Echo Montgomery Garrett, "Branson the Bold," *Success,* November 1992, p. 21.

4. "Still on course: Britain's Virgin Atlantic is probably the most admired small airline in the world. For how much longer?", *The Economist,* January 22, 1994.

5. Echo Montgomery Garrett, *op. cit.*, p. 23.

6. *Ibid.*, p. 24.

7. *Ibid.*

8. *Ibid.*

9. Brian Coleman, "Bookshelf: The Unshaven Face of British Business," *The Wall Street Journal Europe,* November 18, 1994, p. 6.

10. Peter Fuhrman, "Brand-name Branson," *Forbes,* January 2, 1995, p. 42.

11. Harvey Wagner, "The Open Corporation," *California Management Review,* Summer, 1991, p. 58.

12. *Ibid.,* p. 49.

13. *Ibid.,* p. 56.

14. Quoted in Rosabeth Moss Kanter, "Championing Change," *Harvard Business Review,* January–February 1991, p. 120.

15. *Business Week,* March 13, 1995, p. 38.

### Chapter 7

1. Joel Bleeke and David Ernst, "Is Your Strategic Alliance Really a Sale?" *Harvard Business Review,* January–February, 1995, p. 97.

2. Polly Labarre, "The Dis-organization of Oticon," *Industry Week,* July 18, 1994, p. 22.

3. See Oren Harari, "Open the Doors, Tell the Truth," *Management Review,* January 1995, p. 34.

4. Sten Davidsen, "Oticon's Project 330: Improving Competitiveness Danish-Style," August 1994, p. 756.

5. Oren Harari, "Open the Doors, Tell the Truth," *Management Review,* January 1995, p. 33.

6. Richard Rapaport, "Jay Chiat Tears Down the Walls," *Forbes ASAP,* October 25, 1993.

7. See John Seely Brown, "Research that Re-invents the Corporation," *Harvard Business Review,* January–February, 1991, pp. 102–111.

8. *San Jose Mercury News,* August 26, 1991, p. 1.

9. Brown, *op. cit.,* p. 103.

10. Quoted in B. Schlender, "How Toshiba Makes Alliances Work," *Fortune,* October 4, 1993, p. 116.

11. See, for example, Eleanor Westney, "The Japanese Keiretsu in Transition," *Perspectives,* Centre for International Business, University of Toronto, Vol. 2, No. 2, April, 1995.

12. *Ibid.,* p. 118.

13. McKinsey and Co., "Closing the Global Communications Gap." Feasibility study prepared for the International Telecommunication Union, Geneva, 1995.

14. United Nations Conference on Human Rights, Vienna, Austria, 1993; ITU Plenipotentiary Conference, Kyoto, Japan, 1994.

15. McKinsey, "Closing the Global Communications Gap," p. 24.

16. Estimates from World Bank and Independent Commission for Worldwide Telecommunications Development, chaired by Sir Donald Maitland (1984).

17. Press Release ITU/95-3, International Telecommunication Union, Geneva, Switzerland, February 23, 1995.

18. McKinsey, "Closing the Global Communications Gap."

19. ITU Press release.

20. McKinsey, "Closing the Global Communications Gap," p. 25.

21. *Ibid.,* p. 51.

22. Don Gillmor, "Satisfaction," *Saturday Night,* November, 1994, p. 43.

23. "Confident LUKoil Fuels Search for Foreign Money," *Financial Times,* January 15, 1995, p. 16.

### Chapter 8

1. Quoted in *Forbes,* May 26, 1993, p. 45.

2. Quoted in David Ulrich and Dale Lake, *Organizational Capability,* New York: Wiley, 1990, p. 267.

3. Ricardo Semler, *Maverick,* New York: Warner Books, 1993.

4. Ricardo Semler, "Why My Former Employees Still Work for Me," *Harvard Business Review,* January–February 1994, p. 64.

5. *Ibid.,* p. 74.

6. *Ibid.,* p. 64.

7. *Ibid.,* p. 71.

8. Semler, "Why My Former Employees Still Work for Me," p. 65.

9. Ricardo Semler, "Worker's Paradise?" *Report on Business Magazine,* December 1993, p. 40.

10. Business Week, August 1, 1994, pp. 46–47.

11. Robert Haas, "Values Make the Company," *Harvard Business Review,* September–October 1990, p. 134.

12. *Ibid.*, p. 48.
13. "Crunch at Chrysler," *The Economist,* November 12, 1994, p. 81.
14. Management Review, "The Man in Chrysler's Driver Seat," February 1994, p. 30.
15. *Wall Street Journal Europe,* October 6, 1993, p. 1.
16. François Castaing, "Small-Team Responsiveness," *Executive Excellence,* August 1993, p. 10.
17. *Ibid.*
18. "Crunch at Chrysler," *The Economist,* November 12, 1994, p. 81.
19. Robert Lutz, "Implementing Technological Change with Cross-Functional Teams," *Research-Technology Management,* March–April 1994, p. 14 (emphasis added).
20. Gordon Forward and Dennis Beach, "Mentofacturing: a Vision for American Industrial Excellence," *Academy of Management Executive,* 1991, Vol. 5, No. 3, p. 32.
21. Dorothy Leonard-Barton, "The Factory as a Learning Laboratory," *Sloan Management Review,* Fall 1992, p. 24.
22. *Ibid.*
23. Brian Dumaine, "Unleash Workers and Cut Costs," *Fortune,* May 18, 1992, p. 88.
24. Leonard-Barton, "The Factory as a Learning Laboratory."
25. Charlene Marmer Solomon, "HR Facilitates the Learning Organization Concept," *Personnel Journal,* November 1994, p. 56–66.
26. Dumaine, "Unleash Workers and Cut Costs," p. 88.
27. Forward and Beach, "Mentofacturing: a Vision for American Industrial Excellence," p. 32.

### Chapter 9

1. Quoted in "Global Agenda: Toward the Millenium," *Time,* March 13, 1995, p. 45.
2. For a stimulating discussion of this phenomenon, see Kenichi Ohmae, *The Borderless World.*
3. The World Bank, *World Development Report 1994,* New York: Oxford University Press, 1995.
4. James Michaels, "There are More Patels Out There Than Smiths," *Forbes,* March 14, 1994, p. 84.
5. Quoted in Wendy Rohm, "Rupert Murdoch, Global Media Mogul," *Upside,* February 1995, p. 42.
6. "Furnishing the World," *The Economist,* November 19, 1994, p. 83.
7. Quoted in Louis Kraar, "The Kinetic Mr. Kim," *Asia, Inc.,* July 1993, p. 50.
8. Louis Kraar, *ibid.*, p. 55.
9. Reason Foundation, "Mining the Government Balance Sheet," *Policy Insight,* No. 139, April 1992.
10. Kyle Pope, "Strong Finnish: How OY Nokia turned its Smokestack Blues into Cellular Stardom," *Wall Street Journal Europe,* August 19, 1994, p. 1.
11. "From Sausages to Sweaters," *Euromoney,* August 1994, p. 58.
12. Gail Edmondson, "Grabbing Markets from the Giants," *Business Week,* November 18, 1994, p. 156.
13. Joanne Mason, "The Labours of Ollila," *International Management,* July–August 1992, p. 52.

### Chapter 10

1. Michael E. Porter, "America's Green Strategy," *Scientific American,* April 1991, p. 168.
2. Quoted in *Pollution Prevention Review,* Summer 1992, p. 309.
3. Personal communication with the author, Geneva, Switzerland, May, 1992.
4. Southern California Edison, *Environmental Solutions,* Rosemead, California, 1994, p. 1.
5. Quoted in Bruce Smart, *Beyond Compliance: A New Industry View of the Environment,* Washington: WRI 1992, p. 240.
6. In November 1995, for example, fourteen major insurance companies from around the world gathered in Geneva to sign a solemn "Statement of Environmental Commitment" in conjunction with the United Nations Environment Program. While the Statement is unobjectionable and even praiseworthy, I am unaware of *any* of the signatories which has carried the rhetoric into practice to anywhere near the same extent as American Re.
7. SEC Commissioner Richard Roberts, speech to the American Bar Association, 1993 Annual Meeting, New York, August 9, 1993.
8. Personal communication with the author, San Francisco, November 10, 1994.

### Chapter 11

1. Quoted in Michael Marquardt and Angus Reynolds, *The Global Learning Organization,* New York: Irwin, 1994, p. iii.
2. Arie de Geis, "Planning as Learning" *Harvard Business Review,* March–April 1988, p. 71.
3. Quoted in Peter Senge, "The Leader's New Work: Building Learning Organizations," *Sloan Management Management Review,* Fall 1990, p. 8.
4. Ikujiro Nonara, "The Knowledge-Creating Company," *Harvard Business Review,* November–December 1991, p. 96.
5. David Galvin, "Building a Learning Organization," *Harvard Business Review,* July–August, 1993, p. 80.
6. Quoted in Marquardt and Reynolds, *The Global Learning Organization,* p. 219.
7. "Motorola: Training for the Millenium," *Business Week,* March 28, 1994, p. 158.
8. At Motorola, "six-sigma" quality is defined as 3.4 defects per million or fewer.
9. "Motorola: Training for the Millenium," p. 159.
10. Steve Glain, "Samsung Chairman Obsessed with Expansion," *The Wall Street Journal,* March 6, 1995.
11. Quoted in Marquardt and Reynolds, *The Global Learning Organization,* p. 246.
12. *Ibid.,* p. 251.
13. *Ibid.,* p. 254.
14. Quoted in James Brian Quinn, *Intelligent Enterprise,* New York: The Free Press, 1992, p. 266.

### Chapter 12

1. Quoted in Thomas Stewart, "Intellectual Capital," *Fortune,* October 3, 1994, p. 68.
2. See Robert Kaplan and David Norton, "The Balanced Scorecard: Measures that Drive Performance," *Harvard Business Review,* January–February 1992.
3. Robert Kaplan, "Implementing the Balanced Scorecard," *Harvard Business Review,* September–October 1993, pp. 143–147.

4. Skandia AFS, *New Horizons,* April, 1995, p. 3.
5. Skandia AFS, *Visualizing Intellectual Capital in Skandia.* Supplement to the 1994 annual report, Stockholm, 1995.
6. *Skandia AFS: Balanced Annual Report on Intellectual Capital,* 1993, p. 2.
7. *Ibid.*
8. Skandia AFS, Stockholm, 1995.
9. Canadian Imperial Bank of Commerce, *The Generation of Intellectual Capital,* Toronto, 1995, p. 20.
10. *Ibid.*
11. Personal communication with the author, Toronto, April 13, 1995.
12. *Ibid.,* p. 63.
13. The sustainable development ethos first gained widespread international attention in 1987, with the publication of *Our Common Future* by the UN's World Commission on Environment and Development.
14. *Ibid.*
15. E. B. Eddy Group, *A Question of Balance,* 1993.
16. *Ibid.,* p. 2.
17. E. B. Eddy, *A Question of Balance,* August 1994, p. 1.
18. E. B. Eddy Group, *A Question of Balance,* 1993.

# INDEX

# W

# X

# Z